"My overall impression is very positive. It is an original and persuasively argued book that advances discussion in the literature, which the author knows remarkably well. I also find it to be most timely, and likely to be of some practical guidance to readers."

—***Robert M. Stewart***, *California State University, Chico*

THE ETHICS OF HOOKING UP

The Ethics of Hooking Up: Casual Sex and Moral Philosophy on Campus provides a systematic moral analysis of hooking up, or sexual activity between people who barely know each other, frequently while intoxicated, and with little or no verbal interaction. It explores the moral quandaries resulting from this potent combination of sex, alcohol, near-anonymity, and limited communication, focusing in particular on issues involving consent and respect. After delineating common practices involving casual sex on college campuses and exploring the difficulty of reaching mutual consent, author James Rocha argues that respect, kindness, sensitivity, and honest communication are also necessary conditions for morally permissible casual sex.

Key Features

- Provides a rare, systematic examination of the ethics of the hook up practice, which is the dominant mating practice for young people today.
- Analyzes the moral concepts of consent and respect in the context of hooking up, which provides significant moral challenges that highlight how we should obtain consent and show respect to one another.
- Argues for a moral paradigm shift in how young people hook up, emphasizing ways to avoid unintentionally committing grave moral wrongs.
- Situates the philosophy of casual sex in real life hook up practice, enabling us to rethink overly abstracted moral views on casual sex.

James Rocha is Assistant Professor of Philosophy at California State University, Fresno. James specializes in ethics, political philosophy, philosophy of law, and philosophy of race, and he has published in numerous journals, including: *Ethical Theory & Moral Practice, Journal of Applied Philosophy, Social Theory and Practice, The Kennedy Institute of Ethics*, and *Res Publica.*

THE ETHICS OF HOOKING UP

Casual Sex and Moral Philosophy on Campus

James Rocha

Routledge
Taylor & Francis Group
NEW YORK AND LONDON

First published 2020
by Routledge
52 Vanderbilt Avenue, New York, NY 10017

and by Routledge
2 Park Square, Milton Park, Abingdon, Oxon OX14 4RN

Routledge is an imprint of the Taylor & Francis Group, an informa business

Library of Congress Cataloging-in-Publication Data
A catalog record for this title has been requested

ISBN: 978-1-138-50460-8 (hbk)
ISBN: 978-1-138-50461-5 (pbk)
ISBN: 978-1-315-14612-6 (ebk)

Typeset in Bembo
by Taylor & Francis Books

MIX
Paper from responsible sources
FSC www.fsc.org FSC™ C013985

Printed in the United Kingdom
by Henry Ling Limited

For Mona, Jim, and Deanna

CONTENTS

ACKNOWLEDGMENTS

This book began after an independent study with my students Benjamin Dubroc and Lance Middleton. Though the independent study was on the philosophy of war, some off-hand remark after one meeting led to an interesting discussion about the ethics of hooking up. At the time, I probably knew nothing about hook up culture. Yet, early discussions with my students presented hooking up as something that was inherently important in their lives, incredibly confusing, and fraught with significant moral problems. I thank Ben and Lance for alerting me to the importance of taking on this topic.

I also want to thank my earliest readers, Christopher R. M. Phillips and Jon Cogburn. Their initial comments on very early drafts helped immensely to push me in the direction that the book eventually ended up going in. I was also aided by legal discussions regarding consent with Alex DiBona and Ken Levy.

Further invaluable assistance was provided by the team at Routledge, especially Andrew Beck, Marc Stratton, and Lusana Taylor. I was also aided by very helpful comments from blind reviewers. I am very grateful for all of their support.

Early research for the book was aided by support from Louisiana State University. Later research and the writing of the book were aided by funding from California State University, Fresno. I am grateful for the support I received from faculty, staff, and administrators from both universities. I am especially grateful for philosophical conversations with and general support from Jacki Alvarez, Mariana Anagnostopoulos, Honora Chapman, Carolyn Cusick, Andrew Fiala, Saúl Jiménez-Sandoval, Veena Howard, Vadim Keyser, Sergio La Porta, Aaron Lercher, Aldea Mulhern, Robert Maldonado, Jeff Roland, Ed Song, Amine Tais, and Terry Winant. I was also aided in late revisions by research help from David Dunn – I am very grateful for his assistance.

My family also put up with me missing countless family events, and they were always incredibly encouraging and understanding. I want to sincerely thank Deanna Rocha, Jim Rocha, Carmen Constantinescu, Bridget Brown, Derrick Rocha, Greg Brown, Kimi Rocha, Stephanie Fish, Rex Fish, Katherine Rocha, Kyle Rocha, and Savannah Brown.

Finally, Mona Rocha read every word multiple times over, discussed this topic with me endlessly, and provided every bit of support, guidance, and love necessary for me to write this book. Without Mona, this book would have not been possible. I thank her for everything she has done for me.

1

HOOK UP MORALITY

Let's imagine two young adults are about to hook up: they are about to engage in sexual activity without being in a committed relationship. These two individuals barely know each other: maybe they took a class together, but they did not speak much; they may not even know each other's names. They are near strangers: while they somewhat know each other, their relation is distant. Although they have agreed to hook up, each knows there are various activities that could be implied by the vague phrase "hooking up." Perhaps they have the same idea of how far they will go, but they may not. Regardless, they are not likely to discuss their plans and expectations. They also have not established any agreed upon signals to point out if one unintentionally transgresses the other's boundaries – they, instead, will rely on socially established norms (the unwritten social rules that tell us how we should act in these sorts of situations) in the hopes that each will act predictably and properly. Perhaps these young adults are acting from the same social norms, but they also could unknowingly be following completely different guidelines (*unwritten* social rules tend to vary, and many people misunderstand them). Maybe one thinks "no" absolutely means no, while the other thinks that "no" allows for wiggle room. Maybe one thinks silence implies consent, while the other assumes silence expresses a fearful inability to talk. Next, add to this scenario the fact that both have been drinking a good deal of alcohol – not enough to be blackout drunk, but enough to noticeably diminish their reasoning about these already tricky issues.

Clearly hooking up presents some thorny issues, but before looking at them, let me add one final twist: each of these young adults wishes to not only hook up, but also to do so ethically. Neither is a prude: they believe that unmarried sex can be morally permissible. But both would like to ensure that their hook up is morally permissible. They cannot help but notice that their circumstances raise a plethora of moral issues. The alcohol, the lack of verbal communication, not knowing each other well, the vagueness within the "hook up" phrase, and the fact that the planned activity is sexual in nature all add up to make this situation quite complicated, morally speaking. This book aims to discuss these issues, and to try to offer a path for moral agents to work towards ethical hook ups.

The situation described above is not contrived, but is, instead, representative of the hook up practice that social scientists consider to be the dominant mating ritual of young people today.[1] It is estimated that roughly 75–80% of college students have hooked up.[2] Numerous hook ups occur every week around the United States at clubs, bars, parties, and various places where young people run into each other. The social norms associated with hooking up are fairly routine and probably well-known for most participants. These young adults are accustomed to making hook up decisions while intoxicated and with little verbal communication. In spite of the morally frightening aspects of this experience, it is quite possible that hook ups work out fine most of the time. So, we can imagine that hook ups are usually enjoyable and involve no serious moral transgressions in most cases.

The problem for our two imagined hook up participants is that they want to ensure that their hook up is performed morally. Notice that this task is one that moral agents must take on: it is not sufficient for morality that things are likely to work out fine due to fortunate circumstances. Moral agents do what they can to ensure that they do not engage in immoral behavior, especially when a great deal is at stake. A moral agent would only hook up if they knew how to do so permissibly. To summarize: the moral agent wants to ensure that the hook up will be permissible – it is not sufficient for the moral agent that the odds and good luck will likely make the hook up turn out to be permissible since they usually do turn out that way.

With hook ups, a great deal is at stake: the failure cases involve bad sexual interactions, which could involve disrespecting someone, harming someone (emotionally and/or physically), or non-consensual sex. These potential problems could amount to significant moral violations, including causing serious trauma and possibly engaging in sexual assault or rape. The norms associated with hooking up endanger consent and respect in various ways. For example, according to both moral and legal accounts, heavy intoxication, through alcohol or other reason-impairing drugs, can undermine the competence required for consent,[3] and numerous studies have found that hook up participants are routinely intoxicated.[4] Further, the information requirement for consent is difficult to meet through routine hook up practices of using ambiguous phrases – such as the phrase "hooking up" itself[5] – and non-verbal communication.[6] With just a bit of confusion over hook up plans, limits, and/or the withdrawing of consent, the resulting moral transgressions could be quite severe.

Let's consider a brief case to see why a standard hook up could involve unintentional, but severe moral transgressions. Alma and Bradley are well-meaning individuals who are about to hook up. While they have no intention to wrong each other and will follow typical hook up norms, they also have taken no precautions to ensure their hook up is morally permissible. So, they are both somewhat intoxicated, they do not discuss their plans, and they do not know each other well enough to be able to guess what the other expects. They agree to hook up, but Bradley thinks a "hook up" always involves sexual intercourse, while Alma thinks "hook up" rarely implies intercourse and usually implies making out with some level of nudity. At the moment when Bradley, who assumes they agreed to go all the way, initiates sex, Alma is shocked and confused by his presumption. We can assume that Bradley has been in numerous hook ups where the other person did indeed agree to have intercourse with him. We can also assume that Bradley would expect Alma to explicitly withdraw her consent if she did not wish to continue, even while we recognize that her shock and confusion along with her intoxication may make it hard for her to do so.

Here, through a lack of communication, an abundance of alcohol, and a good bit of confusion, Bradley has committed a grave moral transgression by having sex with Alma even though she did not actually consent to sex. Even with well-meaning agents, the norms that structure typical hook ups leave room for grave moral transgressions, especially with respect to consent. Throughout the book, I will argue that it cannot be morally acceptable to simply accept this risk of performing a serious moral transgression just because hook ups usually go fine. A moral agent would, instead, do what they could to avoid such severe transgressions.

There is a question of whether sexual activity requires anything beyond consent to be morally permissible. Let's agree that love is not a requirement for permissible sex since there is nothing morally problematic about enjoying sex for fun. And since hooking up, by definition, excludes people who are committed to each other, it is nearly trivial that hook up participants are not in love. Sex without love can be permissible, and so that doesn't undermine the possibility of moral hook ups.

Respect, though, is a much lower bar. In every human interaction, a certain level of respectful treatment can be assumed as a moral minimum. Part of being a moral agent just is treating other people respectfully. Sometimes, when little is at stake, being respectful comes easy. In more significant human interactions, respect may be more difficult, but it is required nonetheless because it is our way of signaling that we see each other as morally significant beings who are worthy of being treated in dignified manners. So, it is not onerous to expect that hook ups, to be morally permissible, would require respect, but, as we will see, respectful treatment is neither expected within nor implied by current hook up norms.

Agents seeking to morally hook up can act according to the current norms of the hook up practice and usually, due to luck, commit no serious moral transgression. Yet, the intoxicated, incommunicative hook up participant has done nothing to ensure he or she will not seriously violate another person's sexual autonomy. Autonomy refers to the way in which an agent lives according to rules she has set for herself. Sexual autonomy, then, means that the agent is in control over what they are sexually into and the ways they choose to have sexual encounters. Since we should have the right to engage in sexual acts only in the ways we choose for ourselves, it is very important to respect each other's sexual autonomy. One should not rely on luck to ensure that another's sexual autonomy – or one's own – is being respected.

Let's consider Cedric and Donna, who successfully have a consensual, coital hook up while following typical hook up norms. They are both quite intoxicated, did not discuss their plans, but happened to have the same sense of how they hoped to hook up. While Cedric and Donna may consensually hook up, they have done nothing to ensure they treat each other respectfully. Many issues of respect reach beyond mere consent: for example, suppose both Cedric and Donna see the other as mere conquests who they will brag about in unseemly ways to their friends. Neither is being respectful, which is morally problematic even if it is not as immoral as having sex without consent would be. Hence, current hook up practices may often luckily work out as consensual, but it is less likely that they can just luckily work out as respectful. People who wish to respect their hook up partners will have to do some work to establish that respect prior to and after the hook up. People who want to make sure their hook ups are morally permissible will have to take care to ensure their hook ups do not end up in serious moral transgressions and are respectful of the other person.

We have arrived at a position that seems to be at odds with the leading view in the philosophy of sex literature, which finds that casual sex is typically morally permissible.[7] And I do tend to agree with that position as it is usually laid out. There are two methodological differences that explain the apparent disagreement. First, the philosophical literature has concentrated on casual sex in the *abstract*, whereas my discussion will be based on social science studies that examine how young people *actually* hook up. While my analysis will refer to the philosophical literature's discussions on the morality of casual sex, I will also locate my inquiry within the various moral obstacles faced within actual hook ups. The goal is to figure out what the moral requirements are for hooking up as it occurs in real life. This approach comes with limitations. For instance, since the social science studies concentrate (perhaps to an alarming degree) on white, heteronormative, cis, college students, as a result the empirical claims in this book will mostly refer to those kind of hook up participants. Since the social science studies do not include other individuals, it is wrong for the philosopher to generalize beyond those individuals, so I acknowledge that limitation from the start. I will agree that casual sex is morally permissible in the abstract, but we will find that the abstraction loses sight of many of the actual moral problems that make hooking up morally tricky.

Second, the usual, though often unstated, perspective within the philosophy of sex literature is provided from an external or bystander viewpoint.[8] The bystander is not someone trying to make sure their own action will be permissible, as we all must do in real life. The bystander is an external judge who looks from the outside and asks how the action turned out. That means that the bystander tends to evaluate sex acts as a whole, after the fact. As such, philosophers of sex ask whether a given act is morally permissible while fully knowing what the act entailed and how the participants felt about the act. This methodology implicitly assumes a kind of knowledge that actual, real-life participants cannot have in advance of engaging in a hook up. Moral participants must ask themselves, before the hook up begins and without fully knowing what the other person is thinking, how they can ensure the upcoming act will not go wrong. The bystander, instead, asks, after the fact, how the action ended up, given the ability to judge from the sidelines.

The former, holistic perspective is preferable for identifying the overall permissibility of casual sex as well as the major pitfalls that would make it immoral in particular situations. The perspective of the moral agent is preferable for identifying what moral agents should do to make sure that they hook up morally. The bystander may look at typical cases where both people wish to hook up, do not need to communicate much, are able to get intoxicated for the hook up, and yet both succeed in attaining what they want out of the encounter. The bystander then examines the cases after the participants have gotten lucky and successfully hooked up without serious moral trouble. Nevertheless, the apparent ease of their moral hook up was only possible because both people were interested in the same kind of hook up and navigated through it without anything going wrong. The bystander sees the lucky (and perhaps usual) consequence, but does not have to grapple with the moral work necessary to ensure that morally permissible consequence in advance. Thus, to the bystander, it could turn out that a practice is permissible in the abstract even if it takes a good deal of moral work to ensure that the practice is permissible for you in reality.

I am, then, drawing a distinction between assessing a practice from an outsider's perspective and assessing it from the participant's perspective. It is not my intention to claim one is preferable. We learn a lot about ethics by taking the bystander's perspective, including a general sense of which actions, when taken as a whole, can be permissible and which cannot. We also, though, learn a lot about ethics by asking how active agents make sure they are acting morally. The permissibility of a generic action type does not necessarily tell us how to engage in that action permissibly. For example, it might be that there are clear occasions where lying is permissible, such as a lie that is only told to save someone from hurt feelings. It is not as clear to know when you are lying in that permissible fashion and when you are rationalizing your lie for more selfish reasons. Ethics requires figuring out both types of issues. Hence, I am not here disagreeing with the philosophical literature that says casual sex can be morally permissible. I agree with that view. I am instead attempting to figure out how agents can ensure that their own hook ups are morally permissible, which is a different question.

To examine the requirements for morally permissible hook ups, this book is situated in the trends and norms that make up the real-life practice, while also taking seriously the hook up partners' own moral perspectives. Thus, the two main issues that such agents would need clarification on would be how they can ensure the other person is consenting, as well as how they can meet any moral requirements beyond consent, such as respecting their hook up partners.

Various real-life aspects of the current hook up practice endanger both consent and respect. I do believe that there are ways for moral agents to adapt current practices to make hooking up morally permissible. We find these alternative methods by examining the real-life obstacles to moral hook ups, from the perspectives of hook up participants. Therefore, we need to better understand the hook up practice itself.

Hooking Up

Understanding the hook up practice requires first noting the various ambiguities inherent in the phrase "hooking up."[9] To start, there are non-sexual uses. Friends sometimes say, "Let's hook up later," when there is no intention to have any sexual activity at that later time. Yet, at a bar, club, or party, the phrase will have a different meaning that refers to sexual activity. For our purposes, I will only use the sexualized meanings of the phrase, based on the reasonable assumption that context usually makes clear when sexualized meanings are intended. After all, two friends who are not sexually attracted to each other saying, "Let's hook up at the basketball court at 1 pm" is sufficiently different from two near strangers who are sexually attracted to each other saying, "Let's hook up in your car at 1 am."

A "hook up" refers to a sexual encounter between two people who are not in a committed relationship. When someone simply says that they have "hooked up" with someone, there are three places where they are being imprecise. First, the two partners can have any kind of relation with each other except a romantic, committed one. They can be friends, near strangers, or strangers, or somewhere in between. Second, hooking up can involve any activity from kissing to sexual intercourse. Two people can agree to hook up and have different ideas of what activity they agreed to perform. The third vagueness lies in the implications of having hooked up with someone. There is no clear sense of what a hook up means, if anything, after the sexual activity ends. Two people can agree to hook up and have completely different expectations of what follows. While some participants think a hook up can open the door to the possibility of future hanging out or dating, others believe a hook up is necessarily a one-shot encounter that implies that the two partners will have no future interaction, perhaps of any kind (as in, they will ignore each other the next time that they see each other).[10] There is, then, great potential for confusion, and potential moral trouble, in an agreement to hook up: the phrase itself does not entail a singular understanding of what's happening.

Due to these three ambiguities, the phrase, "I hooked up with X," creates an air of mystery where only the speaker and perhaps close friends know the precise meaning.[11] Others can only be certain that the speaker engaged in some kind of sexual activity with someone he or she is not in a committed relationship with. In a way, this ambiguity offers privacy: others can know a person hooks up a lot without knowing whether the person has had a lot of sex with strangers, or even any at all. Yet, one study indicates that, in spite of the ambiguity, there is a surprising amount of unfounded confidence that participants think that they know precisely what others mean by the phrase.[12] Thus, the purposeful ambiguity opens up the door for dangerous confusion: two people can hook up and have very different understandings of what they are doing while confidently assuming they have the same ideas in mind.[13]

While there are many relations that hook up participants could have with each other, including friends, acquaintances, or strangers, hook up participants are often near strangers.[14] I will use "near stranger" to refer to a relation where the agents are familiar, but not very familiar, such as a friend of a friend or a person the agent sees regularly but doesn't talk to, such as a classmate in a large course. In other words, the near stranger relationship lies somewhere between complete strangers and acquaintances. Acquaintances are usually on a first name basis and have short conversations, usually over non-personal issues, such as weather, sports, or entertainment. Though near strangers are likely to know of each other, they are unlikely to have conversations. Unlike complete strangers, there is some kind of connection: near strangers share a class, work in the same building, share a friend, or have some similar connection. Near strangers recognize each other, may know each other's names, but don't normally talk to one another.

The social script for how people typically hook up differs greatly from the better-known social script for dating.[15] When hooking up, individuals do not pair up in advance and plan out an evening as they would for a date. Instead, they usually head out in gendered groups (all men or all women) to a bar, club, or party, to consume alcohol, dance, and have fun. If they meet up with someone they are physically attracted to, and that they know at least distantly, they will likely use non-verbal signals to indicate interest. They will likewise use non-verbal cues to signal their desires, limits, and their agreement to hook up. The alcohol that initiates this process enables the participants to do something (hook up with near strangers while communicating non-verbally) that they may be unable to do while sober.[16]

These typical trends could lead to significant moral difficulties, especially as related to consent. Consent is an agreement that morally transforms the relation between two individuals such that new obligations, responsibilities, permissions, and sometimes rights are created by the very act of agreeing.[17] For this moral transformation to occur, the consenting individuals must make their agreement freely, with adequate information over what they are agreeing to, and while competent enough to obligate themselves. Individuals could not make themselves obligated through a forced or coerced, uninformed, or incompetently made agreement. Thus, an agreement can only amount to consent if it is free, informed, and competent.

It is worth noting that some theorists use "consent" to mean mere agreement, and require that consent only has to meet these requirements (be free, informed, and competent) when it is *valid* or *meaningful* consent.[18] As I will argue in Chapter Two, this usage is neither the norm in the philosophical literature nor is it useful from either a moral or legal perspective. So, I will use "consent" such that it is always valid and meaningful.

The hook up practice includes multiple aspects that challenge these consent requirements. For example, as mentioned, social scientists maintain that a large part of the hook up negotiation and decision-making occurs non-verbally.[19] All of the ambiguity inherent to "hooking up" (the partners' sexual desires and limits, their intentions for the hook up in question, and any other relevant beliefs, feelings, values, etc.) are most likely navigated through non-verbal communication. This non-verbal method of communication greatly problematizes the information requirement for consent.

Further, most hook up participants consume large amounts of alcohol not only during a hook up, but also before meeting their eventual hook up partner.[20] People go to bars, clubs, or parties, begin to drink alcohol, and then seek out someone to hook up with. In a great number of hook ups, the participants are likely intoxicated prior to choosing a hook up partner, during the non-verbal negotiation over how to hook up, and during the hook up itself. This intoxication makes it very unlikely that any of the participants are sufficiently competent to consent.

In addition to the ways in which hooking up problematizes consent, it is inherent to the social trends within hook up culture that participants show few signs of respect for each other. They may not be overly interested in the other person's pleasure, they may not bother to learn each other's names, or they may refuse to acknowledge each other in future encounters. As one telling example, philosopher Howard Klepper argues that when people brag after a sexual encounter, they degrade their former partners by making public a kind of information that was meant to be private.[21] Bragging is one method in which hook up participants regularly disrespect each other, possibly leading to ruined reputations.[22]

The typical hook up involves individuals drinking heavily, communicating non-verbally, and engaging in sexual activity with partners for whom they show little respect. Additionally, the hook up practice is gendered in a fashion that places stricter norms on women. Perhaps the only norm where men risk more stigmatization (as well as being the main norm where men face any real threat of stigmatization) lies in the expectation that individuals within certain settings, such as college, hook up. Research indicates that individuals of both genders who do not hook up could be treated poorly by their peers, unless they are in committed relationships or openly religious, even though there are more virgins among college students than most of them seem to realize (and, of course, some virgins may engage in non-coital hook ups).[23] Yet, men face greater stigmatization than women for not hooking up since our social ideal of masculinity involves excelling at the hook up practice.[24]

Pretty much every other hook up norm subjects women to higher standards just because they are women, while providing almost no room for male stigmatization. The most well-known is the double standard that requires women, but not men, to divine the socially acceptable, but entirely subjective, "correct" number of hook up partners.[25] For men, the goal is simply to maximize and publicize: the more hook ups he tells his friends about, the more highly thought of he will be. Women, on the other hand, must hit a number that is greater than zero, but only barely greater. If their number is too high, the stigma can be quite severe, sometimes leading to women needing to transfer schools to restart their reputations.[26]

One entirely unfair, but common, determination of the "correct" number derives from whether men can infer that a woman is hooking up with multiple partners. For example, according to one study, women are judged negatively for carrying condoms.[27] The thought seems to be that if women are prepared for protected sex, then they must be having too many coital hook ups. This opinion is irrational since the man holding it is surely hoping to have a protected coital hook up with the wisely prepared woman whom he is harshly judging.

In one telling example, a woman is judged punitively for hooking up with just two men who happen to know each other[28] as seen in this exchange between a male student (Kevin) and sociologist Kathleen Bogle (KB):

KB: So it's a no-no to hook up with several people in the same clique?

KEVIN: You are only making yourself trouble … If one girl would hook up with me and then my friend and so on, of course she'd get a reputation.

KB: Even if it was just kissing?

KEVIN: Bad idea. How do you expect these people not to talk [when] they're friends? 'Did you hook up with Susan?' 'Yeah, I hooked up with [her].' 'Yeah, me too.' She would have to realize that these guys are close buddies and of course they are going to know. I'd almost say that would be her fault. I would not put myself in the situation.[29]

Bogle noted that this view represented the opinions of other male students she interviewed.[30] Perhaps these men are judging these women poorly because men, who are known to brag about hook ups, will infer that a woman could only make two men's lists by showing up on a large number of men's lists. Of course, such an inference is evidence of poor critical thinking skills since there are more plausible explanations available: the three of them attend the same parties, take the same classes, have the same friends, etc. Further, their evidence is incredibly anecdotal since it is based only on two sources. Most importantly, their devaluing of a woman for hooking up excessively (according to their determination) confirms that women, and not the men who make and share hook up lists, are judged harshly for having too many hook up partners.

This example also implies that there is a specific hook up norm that requires women to take responsibility for ensuring that male friends shouldn't have overlapping hook up partners. This general, sexist idea – that if there is any kind of moral responsibility in hook ups, it would have to fall on women – is prevalent throughout hook up culture. This case, though, is particularly odd: why should male friends care if their hook up lists overlap, and, if they do care, why would it be incumbent on women to make sure it doesn't happen? Yet, when Kevin in the study above says that it would "almost" be the woman's fault, it is hard to take his hedge seriously since everything else he says clearly lays the blame on her for a rather peculiar transgression.

Women are not only judged for their number, but also for their dress style, their behavior (whether sober or drunk), and even their association.[31] In terms of association, a young woman's reputation is harmed simply by joining a sorority with a reputation for excessive hooking up.[32] Women are treated even worse if they frequently hang out at fraternity houses: fraternity members sometimes refer to such women as "houserats."[33] Mere association is used to imply disapproved behaviors: women who associate with other women who are judged for hooking up excessively or with men who are celebrated for hooking up excessively, are also assumed to be hooking up too much.[34]

While men's behavior is interpreted in a multi-dimensional fashion, women's behavior is almost always construed as sexual.[35] For men, constant intoxication is almost treated as an intrinsic good, but women who drink a lot are thought to be making themselves too sexually available.[36] The drunken behavior of young men can be interpreted variously, often including the idea that drunk men are fun, or at least funny. The drunken behavior of women – such as their dancing, flirting, or acting "wild" – is almost always interpreted as clear proof of their proclivity to hook up with any man.[37] In our society, women are sexually objectified much more than men are. What it means to objectify someone is to treat them as if they are merely an object – to treat them as a body without a mind, replaceable with anyone else who has a similar (or preferable) body. Women are objectified to the extent that much of what they do is taken to necessarily have sexual implications, which quickly leads to the inference that some women are overly sexual. How could one *not* conclude a woman is too sexual if one keeps *interpreting* her every action as sexual?

Merely describing the hook up practice shows it to be thoroughly pervaded by sexism. What it means to act well or poorly within the practice makes it almost impossible for men to fail or for women to succeed. Further, if men and women bring distinct goals into their hook ups, it could provide another problematic aspect of the practice. If, as the case turns out to be, men tend to have a much easier time meeting their typical goals, then we would have another worrisome and gendered power differential within the practice.

Most studies indicate that women have higher hopes that hook ups will lead to relationships than men do.[38] In one telling study, men and women were asked about their "terrible experiences" in hook ups, which 42% of women and 46% of men declared to have had.[39] Most women described terrible experiences that amounted to sexual assault: they were either pressured into changing their mind about hooking up or pressured into going further than they were willing to go. Most men, on the other hand, defined their terrible experiences as hooking up with women who were seeking relationships.[40] Thus, while women risk sexual assault, many men see a woman broaching the relationship question as one of their biggest fears.

Relationship expectations largely divide along gender lines, and men have better odds for meeting their goals. Although about 12% of hook ups turn into relationships,[41] these numbers surely include many men who deviate from the standard male norms by seeking relationships either from the beginning or at least later on. Men who do not wish to end up in relationships surely can avoid them, whereas women who seek relationships (in one study, 63% of women said they would like to meet their husband in college, where hooking up is the most common mating ritual[42]) are surely going to have a much harder time meeting their goal. Of course, women who would prefer to hook up and avoid relationships will also meet their goals. Thus, the majority of males (who wish to avoid relationships) and the minority of males (who wish to end up in relationships) both have positive odds for meeting their goals, while, among women, only the minority group (those who wish to avoid relationships) have the odds in their favor.

As another significant point, men's sexual goals are much more likely to be met in hook ups.[43] Sociologist Lisa Wade argues that women experience significantly fewer orgasms than men enjoy during hook ups.[44] She argues that this is partially due to the fact that hook ups are not as likely to include oral sex for women as they are to include oral sex for men.[45] It is also due to the norms of hook up culture, which prize a man's orgasm much more than a woman's. According to the women Wade interviewed for her study, they felt that "expecting an orgasm from a male hookup partner is demanding or rude."[46] And the men that she interviewed often reported that they felt no interest in giving women pleasure *in a hook up*; these men held onto a distinction whereby they would be interested in sexually pleasing women with whom they were in relationships, but they felt that women's pleasure and orgasms were not necessary parts of hooking up.[47] Therefore, these trends add up to women having a much harder time than men in achieving their sexual goals in their hook ups.

Obviously, these statistics only show gendered trends, and should not be taken to conclude how all women or all men feel. Many women do feel empowered by hooking up, and they see hooking up as part of their sexual liberation.[48] It is very important to take these women at their word.[49] Lots of women will likely feel positive about a portion of their own hook ups, while some women will feel positive about hooking up in general and will have no bad hook ups. It is not necessary to deny that many women feel empowered by hooking up to note that studies show a general trend that allows for the hook up practice to meet men's goals much more than it meets women's goals.

From these norms and statistics, we can see that the hook up practice, as it currently exists, contains so much sexism that it is morally problematic in itself. That does not imply that individuals are sexist just for engaging in the practice, and my focus will be on the morality of individual agents, and not on general trends. Yet, the practice's sexist trends are related to some of the implicit assumptions of what's acceptable for individual men and women. As examples, because hooking up is such a sexist practice, it is easier for men to get away with lying to women and harder for women to have their refusals taken seriously.

We are examining a hook up practice that, through its various norms and due to the related social trends that in part define it, is sexist, problematizes consent, and is disrespectful. A moral analysis of casual sex, therefore, will be very different when directed at the actual social practice. Further, such a real-life-directed moral analysis would be more useful to an ordinary agent who is seeking a way to hook up in a morally permissible fashion.

Analyzing Hook Up Ethics

Our moral assessment of hooking up should incorporate the work done on the morality of casual sex within the philosophical literature. There are two main questions that are asked when judging casual sex's moral permissibility. The first involves determining the requirements to consent to casual sex. The second involves asking what else beyond consent, if anything, is required for casual sex to be permissible. This book follows the structure of this approach by asking what is required for agents to consent to hooking up, and, then, what else, if anything, is required beyond consent for a hook up to be permissible.

Consent, then, is central to the moral assessment of casual sex in general and hooking up in particular. Two individuals can only hook up morally if each consents, since, without consent, the individuals have not gained permission to engage in sexual activity with each other. There is nothing unusual about this requirement: consent is a morally necessary component of most risky human interactions. Since hooking up involves a substantial activity with another person that would involve a grave moral transgression if done without permission, it is clear that hooking up requires consent.

While there is a more or less standardized picture of the main requirements for consent, there is a great deal of disagreement over how these requirements apply to the morality of casual sex. Permissible casual sex must be consensual, which requires an agreement that is, at a minimum, free, adequately informed, and competently made. Yet, the philosophical literature contains a great deal of disagreement over what is required for such an agreement to be freely made, informed, or competently made.

To untangle this debate, it will be necessary to analyze the concept of consent at length in Chapter Two. To begin, I will discuss the ontology of consent, the temporality of different kinds of consent, and the different levels of normative strength for obligations that derive from different kinds of consent. In terms of ontology, I will ask what kind of thing consent is: I will argue that it is an agreement that must exist both in the world (through language or some other type of communicative signaling) and in the minds of the participants (in the sense that they intend to consent). I will then argue that consent can take two temporal forms: advance consent involves an agreement that binds a person to perform some future action, and contemporaneous consent covers an ongoing action where consent can be withdrawn at any time. Next, I will distinguish consent types based on a variety of normative strengths: the fact that people have consented does not yet determine how much morally follows from their consent. Instead, we must examine how instances of consent differ based on the kinds of permissions or rights that the consent creates. In other words, consent differs in terms of normative strength: some instances of consent create stronger obligations and rights, while others create weaker obligations and merely permissions. Finally, I will turn to the three main requirements necessary for obtaining consent: consent must be free, adequately informed, and competently made.

After discussing consent in the abstract, I will turn to how the three main requirements for consent apply to hooking up. In Chapter Three, I will examine the freedom requirement, which may seem to be easily met in typical hook ups. Yet, as argued by feminists such as Onora O'Neill, Sally Haslanger, and Lois Pineau, casual sex in our society typically fits within an aggressive narrative.[50] This narrative involves an aggressor, who is usually male, either refusing to accept another person's refusal to hook up, using aggressive techniques to obtain an agreement to hook up, or using aggressive techniques during the hook up. Some theorists, such as Alan Wertheimer, Douglas Husak, and George Thomas, would argue that this narrative is unproblematic insofar as it is a well-known narrative for most people who engage in casual sex.[51] Against this latter view, I will argue that aggressive techniques can undermine a partner's confidence that they are free to refuse to hook up. I will argue that moral agents can use aggressive techniques but only if they follow strategies that derive from the BDSM community (BDSM is used to reference a variety of sexual activities, including bondage and discipline, dominance and submission, and sadism and masochism). These strategies, importantly, involve having a sober discussion of plans, limits, and ways to withdraw consent.

In Chapter Four, I will continue to examine the practice of using sober discussions prior to hook ups while discussing the information requirement for consent. Some philosophers, such as Alan Soble, argue that the information requirement should be lessened for casual sex since the information to be revealed is often so personal and private that you cannot be required to share it.[52] Against this view, I will argue that hook up consent requires a substantial information requirement since grave moral transgressions are risked by pertinent misunderstandings. Hence, moral agents would seek to have significant pre-hook up conversations to ensure that their partners are adequately informed and severe misunderstandings are avoided.

In Chapter Five, I will examine the competence requirement for consent that is regularly endangered by hook up participants' intoxicated states. Alan Wertheimer argues that intoxication should not undermine consent in sexual contexts because people would prefer a state of affairs where they could have intoxicated sex with strangers: they would choose that state of affairs, and, therefore, they consent to it.[53] Against Wertheimer, I argue that we cannot infer from the fact that many, or even most, people would prefer intoxicated sex with strangers that a given individual is consenting to an intoxicated hook up. I will argue that moral agents should, instead, seek out sober consent to later hook up while intoxicated; moral agents, though, cannot assume that an intoxicated person would have given sober consent.

Having established what it takes to obtain hook up consent in Chapters Two through Five, in Chapter Six, I will examine the view that consent is sufficient for moral permissibility. Many philosophers come close to arguing that consent is sufficient for moral permissibility when it comes to sexual matters.[54] It certainly seems that certain candidates for additional requirements, such as being in love or in a committed relationship, are based on outdated social mores. Yet, sex also brings up tricky issues that consent is inadequate to sufficiently handle. Even consensual sex in our society often involves personal vulnerabilities, the objectification of one's partners, and sexist attitudes. These issues raise moral concerns that occur independently of consent. For example, we have some amount of moral responsibility for the vulnerabilities that we expose in our sexual partners. This responsibility is not due to any kind of consensual agreement to be receptive to each other's vulnerabilities – it derives from a basic responsibility to be decent to people for whom your actions have significant affects. Hooking up would thus require additional moral tools beyond consent.

To locate those additional moral tools, in Chapter Seven I will argue that moral agents must establish that they respect their hook up partners. They can manifest this respect by showing a willingness to be beneficent in the face of exposed vulnerabilities and by providing a basis for trust. Part of accomplishing this task will lie in the pre-hook up conversation. To meet the information requirement for consent, certain factual matters have to be discussed (revealing STDs, discussing desires, etc.). Yet, to be respectful, the conversation both has to be conducted respectfully and has to signal the willingness to be beneficent and trustworthy. Perhaps more importantly, the hook up should occur in situations where vulnerabilities are less likely to be exposed and trust is more easily granted. While this respect requirement will significantly change the hook up practice, it should not be seen as morally controversial: it treats sex like any other activity where there is room for significant vulnerability and disrespectful treatment. Yet, given the significant stakes and the morally dubious nature of how hooking up is currently practiced, respectful treatment may require a very different way to hook up.

The change I am recommending may be so significant that the view begins to look like a *reductio ad absurdum*: if hooking up requires this much change to be permissible, then maybe it is simply impermissible. Many current hook up participants may not be willing to make these changes to a practice that they currently enjoy and that, through good fortune, has never caused them significant moral trouble. The problem is that the current hook up practice leaves quite a bit of room for major moral transgressions, and it is only through good odds that many hook up participants are able to avoid these transgressions. Since moral agents would not rely on luck to avoid engaging in a grave moral error, the practice, as it currently exists, cannot be morally permissible. In the final chapter, Chapter Eight, I will conclude by explaining how I believe hooking up in a morally permissible way may in fact be possible. It will not involve easy changes, and it would involve a practice that looks quite different than it does now. But moral agents should work to develop a new practice that includes a serious and sober pre-hook up conversation, attempts to build trust, and measures to ensure that the hook up occurs in such a way that respectful treatment pervades throughout the activity and even in its aftermath. Though these changes are substantial, they reflect the importance of establishing a method for morally hooking up.

Preliminary Thoughts on Gender

Before getting started, it is worth pausing to make some general remarks about how I will discuss gender in the book. As we have already seen, hook up culture contains a good deal of sexism, which will be worth discussing at various points within the book. Having said that, there are some theorists, such as Nadine Strossen and Katie Roiphe, who express concern that creating strong sexual obligations entails creating stronger obligations for men to act differently in how they engage in casual sex, which thereby treats women as if they need to be protected from their own choices.[55] In other words, to use a straightforward but simplistic example, if I argue that hook up partners have a strong moral obligation to ensure they have each other's consent, that could be read to mean that men in particular have to make sure women are actually consenting when they say "yes." And this latter reading would allegedly be problematic since it treats women as if they do not mean their own words when they say "yes."

In response, I want to make clear that I am not assuming that men and women have different obligations based on their gender. At points in the book, I will use gendered terms to reflect that there are empirical patterns. For instance, in Chapter Three, we will see that empirical research reveals that men are more often aggressors in hook ups, and so it will be useful to refer to the aggressor as male in those discussions. Yet, even in those discussions, I do not intend to imply that women would have different or lessor obligations when they act as aggressors. Further, through much of the book, I will leave gender open-ended to emphasize that the obligations in question are neither being placed more on men nor on women, but simply placed on anyone who engages in hooking up. To display this emphasis, I will often use the singular "they." The singular "they" is an increasingly popular grammar technique where you use "they" as a pronoun that could signify either gender-term ("he" or "she").[56] Thus, "they" in this work will often mean one person who could be either a man or woman.

I further do not intend to weigh in on whether gender traits, such as the sexual aggressiveness of men, are biological or social. The scientific literature suggests that the answer probably falls within a mixture: gender traits are somewhat biological and somewhat social.[57] Instead of weighing in on the nature vs. nurture debate, I will simply point out that regardless of the extent to which some of our traits are biological, we at least have the ability to act against them. And that ability implies a moral responsibility to act against them if they are leading us into immoral behavior. So, I am less interested in whether men or women have certain traits biologically or socially, and more interested in the responsibility to act in the ways that are morally required of them. The question, then, is whether there are any such moral responsibilities for people of either gender, when it comes to hooking up.

Notes

1 See discussions such as Elizabeth L. Paul, Brian McManus, and Allison Hayes, "'Hookups': Characteristics and Correlates of College Students' Spontaneous and Anonymous Sexual Experiences," *Journal of Sex Research* 37, no. 1 (2000); Norval Glenn and Elizabeth Marquardt, *Hooking Up, Hanging Out and Hoping for Mr. Right: College Women on Dating and Mating Today,* An Institute for American Values Report to the Independent Women's Forum (2001); Tracy A. Lambert, Arnold S. Kahn, and Kevin J. Apple, "Pluralistic Ignorance and Hooking Up," *The Journal of Sex Research* 40, no. 2 (2003); Wendy D. Manning, Peggy C. Giordano, and Monica A. Longmore, "Hooking Up: The Relationship Contexts of 'Nonrelationship' Sex," *Journal of Adolescent Research* 21, no. 5 (2006), 459; Kathleen Bogle, *Hooking Up: Sex, Dating, and Relationships on Campus* (New York: New York University Press, 2008); Michael Kimmel, *Guyland: The Perilous World Where Boys Become Men* (New York: Harper Collins, 2008), 190; Teresa M. Downing-Matibag and Brandi Geisinger, "Hooking Up and Sexual Risk Taking Among College Students: A Health Belief Model Perspective," *Qualitative Health Research* 19, no. 9 (2009); Carolyn Bradshaw, Arnold S. Kahn, and Bryan K. Saville, "To Hook Up or Date: Which Gender Benefits?," *Sex Roles* 62 (2010), 661; Leanna Fortunato *et al.*, "Hook Up Experiences and Problem Behaviors among Adolescents," *Journal of Child & Adolescent Substance Abuse* 19 (2010); Jesse J. Owen *et al.*, "'Hooking Up' Among College Students: Demographic and Psychosocial Correlates," *Archives of Sexual Behavior* 39 (2010); Rachel Kalish and Michael Kimmel, "Hooking Up: Hot Hetero Sex or the New Numb Normative?," *Australian Feminist Studies* 26, no. 67 (2011), 137; Elizabeth Armstrong, Paula England, and Alison C. K. Fogarty, "Accounting for Women's Orgasm and Sexual Enjoyment in College Hookups and Relationships," *American Sociological Review* 77, no. 3 (2012), 435; Jennifer Katz and Monica E. Schneider, "Casual Sex During the First Year of College: Prospective Associations with Attitudes about Sex and Love Relationships,"

Archives of Sexual Behavior 42 (2013); Melissa A. Lewis *et al.*, "What is Hooking Up? Examining Definitions of Hooking Up in Relation to Behavior and Normative Perceptions," *Journal of Sex Research* 50, no. 8 (2013), 757; Herbert W. Helm Jr., Stephanie D. Gondra, and Duane C. McBridge, "Hook-Up Culture Among College Students: A Comparison of Attitudes Toward Hooking-Up Based on Ethnicity and Gender," *North American Journal of Psychology* 17, no. 2 (2015), 221–232; Spencer B. Olmstead *et al.*, "Hooking Up and Risk Behaviors Among First Semester College Men: What is the Role of Precollege Experience?," *The Journal of Sex Research* 52, no. 2 (2015), 187; Lisa Wade, *American Hookup: The New Culture of Sex on Campus* (New York: W. W. Norton & Company, 2017), 19.

2 Gary Gute and Elaine M. Eshbaugh, "Personality as a Predictor of Hooking Up Among College Students," *Journal of Community Health Nursing* 25 (2008), 35; Fortunato *et al.*, "Hook Up Experiences," 263; Lewis *et al.*, "What is Hooking Up?," 757; Molly K. Bachtel, "Do Hookups Hurt? Exploring College Students' Experiences and Perceptions," *Journal of Midwifery & Women's Health* 58, no. 1 (2013), 41–42; Martin A. Monto and Anna G. Carey, "A New Standard of Sexual Behavior? Are Claims Associated with the 'Hookup Culture' Supported by General Social Survey Data?," *Journal of Sex Research* 51, no. 6 (2014); Wendasha Jenkins Hall and Amanda E. Tanner, "US Black College Women's Sexual Health in Hookup Culture: Intersections of Race and Gender," *Culture, Health & Sexuality* 18, no. 11 (2016), 1265.

3 Laurence Thomas, "Sexual Desire, Moral Choice, and Human Ends," *Journal of Social Philosophy* 33, no. 2 (2002), 183; Alan Wertheimer, *Consent to Sexual Relations* (Cambridge: Cambridge University Press, 2003), 235–236; Thomas A. Mappes, "Sexual Morality and the Concept of Using Another Person," in *The Philosophy of Sex: Contemporary Readings*, eds. Alan Soble and Nicholas Power (New York: Rowman and Littlefield, 2008), 233–234; Downing-Matibag and Geisinger, "Sexual Risk," 1196, 1203; John Kleinig, "The Nature of Consent," in *The Ethics of Consent*, eds. Franklin G. Miller and Alan Wertheimer (New York: Oxford University Press, 2010), 13–14; Tom Dougherty, "Sex, Lies, and Consent," *Ethics* 123 (2013), 722.

4 Paul *et al.*, "Hookups," 83–85; Glenn and Marquardt, *Hanging Out,* 15–16; Lambert *et al.*, "Pluralistic Ignorance," 129; Joan McGregor, *Is it Rape? On Acquaintance Rape and Taking Women's Consent Seriously* (Burlington: Ashgate, 2005), 147; Bogle, *Hooking Up*, 30, 47, 63–64, 166–168; Gute and Eshbaugh, "Personality," 27–28, 35–36; Kimmel, *Guyland,* 199; Downing-Matibag and Geisinger, "Sexual Risk," 1196, 1203; Lisa Menegatos, Linda C. Lederman, and Aaron Hess, "Friends Don't Let Jane Hook Up Drunk: A Qualitative Analysis of Participation in a Simulation of College Drinking-Related Decisions," *Communication Education* 59, no. 3 (2010); Owen *et al.*, "Correlates," 658–659; Kalish and Kimmel, "Hot Hetero Sex or the New Numb Normative?," 143; Jesse Owen and Frank D. Fincham, "Young Adults' Emotional Reactions after Hooking Up Encounters," *Archives of Sexual Behavior* 40 (2011), 328; Jesse Owen, Frank D. Fincham, and Jon Moore, "Short-Term Prospective Study of Hooking Up Among College Students," *Archives of Sexual Behavior* 40 (2011), 337, 338–339; Julie A. Reid, Sinikka Elliott, and Gretchen R. Webber, "Casual Hookups to Formal Dates: Refining the Boundaries of the Sexual Double Standard," *Gender & Society* 25, no. 5 (2011), 556; Melina M. Bersamin *et al.*, "Young Adults and Casual Sex: The Relevance of College Drinking Settings," *Journal of Sex Research* 49, no. 2–3 (2012); Lewis *et al.*, "What is Hooking Up?," 764–765; Allyson L. Dir, Melissa A. Cyders, and Ayca Coskunpinar, "From the Bar to the Bed via Mobile Phone: A First Test of the Role of Problematic Alcohol Use, Sexting, and Impulsivity-Related Traits in Sexual Hookups," *Computers in Human Behavior* 29 (2013); Bachtel, "Do Hookups Hurt?," 42; Megan Manthos, Jesse Owen, and Frank D. Fincham, "A New Perspective on Hooking Up Among College Students: Sexual Behavior as a Function of Distinct Groups," *Journal of Social and Personal Relationships* 31, no. 6 (2014), 824–825; Olmstead *et al.*, "Hooking Up and Risk Behaviors," 188; Patricia N. E. Roberson,

Spencer B. Olmstead, and Frank D. Fincham, "Hooking Up During the College Years: Is There a Pattern?" *Culture, Health & Sexuality* 17, no. 5 (2015), 578, 586, 587; Tara E. Sutton and Leslie Gordon Simons, "Sexual Assault Among College Students: Family of Origin Hostility, Attachment, and the Hook-Up Culture as Risk Factors," *Journal of Child and Family Studies* 24, no. 10 (2015); Wade, *American Hookup*, 28–31, 43–45, 70–91.

5 Glenn and Marquardt, *Hanging Out*, 5, 13, 22; Bogle, *Hooking Up*, 28–29, 85–88; Lewis *et al.*, "What is Hooking Up?,"; Fortunato *et al.*, "Hook Up Experiences," 262–263; Owen *et al.*, "Correlates," 653; Kimmel, *Guyland*, 196; Armstrong *et al.*, "Women's Orgasm," 435; Rachel Kalish, "Masculinities and Hooking Up: Sexual Decision-Making at College," *Culture, Society & Masculinities* 5, no. 2 (2013), 147; Wade, *American Hookup*, 40; Allison B. Wolf, "A Hookup of Her Own," *International Journal of Applied Philosophy* 30, no. 2 (2017), 191.

6 Monica Moore, "Courtship Signaling and Adolescents: 'Girls Just Wanna Have Fun'?" *The Journal of Sex Research* 32, no. 4 (1995); Douglas N. Husak and George C. Thomas III, "Rapes without Rapists: Consent and Reasonable Mistakes," *Philosophical Issues: Social, Political, and Legal Philosophy* 11 (2001), 88, 93–94, 98; Lambert *et al.*, "Pluralistic Ignorance," 129; Bogle, *Hooking Up*, 33–39.

7 Alan H. Goldman, "Plain Sex," *Philosophy and Public Affairs* 6, no. 3 (1977); Wertheimer, *Consent to Sexual Relations*, see esp. 140; Alan Soble, *Sexual Investigations* (New York: New York University Press, 1996), 27–28, 33–43; David Archard, *Sexual Consent* (Boulder: Westview Press, 1998), see esp. 2; Mappes, "Sexual Morality," 229–249; Igor Primoratz, *Ethics and Sex* (London: Routledge, 1999); Igor Primoratz, "Sexual Morality: Is Consent Enough?" *Ethical Theory and Moral Practice* 4, no. 3 (2001): 201–218; Thomas, "Sexual Desire," 181–182.

8 For accounts that provide such a viewpoint, see: Primoratz, "Sexual Morality;" Anthony Ellis, "Casual Sex," *International Journal of Moral and Social Studies* 1, no. 2 (1986); Mappes, "Sexual Morality," 229–249; Raja Halwani, "Are One Night Stands Morally Problematic?," *International Journal of Applied Philosophy* 10, no. 1 (1995); Alan Soble, "Sexual Use," in *The Philosophy of Sex: Contemporary Readings*, eds. Alan Soble and Nicholas Power (New York: Rowman and Littlefield, 2008), 259–289; and David Benatar, "Two Views of Sexual Ethics: Promiscuity, Pedophilia, and Rape," in *The Philosophy of Sex: Contemporary Readings*, eds. Alan Soble and Nicholas Power (New York: Rowman and Littlefield, 2008), 325–336.

9 See footnote 5 above.

10 This ambiguity also comes up in the literature. For a few theorists who argue that a hook up can result in a relationship, see: Paul *et al.*, "Hookups," 81; Bogle, *Hooking Up*, 29; Wade, *American Hookup*, 46, 145–146, 235. More on this position below. For a contrary position, see Allison B. Wolf who says that a hook up implies that "nothing further should be expected" (Wolf, "Hookup of Her Own," 191).

11 Glenn and Marquardt, *Hanging Out*, 5, 13, 22; Bogle, *Hooking Up*, 28–29, 85–88; Kimmel, *Guyland*, 198; Wade, *American Hookup*, 40; Wolf, "A Hookup of Her Own," 191.

12 Lewis *et al.*, "What is Hooking Up?," 764–765.

13 Fortunato *et al.*, "Hook Up Experiences," 263; Wade, *American Hookup*, 215.

14 Paul *et al.*, "Hookups," 76; Bogle, *Hooking Up*, 30–31; Downing-Matibag and Geisinger, "Sexual Risk," 1200. For a contrary position, some studies indicate that hook up partners are more likely friends than they are either strangers or acquaintances. Yet, these studies do not seem to have anything that closely resembles a "near stranger" category. For example, Manning *et al.* suggest friends are more common hook up partners than strangers, but their data concerns participants younger than college, and their options were: friends, exes, or strangers (Manning *et al.*, "Relationship Contexts," 468–470). Fortunato *et al.* also concentrated on adolescents younger than college, and showed that, for that group, friends (48%) were more common partners than

acquaintances (23%) and strangers (6%) (Fortunato *et al.*, "Hook Up Experiences," 263). Since neither study looked at college students, and both studies lacked a near stranger category, these results do not undermine the other studies that suggest that near stranger is the most common category for college-aged hook up participants.

15 Paul *et al.*, "Hookups;" Glenn and Marquardt, *Hanging Out*; Bogle, *Hooking Up*; Downing-Matibag and Geisinger, "Sexual Risk," 1196; Monto and Carey, "A New Standard," 606; Owen *et al.*, "Correlates," 653; Kalish and Kimmel, "Hooking Up: Hot Hetero Sex or the New Numb Normative?," 137; Wade, *American Hookup*.

16 Paul *et al.*, "Hookups," 77, 83–85; Glenn and Marquardt, *Hanging Out*, 15–16; McGregor, *Is it Rape?*, 147–149; Bogle, *Hooking Up*, 30, 47, 63–64, 166–168; Kimmel, *Guyland*, 199; Bradshaw *et al.*, "To Hook Up or Date," 663; Kalish and Kimmel, "Hooking Up: Hot Hetero Sex or the New Numb Normative?," 143; Reid *et al.*, "Casual Hookups," 556; Olmstead *et al.*, "Hooking Up and Risk Behaviors," 1881; Roberson *et al.*, "Is There a Pattern?," 578.

17 Alan Wertheimer, "Consent and Sexual Relations," in *The Philosophy of Sex: Contemporary Readings*, eds. Alan Soble and Nicholas Power (New York: Rowman and Littlefield, 2008), 291; Heidi M. Hurd, "The Moral Magic of Consent," *Legal Theory* 2, no. 2 (1996), 121, 123–124, 137; Archard, *Sexual Consent*, 3, 5–6; John Kleinig, "The Nature of Consent," in *The Ethics of Consent*, eds. Franklin G. Miller and Alan Wertheimer (New York: Oxford University Press, 2010), 4; Tom Dougherty, "Sex, Lies, and Consent," *Ethics* 123 (2013), 722; Tom Dougherty, "Yes Means Yes: Consent as Communication," *Philosophy & Public Affairs* 43, no. 3 (2015), 226, 232–233.

18 For the most explicit usage of "consent" in this fashion, see Joel Feinberg, "Victims' Excuses: The Case of Fraudulently Procured Consent," *Ethics* 96, no. 2 (1986), 333–334.

19 See footnote 6 above.

20 Paul *et al.*, "Hookups," 77, 83–85; Glenn and Marquardt, *Hanging Out*, 15–16; Lambert *et al.*, "Pluralistic Ignorance," 129; McGregor, *Is it Rape?*, 147; Susan Gardner and Laura Choate, "The College Experience for Women: Progress and Paradox," in *Girls and Women's Wellness*, ed. Laura Choate (Alexandria: American Counseling Association, 2008), 126–127; Bogle, *Hooking Up*, 30, 47, 63–64, 166–168; Bradshaw *et al.*, "To Hook Up or Date," 663; Dir *et al.*, "From the Bar to the Bed;" Wade, *American Hookup*, 28–31.

21 Howard Klepper, "Sexual Exploitation and the Value of Persons," in *The Philosophy of Sex: Contemporary Readings*, eds. Alan Soble and Nicholas Power (New York: Rowman and Littlefield, 2008), 251–254.

22 Bogle, *Hooking Up*, 88–89, 96–127, see esp. 112–115; Glenn and Marquardt, *Hanging Out*, 16–17, 21–22; Paul, *et al.*, "'Hookups," 80–82; Ayres A. Boswell and Joan Z. Spade, "Fraternities and Collegiate Rape Culture: Why Are Some Fraternities More Dangerous Places for Women?" *Gender and Society* 10, no. 2 (1996), 134, 141; Eleanor Maticka-Tyndale, Edward S. Herold, and Martin Oppermann, "Casual Sex Among Australian Schoolies," *The Journal of Sex Research* 40, no. 2 (2003), 165; Wade, *American Hookup*, 34.

23 Glenn and Marquardt, *Hanging Out*, 13; Bogle, *Hooking Up*, 82–85, 161–162; Lambert *et al.*, "Pluralistic Ignorance;" Kalish, "Masculinities and Hooking Up;" Wade, *American Hookup*, 91–112.

24 Glenn and Marquardt, *Hanging Out*, 26–27, 28; Bogle, *Hooking Up*, 25, 69–71, 126; Manning *et al.*, "Relationship Contexts," 463; Wade, *American Hookup*, 56; Wolf, "A Hookup of Her Own," 195.

25 Mary Crawford and Danielle Popp, "Sexual Double Standards: A Review and Methodological Critique of Two Decades of Research," *The Journal of Sex Research* 40, no. 1 (2003); Bogle, *Hooking Up*, 96–127; Glenn and Marquardt, *Hanging Out*, 21–22; Boswell and Spade, "Collegiate Rape Culture," 141; Maticka-Tyndale *et al.*, "Sex Among Schoolies," 165; Michael W. Wiederman, "The Gendered Nature of Sexual Scripts," *The Family Journal: Counseling and Therapy for Couples and Families* 13, no. 4 (2005),

497–500; Manning *et al.*, "Relationship Contexts," 463, 475; Fortunato *et al.*, "Hook Up Experiences," 262–263; Kimmel, *Guyland*, 192, 197; John Draeger, "Can Girls Go Wild With Self-Respect?" in *College Sex: Philosophy for Everyone*, eds. Michael Bruce, Robert M. Stewart, and Fritz Allhoff (West Sussex: Wiley-Blackwell, 2010), 198–208; Reid *et al.*, "Casual Hookups,"; Owen *et al.*, "Hooking Up Among College Students," 338–339; Kalish, "Masculinities and Hooking Up," 154–155; Jenkins Hall and Tanner, "US Black College Women's Sexual Health," 1268; Heather H. Kettrey, "What's Gender Got to Do With It? Sexual Double Standards and Power in Heterosexual College Hookups," *The Journal of Sex Research* 53, no. 7 (2016); Wolf, "A Hookup of Her Own," 195–196. For a view that the double standard problem is becoming alleviated (based on the reported attitudes towards hooking up for both men and women), with women in particular holding more egalitarian and less gendered views, see Rachel Allison and Barbara J. Risman, "A Double Standard for 'Hooking Up': How Far Have We Come Toward Gender Equality?" *Social Science Research* 42 (2013), esp. 1201. Lisa Wade reinforces this view, at least in part, by noting that most students will not explicitly endorse this double standard about hooking up (Wade, *American Hookup*, 69). Yet, it could be that they will no longer openly endorse this view, but there is plenty of evidence, including in Wade's own findings (see 170–176, 212), that they largely act according to it.

26 Bogle, *Hooking Up*, 88–89, 96–127, see esp. 112–115; Glenn and Marquardt, *Hanging Out*, 16–17, 21–22; Paul *et al.*, "Hookups," 80–82; Boswell and Spade, "Collegiate Rape Culture," 134, 141; Maticka-Tyndale *et al.*, "Sex Among Schoolies," 165; Manning *et al.*, "Relationship Contexts," 463; Robyn L. Fielder *et al.*, "Sexual Hookups and Adverse Health Outcomes: A Longitudinal Study of First-Year College Women," *Journal of Sex Research* 51, no. 2 (2014), 139–140.

27 Crawford and Popp, "Sexual Double Standards," 24.

28 Bogle, *Hooking Up*, 105–108.

29 Ibid., 108. Insertions are hers.

30 Ibid., 107.

31 Bogle, *Hooking Up,* 96–127; Glenn and Marquardt, *Hanging Out,* 21–22; Crawford and Popp, "Sexual Double Standards," 22–25; Reid *et al.*, "Casual Hookups," 556.

32 Bogle, *Hooking Up,* 180.

33 Ibid., 109.

34 Ibid., 110.

35 Ibid., 111–112; Crawford and Popp, "Sexual Double Standards," 22–25.

36 Bogle, *Hooking Up,* 111.

37 Ibid., 111–112.

38 Boswell and Spade, "Collegiate Rape Culture," 139; Glenn and Marquardt, *Hanging Out,* 15–19; Bogle, *Hooking Up*, 29, 39, 42–43, 76, 179–180; Lambert *et al.*, "Pluralistic Ignorance," 130; Peter K. Jonason, Norman P. Lin, and Margaret J. Cason, "The 'Booty Call': A Compromise Between Men's and Women's Ideal Mating Strategies," *Journal of Sex Research* 46, no. 5 (2009), 460, 466; Owen and Fincham, "Young Adults," 322; Bradshaw *et al.*, "To Hook Up or Date," 663, 667; Kalish and Kimmel, "Hooking Up: Hot Hetero Sex or the New Numb Normative?," 144; Reid *et al.*, "Casual Hookups," 547; Bachtel, "Do Hookups Hurt?," 45; Fielder *et al.*, "Adverse Health Outcomes," 132; Wolf, "A Hookup of Her Own," 196. For a contrary position, see Wade, *American Hookup*, 144. Wade notes that 71% of men and 67% of women wished for "more opportunities to find a long-term partner."

39 Lambert *et al.*, "Pluralistic Ignorance," 130.

40 Ibid.

41 Paul *et al.*, "Hookups," 81. For more general information on hook ups leading to relationships, see Bogle, *Hooking Up*, 29; Wade, *American Hookup,* 46, 145–146, 235.

42 Glenn and Marquardt, *Hanging Out*, 4.

43 Laura Backstrom, Elizabeth A. Armstrong, and Jennifer Puentes, "Women's Negotiation of Cunnilingus in College Hookups and Relationships" *Journal of Sex Research* 49, no. 1 (2012); Wade, *American Hookup*, 157–179.
44 Wade, *American Hookup*, 158.
45 Ibid., 162. See also: Backstrom *et al.*, "Women's Negotiation of Cunnilingus."
46 Wade, *American Hookup*, 168.
47 Ibid., 169–170.
48 Hanna Rosin, "Boys on the Side," *The Atlantic* (September 2012), last accessed 1 August 2018 at: www.theatlantic.com/magazine/archive/2012/09/boys-on-the-side/309062/; Kate Taylor, "Sex on Campus: She Can Play That Game, Too," *New York Times* (July 12 2013), last accessed 1 August 2018 at: www.nytimes.com/2013/07/14/fashion/sex-on-campus-she-can-play-that-game-too.html; Nancy Bauer, *How to Do Things with Pornography* (Cambridge: Harvard University Press, 2015), 14–15, 44–46; Wade, *American Hookup*, 67.
49 Bauer, *How to Do Things with Pornography*, 45–46.
50 Onora O'Neill, "Between Consenting Adults," *Philosophy and Public Affairs* 14, no. 3 (1985), 254; Sally Haslanger, "On Being Objective and Being Objectified," in *A Mind of One's Own*, eds. Louise Anthony and Charlotte Witt (Boulder: Westview Press, 1993), 99; Lois Pineau, "Date Rape: A Feminist Analysis," in *Date Rape: Feminism, Philosophy, and the Law*, ed. Leslie Francis, 1–26 (University Park: The Pennsylvania State University Press, 1996), 6–9, 22.
51 Wertheimer, *Consent to Sexual Relations*, 152–155; Husak and Thomas III, "Without Rapists," 88, 93–94, 98.
52 Soble, "Sexual Use," 270.
53 Alan Wertheimer, "Intoxicated Consent to Sexual Relations," *Law and Philosophy* 20, no. 4 (2001), 378–379; Wertheimer, *Consent to Sexual Relations*, 236–238.
54 Goldman, "Plain Sex;" Archard, *Sexual Consent*, see esp. 2; Mappes, "Sexual Morality," 229–249; Soble, *Sexual Investigations*, 27–28, 33–43; Primoratz, *Ethics and Sex*; Primoratz, "Sexual Morality: Is Consent Enough?," 201–218; Thomas, "Sexual Desire," 181–182; Wertheimer, *Consent to Sexual Relations*, see esp. 140.
55 Nadine Strossen, "A Feminist Critique of 'The' Feminist Critique of Pornography," *Virginia Law Review* 79, no. 5 (1993), 1147–1151; Katie Roiphe, *The Morning After: Sex, Fear, and Feminism on Campus* (Boston: Little, Brown, and Company, 1993), 53–54, 62, 67–69, 163.
56 Here are a few different sources in favor of the singular "they." First, the American Dialect Society named the singular "they" the 2015 Word of the Year (American Dialect Society, "2015 Word of the Year is Singular 'They,'" (8 January 2016), last accessed 4 January 2019 at: www.americandialect.org/2015-word-of-the-year-is-singular-they; Katy Steinmetz, *Time* (9 January 2016), "This Pronoun Is the Word of the Year for 2015," last accessed 4 January 2019 at: http://time.com/4173992/word-of-the-year-2015-they/.). Second, the singular "they" was added to the Associated Press Stylebook in 2017 (Travis M. Andrews, *The Washington Post* (28 March 2017), "The Singular, Gender-Neutral 'They' Added to the Associated Press Stylebook," last accessed 4 January 2019 at: www.washingtonpost.com/news/morning-mix/wp/2017/03/28/the-singular-gender-neutral-they-added-to-the-associated-press-stylebook/?noredirect=on&utm_term=.59bbcca64a4d.) For scholarly discussions of the singular "they," see: Julie Foertsch and Morton Ann Gernsbacher, "In Search of Gender Neutrality: Is Singular 'They' a Cognitively Efficient Substitute for Generic 'He'?," *Psychological Science* 8, no. 2 (1997), 106–111; Mark Balhorn, "The Rise of Epicene They," *Journal of English Linguistics* 32, no. 2 (2004), 70–104; Darren K. LaScotte, "Singular They: An Empirical Study of Generic Pronoun Use," *American Speech* 91, no. 1 (2016), 62–80.
57 For instance, see: Brenda K. Todd *et al.*, "Sex Differences in Children's Toy Preferences: A Systematic Review, Meta-Regression, and Meta-Analysis," *Infant and Child Development* 27, no. 2 (2018).

2

CONSENT

As consent is an essential part of the moral assessment of hooking up, we shall begin with a conceptual analysis of consent in this chapter prior to looking at the requirements for hook up consent in the following three chapters. Thus, this chapter mostly involves an analysis of consent independent from the specific issues that surround contemporary hook ups.

What distinguishes consent as a unique type of agreement is that consent transforms the moral standing between two people.[1] Consent is an agreement made between two or more people where the fact that the agreement has been made creates new moral relations between the parties. When an agent gives consent, she thereby creates for another agent at least a moral permission (and at most a right) to behave (or not behave) in a certain way, and she creates for herself a moral obligation to be bound by that newly created moral permission (or possibly right). Consent, in effect, creates moral permissions (or rights) and obligations between agents who have freely chosen to take on these new moral relations with respect to each other. To understand what consent is and how it works, we must remember that consent essentially has this power to create new moral obligations.

As noted in Chapter One, my usage of "consent" in this fashion is not without controversy. For instance, some theorists, such as Joel Feinberg, use "consent" to mean that the person merely agrees, and presumably there would be no moral transformation unless the consent is also valid.[2] However, much of the literature uses "consent" to mean the substantial kind of agreement where there is such a moral transformation, such that "valid consent" would be used just for emphasis, rather than for picking out a different type of agreement.[3] For the most part, this distinction is largely semantic: different theorists are using the word in different but related fashions. There are, however, two questions that can determine which usage we ought to adopt: which one better captures ordinary usage and which one makes more sense from a moral and/or legal perspective.

Debating ordinary usage often comes down to differences in intuition, though there are some notable points on both sides. It is my view that ordinary usage makes "valid consent" a form of emphasis, but it doesn't always seem to be used merely as emphasis. We do sometimes say things like, "Was his consent informed?" or "When she consented, was she free to say no?" On the one hand, I think these may just be casual ways of making a more complex point: sometimes what appears to be consent turns out later not to be.

Importantly, much of ordinary usage supports the view that consent is always morally significant. First, notice how rarely we say "valid consent" even when we clearly mean it. Doctors, lawyers, business people, social scientists running experiments, the police, etc. can all simply ask: "Do you consent?" Even in very serious contexts, people rarely see the need to include "validly" or "meaningfully" in that essential question. Second, failure cases are rarely referred to as if they were ultimately consensual. I do not think it sounds right to say, "Lisa consented to sell her car even though she didn't realize what she was doing when she signed a blank piece of paper that we later printed a contract on." Nor do I think it makes sense to say, "The school's rules say you must obtain consent for sex, but it doesn't say it must be valid consent – so forcing someone to consent will be fine." When the conditions for consent are not met, we tend to not use the word. Using "consent" in these cases where the requirements for consent fail sounds completely foreign, and I believe we would think someone did not know what the word meant if they used it in those sorts of failure cases. While I think it is harder to explain away these latter counter-examples, I do not want to hang my case entirely on ordinary usage.

More importantly, I believe there are practical considerations, related to morality and the law, which are signaled by the last two examples of failure cases. Suppose we thought, as Feinberg and others seem to, that consent has no standards, but valid consent has standards such as that it be free, informed, and competent. It would follow that people could receive consent, in this sense, without having any moral permission to act. That provides for a confusing set of circumstances that could actually be dangerous in situations where consent is important. One person could ask if another person "consents to sex," and the other person could honestly say, "Yes, I consent," but have in mind that they are not giving *valid* consent. Should we say the first person acts wrongly even though they obtained explicit consent? It does not seem to be a moral violation given that they asked and they received an unwavering, affirmative response. Further, we would have to say of completely empty agreements that they still count as consent: a person consents, in this sense, while half-asleep because they mouth "yes" without knowing what is going on. Even if we granted, for the sake of argument, that ordinary usage followed the Feinberg usage, there would still be some people who think of consent as conveying permission, and that would leave room for this kind of dangerous confusion. It is much cleaner – and even safer – to use "consent" to mean that you have obtained a moral permission. We can use "mere agreement" to convey an agreement that lacks that moral permission. Finally, we can use "valid consent" or "meaningful consent" just for emphasis (though these modifiers would be technically redundant since valid and meaningful consent is just consent). That is the usage that I will follow: "consent" entails a moral transformation that must meet standards, such as being free, informed, and competent.

Given this substantial sense of consent, it will be necessary to ask what kind of entity consent is. I will thus begin with a brief discussion of the ontology of consent. I will argue that consent is a mental entity whose full realization requires an external performance that conveys the agreement to another person. Once we have the ontology, we will be able to distinguish different kinds of consent based on how they apply temporally: consent that is cemented in advance and consent that is contemporaneous with the performance of the action. We will then be able to turn to normative distinctions based on consent's strength. Since consent transforms the moral parameters between agents, we should be able to distinguish instances of consent based on how much moral transformation they create. I will finish this chapter with a discussion of the requirements necessary for consent.

Consent Ontology

When we ask about the ontology of consent, we are seeking to figure out what type of thing consent is. There are three standard options for the ontological status of consent. We could think of consent as something mental (a mental state), such as the decision to uphold one's end of the agreement or the intention to do so. We can call this, "the mental state conception."[4] Another conception holds that consent is an external performance: consent consists in behavioral cues that an agreement has been cemented, such as a signature, shaking hands, or a verbal agreement. We can refer to this as, "the performative conception."[5] Finally, under the "hybrid conception," we could argue that consent is a hybrid of those two views, and consists of both the mental state and the performance.[6] This question is not purely academic since we want to know what consent would have to be so that it can create new moral obligations. Fortunately, the moral transformation that constitutes consent will establish that only the hybrid conception can fully explain the ontology of consent. For consent to create moral obligations, it must have both mental and performative aspects.

The mental aspect is necessary because one cannot imagine a case where an agent created moral obligations for herself through consent without a mindset that included an intention to take on the new obligations. Try to imagine a performance of consent that lacks such a mindset. Suppose, to make the performance seem as consensual as possible, Biff utters the words, "I consent to walk your dog." If Biff's mindset is attuned to a different state of affairs (he thinks he is in a movie, with hidden cameras, where this is his line), then no moral transformation has taken place – he is not obligated to walk the dog. Such a performance may lead the listener, Abby, to form a reasonable belief that consent has been given – Abby reasonably believes that Biff is obligated to walk her dog. But it certainly isn't the case that Biff consented. The mere performance has simply led to confusion, but it is not sufficient to generate consent.

It may be that Biff's performance, even if it doesn't count as consent, is sufficient to provide Abby with a legal permission to act, and often consent theorists are primarily interested in the law. Because it is reasonable for Abby to assume that Biff actually consented (why would she infer that he is in a movie when there are no cameras?), it may be legal for her to act as if he did.

In this book, we are interested primarily in moral permission. Yet, it still makes sense to think that Abby is morally allowed to act on Biff's consent even though he did not mean to consent, just as it makes sense to think she would be legally permitted. Abby does nothing wrong since her incorrect belief that Biff consented is perfectly reasonable. Her reasonable belief permits her to act as if she has his consent, but it still does not seem that Biff is morally obligated since he did not mean to consent. We may have a case of moral permission without moral obligation: Abby is not wrong to expect Biff to walk the dog, even though Biff is not obligated to walk the dog. This situation could be morally possible since Abby's moral permission merely implies that she has not wronged Biff by expecting him to walk the dog. She still doesn't have a moral right to have Biff walk her dog. Abby has a permission to drop off the dog, and Biff has a permission to refuse the task. There is no moral obligation because Biff could not purposely create such an obligation for himself without any intention to do so. Consent is a purposeful creation of new obligations for oneself, and Biff did not intend to create an obligation when he thought he was in a hidden-camera movie. At least a portion of consent must consist in a mental state since the performance can at best create permissions, but it cannot create the obligation that occurs in consent's moral transformation.

The mental requirement is not sufficient for consent since an intention is not yet an agreement. Imagine Biff intends to agree to walk Abby's dog while she is away, but forgets to tell Abby that he will do so. Once Abby leaves, the question is whether Biff is morally obligated to walk her dog. There may be an intuition that he is since Biff has already made the intention to walk the dog, and intentions imply commitments: you cannot really intend to do something if you aren't going to do it when the opportunity arises (assuming you retain the intention). What it means to intend to perform some action is that you will do what's in your power to perform that action. By intending to walk Abby's dog, Biff has committed himself to do so, even if Abby doesn't know that he has.

While it is true that Biff is committed, his commitment is practical, not moral. Biff will walk the dog provided that he is able to and continues to retain the intention – that is just how intention works. The practical commitment just falls out of having an intention. In one sense, this commitment is stronger than a moral one since the agent cannot intend to walk the dog and fail to try to walk the dog at the same time. Yet, in another sense, this commitment is weaker because of the relatively low escape cost: if Biff changes his intention, he is no longer practically committed at all. A moral commitment applies regardless of whether the agent changes his mind. In this case, where Biff never told Abby, if Biff changes his mind, he has done nothing wrong.

The intention, then, is not sufficient to create consent's moral transformation. Nor would an intention alone provide the correct ontological structure since an intention is not an agreement. While the intention is the first step, agreements can only be cemented by performances, whether verbal or behavioral, that convey the intention to agree. A performance is necessary for any agreement, and therefore necessary for consent.

The hybrid view best explains consent's ontology. The mental state is necessary for the purposeful moral transformation. The mental state does not suffice since consent is a type of agreement, which implies that an external interaction with others is necessary. Hence, combining both aspects in a hybrid account obtains the correct ontological status.

We could continue with ontological questions by asking what specific kinds of mental states and performances consent consists in. Unfortunately, this search is unlikely to be very fruitful. First, quite a large variety of performances could occasion consent. There is a plethora of both verbal tokens (ranging from "Okay" to "Yes, I consent") and non-verbal ones (ranging from a lack of dissent to clear non-verbal cues, such as a nod or thumbs up). As there are so many real-life instances of consent established through these various tokens, it is not worthwhile to shift through them to seek a definitive or exhaustive list.

When it comes to the mental aspect, we can probably find more guidance, but we should avoid being too precise.[7] Consent at least includes the intention to agree and an understanding that a moral obligation is being accepted. The intention to agree is necessary since it would not count as consent if the agent did not intend to agree. The agent also has to understand that she is taking on a new moral obligation because without that understanding, she cannot purposely create a moral obligation for herself. That of course doesn't imply that all moral obligations must come from purposeful actions. Consent in particular cannot happen accidentally: it involves an agent doing something with the understanding that in doing it she is creating a new moral obligation for herself. The point is that if I'm going to purposely create a moral obligation, I must both intend to do so and understand what I'm doing.

Since the ontological status should leave available any possibly correct uses, we should not settle ontology beyond the fact that the hybrid position is correct. Consent involves both mental and performative aspects, and the mental aspect involves at least an intention (to agree) and an understanding (that moral obligations are being created).

Temporality of Consent

As another foundational issue for consent, theorist Leo Katz points out that we need to distinguish advance from contemporaneous consent.[8] Advance consent implies an agreement to perform a certain action at a later moment in time: the consent is given first, but is binding later on. Contemporaneous consent implies an agreement to continue an action while that action is ongoing. With contemporaneous consent, the consent is binding not prior to the activity, but only while the activity is occurring. Thus, contemporaneous consent is usually required for activities that involve ongoing interaction that could, at each step, endanger the moral permissibility of the next step.

Consider the consent of boxers. At any given moment in the boxing match, a boxer might get hit so hard that her consent cannot be thought of as allowing for any additional punches. For example, if she has been knocked out, is clearly injured, or has thrown in the towel, then her previous consent to fight no longer makes future punching permissible. Withdrawing contemporaneous consent ends the consent without any moral failure since there is no obligation to continue the event. If a boxer consents at time 1 (t1) to fight all the way until time 12 (t12), she is in fact consenting insofar as the activity continues. If at t6 she refuses to continue, she has not failed any obligations for t7 through t12 since her consent at t1 no longer applies.

Advance consent is different. An instance of advance consent involves an agent saying at t1 that they agree to perform an action at t2. The agent then becomes morally obligated to perform the action at t2. If between t1 and t2, the agent changes their mind and fails to act as agreed at t2, then they have committed a moral infraction since they have failed their moral obligation that they intentionally created through their consent. Thus, revoking advanced consent entails failing the moral obligation that the consent created.

It remains to be settled which agreements count as advance consent and which ones count as contemporaneous consent. Surgery looks like boxing (the harms that require consent are ongoing throughout the activity), but no one thinks that surgeons should have to continually check with their patients to make sure they want to continue. Therefore, surgery must occur with advance consent: the patient must agree to see it through and waive any right to stop in the middle of the activity. On the other hand, sex appears to involve contemporaneous consent since something could happen in the middle that could create a legitimate reason to change one's mind. Hence, this temporality distinction will be important for discussing hook up consent.

Normative Consent Division

Having described the ontology and temporality of consent, the next task is to examine the normativity of consent. In looking at consent's normativity, we are discussing how strong the moral obligations are that consent creates. Although levels of normative strength are mostly overlooked in the consent literature, it can be quite useful to draw these distinctions. Consent provides a transfer of normativity so that one person's action becomes permitted and another's obligated. There is no reason to assume that different instances of consent transfer the same amount of normativity; the obligations created by consent could differ in normative strength.

There are two, largely related, dimensions across which we can measure consent's normative strength. The first concerns the amount of normativity that the consent transfers. When A consents to give a permission to B, how much does B gain from A's consent? Let's call this the "transfer level of normative strength." The second concerns how much recognition is mandated by the consent. When two people consent, how many third parties must respect the claims that result from their consent? Is it just the two people or could it be more? Let's call this the "recognition level of normative strength."

Transferring Claims

When A consents to B, A transfers over moral permissions of some kind to B (and usually vice versa, but it will be simpler to concentrate on one direction). The transfer level of normative strength measures how much is handed over in this transfer. We can use the work of Leo Katz to observe that not all cases of consent fully transfer in this sense, which shows that there are distinct transfer levels.

Katz argues that there are secondary rights that do not always transfer in instances of consent.[9] Secondary rights are rights that are not directly agreed to, but that seem to be implied by the agreement. Let's begin with a simple example: if I consent to lend you my car, I cannot claim that you have no permission to use my car keys. Even though we never discussed the car keys, my consent to lend you my car implied a secondary right to my car keys.

Katz's list of secondary rights begins with necessity and duress rights. Necessity and duress rights refer to things a person has to do in order to fulfill the consent, even if those things are seemingly immoral and illegal.[10] In other words, if you have given me consent to drive your car to Vegas and your consent fully transfers necessity and duress rights, then I have the right to do whatever it takes to drive to Vegas, even if it is immoral and illegal. As we can see from this quick example, these rights are complicated. To transfer them, you must first have them. Usually, when you lend out your car, you do not have the right to do whatever it takes to drive somewhere (you would only have these secondary rights in some kind of extreme emergency situation). Your consent cannot transfer necessity and duress rights that you did not originally have. The question is whether your consent always transfers such rights when you have them.

Second, Katz argues that self-help rights give the person the right to help herself to the necessary means to fight off an attack against her rightful action.[11] If you lend me your car and it is your right to defend your car against carjackers, then a transfer of self-help rights would allow me to defend your car against carjackers as well. Or, to be more picturesque, suppose you are in an action-movie like scenario and you have the right to fight off anyone who tries to prevent you from making a delivery of some world-saving item to Vegas. You then consent to let me make the delivery for you. I then would obtain the same self-help rights to fight off anyone who tries to stop me from saving the world.

Finally, Katz argues that due care rights give the right to insist that others take due care with respect to your interests.[12] In this case, driving that world-saving item to Vegas is important enough that you could ask everyone to stay off the freeway until you have made your delivery. If you consent to let me make the delivery, then I would similarly be able to ask everyone to stay off the road until I succeed in my task.

As we can see in these quick examples, it is probably rare that we have these secondary rights in the first place. Yet, we can learn more by using Katz's own strategy[13] to show a case where there are secondary rights, but they are not transferred in consent. This strategy, if successful, shows that there are different levels of normative strength based on what consent transfers.

Juanita and Margaret have just been in a car accident. Long ago, Margaret saved Juanita's life, at which point Juanita agreed to perform one huge favor for Margaret. The car accident leaves Margaret fine, but Juanita's (non-driving) leg is badly mangled. In spite of Juanita's painful situation, Margaret chooses this moment to call in her favor. They were driving to a World Series poker tournament, which Margaret had always dreamed of winning, and she's already paid the $10,000 buy-in. Margaret knows that the casino is slightly out of the way for going to the hospital, but it is plausible that Juanita could get Margaret to the casino and still make it to the hospital in time for treatment. If they go to the hospital first, Margaret will be considerably late for her tournament, which will lead to a large deduction of her chips, making her dream of winning the World Series much more improbable. So, Margaret calls in her favor – this is the World Series, and poker is her life. Juanita understands the importance of poker to Margaret, and she wants to do her friend this huge favor, so she is happy to consent to driving to the casino first.

Now, it seems clear that Juanita has a certain number of secondary rights that derive from her strong need for medical treatment. For example, she can, on the way to the hospital, drive a bit more carelessly and above the speed limit due to her necessity and duress rights.[14] We can be warranted to break the law when necessary to avoid severe harm to ourselves. Similarly, based on her due care rights, she will be able to shift the burden of safe driving onto others since they can be expected to take due care to protect Juanita's strong medical need.[15]

Juanita's rights allow her to take illegal action and shift risk onto others for the sake of getting to the hospital, but it is not clear that Juanita can transfer these rights to Margaret through her consent. Technically, she is still on her way to the hospital – she is just stopping at the casino first. But surely Margaret cannot use Juanita's secondary rights to endanger others to get to a poker game (even if it is a very important one). As Katz argues, the point of these secondary rights is that we can justify putting bystanders at risk as long as the potential damage to ourselves is severe and probable.[16] Juanita has that probable, severe potential for damage to herself due to her mangled leg. It would be justified for Juanita to ask bystanders to take some of her risk away, but those bystanders have no reason to subsume risk for the sake of Margaret making her poker tournament. Juanita cannot use her consent to transfer her secondary rights onto Margaret's less severe problem.

Notice though that this case would be quite different if Juanita asked Margaret to drive her to the hospital, and Margaret consented to do that. In this case, we would have Juanita's secondary rights clearly transferring to Margaret: by acting on Juanita's behalf, Margaret gets the necessity and duress rights to break the law, and she gets the due care rights to shift the burden of risk onto bystanders. In this case, all of Juanita's rights transfer to Margaret, and we can consider their consent to fully transfer. Thus, we can see from the big difference between these two cases that there is a normative distinction within consent between full transfer instances and instances that only partially transfer the relevant claims.

We can then distinguish the normative strength between consent that fully transfers (and all secondary rights pass to the other party to the consent) and consent that only partially transfers. The level of normativity tracks how many implied claims transfer from one party to the other consenting party. Returning to a simpler example, if I consent to lend you my car, then we can judge the transfer strength of our consent by how many of my claims transfer to you. Under certain, extreme conditions, all my claims transfer to you: whatever I can do with my car and whatever rights I have with respect to my car would all become yours. Under more standard conditions, when I loan you my car, certain claims transfer and others do not. While you are welcome to use the keys, the gas, the radio, and probably the trunk (even if we did not make any of these components explicitly part of the deal), you cannot choose to paint the car or change the radio presets (even if these actions were not explicitly prohibited). Consequently, we can distinguish transfer levels of consent through the amount of implied claims that transfer from one consenting party to the other.

Recognizing Others' Consent

Consent is an agreement between certain parties, which means there are third parties that are not part of the consent. We can ask whether third parties ought to respect others' consent. Perhaps the intuitive answer is: well, of course, everyone should respect others' consensual agreements. The first point to note against this intuitive answer is that it, at the very least, requires further justification. Consent, by definition, is a way to create new moral obligations between the consenting parties. There is nothing inherent within consent that entails that third parties must respect the agreement – it is clearly the consenting parties who are morally obligated to respect it. More importantly for current purposes, we will see that cases will differ in terms of how much third parties ought to respect other people's consensual agreements. Thus, we will be able to distinguish the normative strength of consent along this second measure: the stronger consent is, the more third parties are obligated to recognize and respect it. We can refer to this as the recognition level of consent.

To make this recognition measure of normative strength clear it is important to distinguish it from the transfer measure. On the transfer measure of consent's normative strength, one of the secondary rights in question is due care rights. When due care rights are transferred, third parties are morally required to take due care for the second party to the consent just as they would for the first party. In other words, if I have due care rights to ask others to pave the way for my emergency delivery and I transfer those due care rights to you through consent, then third parties are morally obligated to pave the way for you. Yet, this transfer is of existing due care rights that already belonged to me. Third parties are not being obligated to provide due care *because of the consent.* Third parties instead were already obligated to provide due care. Therefore, for this measure of normative strength, we want to concentrate on whether third parties ought to respect the consent itself (as opposed to respecting my original due care rights that happened to transfer through consent).

We can imagine cases where the consent of other people gives third parties reasons to recognize and respect the consent, and cases where it does not. Since our intuitions probably lean towards the former type of cases, let's try to develop a simple case of the latter type. Suppose that on Friday, Carter consents to sell his car to Dominique on Tuesday. Eliza is aware of this deal, but she is willing to offer more money for the car on Monday. Were Carter to take Eliza's deal on Monday, he would be morally wronging Dominique. But would Eliza be wronging Dominique? In this case, the moral obligations in question (Carter's obligation to provide the car and Dominique's obligation to pay the money) are only created by consent. Since Eliza made no consent, it does not seem that she is made morally obligated through *their* consent. Eliza is simply acting out of her best self-interest to try to interrupt their deal so she can buy the car.

Perhaps someone might think there is a general requirement that we all morally ought to respect the consent of others at all times. Yet, sometimes the consent of two people could harm third parties. It would be strange for third parties to have to accept harms just because of the agreements of others, especially where they have no say in that agreement. If Carter's and Dominique's car deal would significantly harm Eliza and Eliza had no say in the making of the deal, then it is not clear why Eliza should not be permitted to try to stop the deal.

An unwavering, general requirement would require one of two options, neither of which is plausible. The first is that no agreement counts as consensual if it could harm third parties. This idea would make consent nearly impossible: almost every consensual agreement could harm third parties in unexpected or even sometimes in intentional ways. When Carter and Dominique make their car deal, they are preventing everyone else in the world from buying Carter's car from him. To use another example, consider when a landowner sells land to a corporation that plans to build a factory that will pollute the land of its neighbors. The deal harms third parties, who have the right to petition the landowner or even the government to try to prevent the deal. Of course, there are always possible harms to third parties in any deal, even if we sometimes have difficulty spotting them. So unless we are to rule out consent as unrealistic, this option is not plausible.

The other option for the general requirement is to simply demand that third parties always respect consent, even when they are harmed by it. Perhaps strict libertarians would adopt such a view. Libertarians, whom we will discuss more later on, believe that morality can be reduced to the importance of self-ownership (we all own ourselves), liberty (we are free to do what we want with ourselves and anything else we own), and consent (we extend our liberty by consenting with others). Since consent is so foundational for libertarians, we can imagine that strict libertarians might accept the view that the consent of others ought to always be respected.

I'm skeptical of this strong view. To start, it seems like when a third party realizes they are going to be harmed, then it is reasonable for them to try to interrupt the deal. Further, if they are going to be seriously harmed by a deal that they had no say in, then it would be reasonable for them to ask for others to assist them in stopping the deal. Families whose children will become seriously ill due to the pollution have the right to turn to friends, family, the media, and even the government to try to interfere with the deal that could significantly harm or even kill their children. And, if they have the right to try, then they also have the right to succeed: a right to try does not make sense if the attempt could not rightfully come to fruition.

It does not seem like there should be a general requirement that all consent should be respected. We might think there should be a *prima facie* requirement that all consent should be respected. A *prima facie* requirement would imply that we ought to assume the requirement is in place until something shows up to overrule it. So, there could be a *prima facie* requirement to respect consent, unless, let's say as an example, we discover that third parties will be harmed and have a right not to be harmed. I will neither argue for nor against such a *prima facie* requirement. It is sufficient for current purposes that the *prima facie* requirement implies that consent comes in degrees depending on other factors, such as how much third parties have the right to object. If there is a *prima facie* requirement, then third parties may have a right to object and may not. If there is no such *prima facie* requirement, it is because there are likely degrees at which third parties can object. Hence, there likely are recognition levels for consent either way.

To further indicate that there are recognition levels of normativity for consent, let's look at two different types of cases. Generally speaking, it would seem in cases of advance business consent, third parties have less obligation, if any, to recognize the consent. That is partially because they might be harmed by some other party's business deal. There is another reason. If we return to our case of Carter selling his car to Dominique, I believe it is intuitive that Eliza does nothing wrong in trying to interfere before the sale happens (though Carter does wrong by changing his mind). Part of the basis for this intuition is that business deals are meant to be competitive until they are completed. When two business people make a deal that is not yet completed, it is commonly accepted that other business people can attempt to better the deal until the contract is officially signed. Yet, the consent occurs when they agree they will sign the contract. So, we think business deals are consensual agreements where third parties can try to talk the parties out of their consent, at least until the consent is in writing.

Notice that sexual consent is different. When two people consent to have sex, their consent is contemporaneous and so either acts within their rights to withdraw consent. Yet, it would normally be heavily improper for any third party to try to interrupt the deal. We can imagine some rare exceptions: a spouse who attempts to prevent their spouse's adultery may qualify.[17] However, in most cases, the very attempt to interfere with other people's sexual consent is almost certainly immoral. Obviously it would be immoral to physically interfere with people about to have consensual sex. Yet, even a verbal attempt to talk them out of it would be clearly improper and would also be a significant interference with their privacy. Sexual consent usually puts third parties morally out of bounds. And so sexual consent is the type of consent that third parties seem to be required to recognize.

One might wonder about a case where the sexual exchange was itself a business transaction: what if one John wants to offer a better deal to a prostitute who is already engaged with another John? Such a case draws on competing intuitions since it is a business deal (and so third parties can interfere) and a sexual interaction (and so third parties cannot interfere).[18] My intuition is that, in such a case, the sexual issues are more significant and trump the business ones. The reason business deals allow for third party interference is that business is a system made up of free competition where all parties act out their own self-interests. Sex, however, involves a world that is typically very private, and once a sexual exchange is initiated, that right to privacy trumps the value of competition. Importantly, the general idea that we can make interests compete by drawing out complicated cases further establishes that consent normativity is complex and comes with layers of difference.

Thus, we can see that there are reasons to distinguish consent along different lines of normative strength. We first saw that there is a measure of how much transfers in a consensual transaction. We now can see that there is also a measure of how much third parties become morally obligated to recognize the consent. Some of what goes into issues of normative strength are clearly the other moral issues surrounding the consent. Another part, though, is how high the requirements are for a given agreement to count as consent. Accordingly, we will finish this chapter by looking at the standard requirements for consent.

Consent Requirements

While there are some contentious requirements for consent, three requirements are fairly non-contentious. Most theorists in the consent literature agree that consent must be freely formed, adequately informed, and made by competent persons. Each of these standard conditions will be relevant to determining whether hook up culture is conducive for consent. It will be useful here to discuss each one before turning to our larger discussions of them within hook up culture in the following three chapters.

Free Consent

That an agreement must be free to be consensual should be clear: a person who is forced to agree cannot be said to be purposely taking on new moral obligations.[19] "Unfree consent" is a contradiction.[20] The freedom requirement can be laid out in a negative fashion: an agreement is freely made provided that it is neither forced, coerced, involves brainwashing, nor otherwise manipulated against the person's will. No one would think an agreement could be consensual if it is forced – meaning someone literally made the person agree, say by raising her hand at an auction against her will. Such an agreement would fail the mental requirement, and thus could not qualify as consent under the hybrid conception. Nor is there any way a completely brainwashed agreement could be consensual: a choice brought on by brainwashing also lacks the intention to consent, and so cannot count as an agent purposely taking on new moral obligations for themselves.

Coercion is a bit trickier. Coercion involves the use of a threat to make someone choose in a way that serves the coercer's ends.[21] There are certainly instances of coercion, such as ones that threaten extreme physical violence, that we can all agree undermine consent, whereas lesser instances of coercion may be consistent with consent. This determination largely depends on the severity of the threat, the wrongness of the coerced action, and the possibility that the coerced action would be independently chosen without coercion. When your life is threatened, you can agree to almost anything without being held responsible. If the agent cannot be held responsible, then no obligation has been created, and, therefore, consent was not realized. However, even when the threat is as severe as death, we think there is room for some doubt that you are blameless if what you are asked to do is to kill or torture others. Such a case would at least be contentious.

We could build a coerced case of consent by making the threat sufficiently weak compared to what was asked of you. Suppose someone threatened to step on an ant unless you gave them a ride to the airport on Tuesday. If you don't have a pathological fear of untimely ant deaths, then your agreement provides sufficient evidence that you would independently agree were you not coerced. Your agreement exhibits your intention to create for yourself an obligation to take the person to the airport more than it exhibits a fearful submission. You have consented while someone is coercing you.

While coercion usually undermines consent, it could turn out that the hook up culture is filled with borderline cases where coercion and consent might be considered to be consistent. Many societies seem to be more likely to count non-violent coerced agreements as consensual when sex is involved – problematically, rape laws in the US tend to allow a significant amount of non-violent coercion to be consistent with so-called "consensual sex."[22] I will not, however, take for granted that either social customs or the law track what's morally permissible when it comes to borderline coercive hook up consent. Instead, we will examine these sorts of cases at length in the next chapter on aggressive hook ups. For now, it is sufficient to note that the freedom requirement can be tricky when it comes to coercion, and this issue may be a common hurdle for hook up consent.

Informed Consent

The second standard condition is that consent must be adequately informed.[23] It is fairly uncontroversial that for an agreement to count as consensual, it must be adequately informed over the content of the agreement and what it will likely entail. If a person lacks information, either because it is being withheld or someone is being deceitful, then the agent lacks the information necessary to purposely take on a new moral obligation. "Informed consent" is redundant insofar as the information is necessary for the moral transformation, and thus the consent, to be possible.[24] You can't obligate yourself if you don't really know what you are obligating yourself to do.

The question is how much information is required. Although we sometimes talk as if consent should be "fully informed," that is impossible. There are numerous insignificant details that cannot be covered before two individuals come to an agreement. Let's return to Abby asking Biff to walk her dog. If Abby's dog bites, then Biff clearly needs that information prior to consenting. There are many other details that would be overwhelming and unnecessary. Abby doesn't need to give Biff a detailed history of all previous walks so that Biff could calculate the percentage chance that minor issues could come up based on past experience (such as a 4.2% chance that Peppy will find a bunny and chase it for a few seconds). Full information cannot be required because it may be undesired, unnecessary, and even impossible.[25]

Philosophers Neil Manson and Onora O'Neill argue that we ought to seek *adequately* informed consent, which is determined by the purposes at hand.[26] Even this lower standard can be difficult to meet since passing the right information is much more complex than it seems. Consent has propositional content. That means that both the initial proposal and the response of whether to agree each take propositional form: we exchange sentences that are meant to convey our mental ideas of what we are agreeing to.[27] This transition from mental content to expressed words, and then back again, allows for a good amount of room for error. Manson and O'Neill refer to consent as being "referentially opaque" in that we cannot see into the other person's mental states, but must make inferences based on what is said and how we understand the words being used.[28] Words have multiple meanings and different individuals use and interpret phrases in different ways. Perhaps most importantly, sentences used in a consensual exchange will allow for a plethora of inferences, with different individuals inferring different things from the same sentences. It is almost never a simple fact to say what exactly is consented to, and we cannot assume both individuals have the same understanding of what they've agreed upon.[29]

Even something as simple as a dog walk could cause confusion. Abby may assume that everyone knows that a proper dog walk involves giving the dog a chance to explore, taking the dog to new places, and staying out for at least an hour. Biff may think of a dog walk as going around the block once and being back home in 10–15 minutes tops. Which type of walk has Biff consented to? Without a full appreciation of the differences between their mutually exclusive understandings, it is unclear what their consent consists of. Thus, it is both necessary to gain this information for the consent to be adequately informed, and it is unlikely that the information would be discussed, given both agents' entrenched assumptions over what a proper dog walk looks like.

Though the adequately informed requirement can be difficult to meet, it is not quite impossible since we usually obtain consent in situations where either not much is at stake, we know the persons we are dealing with, and/or there are sufficiently strong social or legal rules to protect against serious misunderstandings. If things are not very serious, and misunderstandings would not cause grievous harm, then the requirement can be relaxed. If we know each other very well, then we can more easily line up our inferences. Finally, we may find ourselves in heavily regulated practices where information conditions are largely maintained externally, such as in medical or legal settings. Some scholars, such as Douglas Husak and George Thomas, think that we have social rules for sexual agreements that are sufficiently well established to ensure that sexual consent is usually adequately informed,[30] but I will argue that things are not quite that simple when we discuss the information conditions for hooking up in Chapter Four.

Competent Consent

The third and final standard condition for consent is that the agents must be competent.[31] If a person is not competent to take on moral obligations either because of some general deficiency or a situational problem, then, by definition, they cannot be competent to consent. That there are competence conditions for consent is trivial insofar as there are competence conditions for taking on moral obligations.

We should not assume from the beginning that competence always requires adulthood.[32] Teenagers and even young children can make some consensual agreements. A child who agrees to wash the dishes instead of doing lawn work becomes morally obligated to wash the dishes, and so is old enough to give consent. Some situations may be so grave that children cannot give consent, but they can consent to mundane matters at quite early ages. The same point would also apply for most mental illnesses and disabilities.[33] In instances where the person is competent enough to have moral obligations and to engage in agreements, she is likely competent enough to consent.

On the other hand, any individual could be put in a situation where she is no longer sufficiently competent to consent. The clearest examples would involve substances that remove the ability to be rational. Any drugs that make people unable to reason and deliberate well would render those agents unable to purposely take on new moral obligations, and thus unable to consent.[34] Since we are often under the influence of substances that affect us in various ways, such as caffeine or energy drinks, being on a substance that affects mental thinking is not enough to prevent the ability to consent.[35] What matters, as with all of these conditions, is whether the agent is in a position to purposely accept a new moral obligation. If her rationality is too impaired for her to take on a new moral obligation, then she cannot consent.

With reason-inhibiting substances, there is usually a large gray area. Many drugs, alcohol included, start inhibiting rationality soon after being ingested, but it is only after a great deal of ingestion that rationality is so inhibited as to undermine the possibility of consent. While consent is almost surely possible at the early stages, there will always be a large gray area where it is uncertain whether reason is so inhibited that an agreement is unable to count as consensual. When discussing hook ups, we will have to deal with the problem that almost all hook ups are agreed upon within this inebriated gray area. For now, it is sufficient to note that reason-inhibiting substances can undermine consent, but do not always do so. Consequently, even this standard requirement of competency allows a good deal of room for controversy in particular instances.

Conclusion

The goal of this chapter was to orient us generally as to the various aspects of consent. For the next few chapters (Chapters Three–Five), we will closely examine specific consent issues and how they apply to hooking up. As such, it was important for us here to delve into a general analysis of consent, since this grounding discussion will provide a conceptual framework for future chapters. To that end, in this chapter, we covered several conceptual issues for consent: ontology, temporality, normativity levels, and requirements.

In terms of ontology, we argued for a hybrid view that combines two essential aspects of consent. The first is a mental aspect: consent begins with an intention to make an agreement combined with an understanding that this agreement entails the agent will be morally obligated by what is agreed upon. The second is the performative aspect: consent requires agents perform certain behaviors that indicate to the other consenting parties their intentions to give and uphold their agreements.

Next, we saw that there is a temporal distinction for consent. Some instances of consent are given in advance such that the agent agrees to do something in the future. Other instances are contemporaneous and cover the action as it occurs, and these instances of consent can be legitimately revoked during the action.

We also saw that consent has different levels of normative strength. This normative strength can be measured in two ways. First, there is a measure of how many claims transfer from one person to another. In the strongest cases, when A consents to B, B obtains all the associated claims that A had. In weaker versions, A can consent to B, but B obtains only partial claims or almost no claims at all from A. Second, there is a measure of how much third parties must respect consent. In the strongest cases, third parties must fully respect the consent of other individuals, but in weaker cases perhaps no third parties need to respect the consent.

We next turned to the standard requirements for consent. At a minimum, consent requires that the parties are free, adequately informed, and competent. While there are more controversial requirements for consent, we will not have to weigh in on them because they are unlikely to be important for hook up consent. For example, some theorists argue that there are things you could never consent to. Robin West holds that a person could not give consent to trade or sell babies, sex, freedom, or lives.[36] Leo Katz similarly believes that you cannot consent to sell babies or sex, and adds bodily organs.[37] We do not have to weigh in on these issues, though, since we will assume that hooking up is something we can uncontroversially consent to.

Hook up consent, nonetheless, will allow for tricky issues along the three standard requirements. First, hook up practices, such as refusing to take no for an answer, can be so aggressive that we can question whether both parties feel sufficiently free to refuse. We will examine the freedom requirement for consent in the next chapter. Hook ups are also often negotiated with vague phrases and non-verbal communication, which seems to undermine the information requirement for consent, as we will discuss in Chapter Four. Finally, the competency requirement will be examined in Chapter Five with respect to the various amounts of alcohol and possibly drugs taken during routine hook ups.

Notes

1 Heidi M. Hurd, "The Moral Magic of Consent," *Legal Theory* 2, no. 2 (1996), 121, 123–124, 137; David Archard, *Sexual Consent* (Boulder: Westview Press, 1998), 3, 5–6; Alan Wertheimer, "Consent and Sexual Relations," in *The Philosophy of Sex: Contemporary Readings*, eds. Alan Soble and Nicholas Power (New York: Rowman and Littlefield, 2008), 291; John Kleinig, "The Nature of Consent," in *The Ethics of Consent*, eds. Franklin G. Miller and Alan Wertheimer (New York: Oxford University Press, 2010), 4; Tom Dougherty, "Sex, Lies, and Consent," *Ethics* 123 (2013), 722; Tom Dougherty, "Yes Means Yes: Consent as Communication," *Philosophy & Public Affairs* 43, no. 3 (2015), 226, 232–233.

2 Joel Feinberg, "Victims' Excuses: The Case of Fraudulently Procured Consent," *Ethics* 96, no. 2 (1986), 333–334; Thomas Mappes, "Sexual Morality and the Concept of Using Another Person," in *The Philosophy of Sex: Contemporary Readings*, eds. Alan Soble and Nicholas Power (New York: Rowman and Littlefield, 2008), 235; Dougherty, "Yes Means Yes," 226. I believe part of the reason that Feinberg in particular adopts this view is that he is dealing with the oddities of rape law. To put it simply, we tend to think of rape as sexual intercourse without consent. As we will see in later chapters, however, rape law tends to ignore a certain amount of non-consensual sex. For instance, purposeful deception surely undermines consent, but the law allows, with only a few exceptions, a significant amount of purposeful deception to obtain sexual agreements (See Jane E. Larson, "Women Understand So Little, They Call My Good Nature 'Deceit:' A Feminist Rethinking of Seduction," *Columbia Law Review* 93, no. 2 (1993); Steven J. Schulhofer, *Unwanted Sex: The Culture of Intimidation and the Failure of Law* (Cambridge: Harvard University Press, 1998), 112, 152–159; Alan Wertheimer, *Consent to Sexual Relations* (Cambridge: Cambridge University Press, 2003), 18, 193). So, looking at the law's seeming oversight, Feinberg concludes the "sex without consent" definition must imply that rape means sex without any agreement whatsoever, but valid consent is not (legally) necessary for sex (334). And so he takes "consent" to mean mere agreement. I think it is more plausible that rape law has a history of being sexist and is not theoretically well grounded, as seen by the fact that business law makes no similar usage of "consent" as mere agreement (in business, you cannot deceive the other party and receive consent in any legal sense). Further, judges attempt to defend this oddity of rape law with typically sexist responses, such as the idea that the woman would still have enjoyed the sex if she was merely deceived and so it should not count as rape (See Schulhofer, *Unwanted Sex*, 156). Instead of changing the meaning of "consent" to maintain the idea that rape is sex without consent, we could either refine that idea, acknowledge that rape law is imperfect, or both.

3 For examples, see: Hurd, "Moral Magic"; Wertheimer, "Consent and Sexual Relations," 291; Kleinig, "The Nature of Consent," 4; Wertheimer, *Consent to Sexual Relations*, 119–120; Leo Katz, "Choice, Consent, and Cycling: The Hidden Limitations of Consent," *Michigan Law Review* 104, no. 4 (2006), 628; Robin West, "Sex, Law, and Consent," in *The Ethics of Consent*, eds. Franklin G. Miller and Alan Wertheimer (New York: Oxford University Press, 2010), 221.

4 Hurd, "Moral Magic," 121–146, 124–126, 135–138.

5 Archard, *Sexual Consent*, 4; Wertheimer, *Consent to Sexual Relations*, 146–162.

6 Douglas N. Husak and George C. Thomas III, "Rapes without Rapists: Consent and Reasonable Mistake," *Philosophical Issues: Social, Political, and Legal Philosophy* 11 (2001): 86–117, 90–92; Dougherty, "Yes Means Yes." Although Dougherty claims to hold the performative conception, he in fact rules out the pure performative conception, as it is described here, as a view that "everyone should agree" is unacceptable (229). He argues in a footnote that Wertheimer may have once held the performative view, but eventually gave it up (229n15). Dougherty thus only allows two views: the mental

state conception and the hybrid, which he refers to as the "performative." Dougherty's own view is actually a hybrid conception if we allow for the conceptual possibility of all three views (229–230).

7 For instance, I do not believe it is fruitful to discuss whether consent involves a *de re* or *de dicto* intention, as is discussed by Heidi Hurd in "Moral Magic," 127–133. There are surely real-life examples of both kinds of consensual intentions. Suppose two women consent to sleep with men in dark rooms. The first woman gives *de dicto* consent: she intends to sleep with this man in the dark room, whoever he is. The next woman entered the dark room believing that her husband was in it, and gives *de re* consent to sleep with the man in the dark room. This latter woman has only consented if the man is in fact her husband. Since both *de dicto* and *de re* cases are possible in real life, we wouldn't want to rule out either from the ontology of consent.

8 Katz, "Choice, Consent, and Cycling," 652.

9 Ibid., 631–658.

10 Ibid., 642, 655.

11 Ibid., 641, 654.

12 Ibid., 641, 655.

13 Ibid., 631–652.

14 Ibid., 642, 655.

15 Ibid., 650–651.

16 Ibid., 650–651.

17 I thank a blind reviewer for pointing this exception out to me.

18 Thanks to Mona Rocha for suggesting this objection.

19 Wertheimer, "Consent and Sexual Relations," 295, 302–304; Archard, *Sexual Consent*, 50–53; Mappes, "Sexual Morality," 231–232, 235–241; Kleinig, "The Nature of Consent," 13–16; Tom L. Beauchamp, "Autonomy and Consent," in *The Ethics of Consent*, eds. Franklin G. Miller and Alan Wertheimer (New York: Oxford University Press, 2010).

20 Contrary to this point, and as mentioned previously, Joel Feinberg sometimes speaks as if we could have *involuntary consent*. He likewise thinks that "informed consent" is not redundant. See Feinberg, "Victims' Excuses," 333–334.

21 For theories of coercion, see: Robert Nozick, "Coercion," in *Philosophy, Science, and Method: Essays in Honor of Ernest Nagel*, eds. S. Morgenbesser, P. Suppes, and M. White (New York: St. Martin's Press, 1969), 440–472; Joseph Raz, *Morality of Freedom* (Oxford: Oxford University Press, 1988), 148–149; Michael Gorr, "Toward a Theory of Coercion," *Canadian Journal of Philosophy* 16 (1986), 386; Martin Gunderson, "Threats and Coercion," *Canadian Journal of Philosophy* IX (1979), 253; Cheyney C. Ryan, "The Normative Concept of Coercion," *Mind* 89 (1980), 483; Onora O'Neill, "Which Are the Offers You Can't Refuse?" in *Bounds of Justice* (Cambridge: Cambridge University Press, 2005), 81; Beauchamp, "Autonomy and Consent," 69.

22 Schulhofer, *Unwanted Sex*, 82, 114–136; Igor Primoratz, "Sexual Morality: Is Consent Enough?" *Ethical Theory and Moral Practice* 4, no. 3 (2001), 211.

23 For more on the information requirement, see: Mappes, "Sexual Morality," 231–232; Wertheimer, "Consent and Sexual Relations," 295, 304–305; Archard, *Sexual Consent*, 46–50; Wertheimer, *Consent to Sexual Relations*, 193–214; Neil Manson and Onora O'Neill, *Rethinking Informed Consent in Bioethics* (Cambridge: Cambridge University Press, 2007); Kleinig, "The Nature of Consent," 16–17; Dougherty, "Sex, Lies, and Consent."

24 Manson and O'Neill, *Rethinking Informed Consent*, 88–89. For a contrary position, see Feinberg, "Victims' Excuses," 333–334.

25 Wertheimer, *Consent to Sexual Relations*, 190; Manson and O'Neill, *Rethinking Informed Consent*, 84–90.

26 Manson and O'Neill, *Rethinking Informed Consent*, 87–88.

27 Ibid., 42–43.
28 Ibid., 45.
29 Onora O'Neill, "Between Consenting Adults," *Philosophy and Public Affairs* 14, no. 3 (1985): 255–256; David M. Adams, "Date Rape and Erotic Discourse," in *Date Rape: Feminism, Philosophy, and the Law*, ed. Leslie Francis (University Park: The Pennsylvania State University Press, 1996), 38–39; Manson and O'Neill, *Rethinking Informed Consent*, 45–48; Patricia Marino, "The Ethics of Sexual Objectification," *Inquiry* 51, no. 4 (2008), 355, 357. As one particular example, Backstrom *et al.* show that expectations vary widely over whether a hook up agreement should be presumed to include cunnilingus, or only include fellatio. See Laura Backstrom, Elizabeth A. Armstrong, and Jennifer Puentes, "Women's Negotiation of Cunnilingus in College Hookups and Relationships," *Journal of Sex Research* 49, no. 1 (2012), 6–9.
30 Husak and Thomas, "Rapes without Rapists."
31 For more on the competence requirement, see: Mappes, "Sexual Morality," 233; Hurd, "Moral Magic," 140–142; Wertheimer, "Consent and Sexual Relations," 295, 305–306; Archard, *Sexual Consent*, 44–46; Wertheimer, *Consent to Sexual Relations*, 215–257; Kleinig, "The Nature of Consent," 13–14.
32 For more on age and competence, see Archard, *Sexual Consent*, 116–129; Wertheimer, *Consent to Sexual Relations*, 216–222; David Benatar, "Two Views of Sexual Ethics: Promiscuity, Pedophilia, and Rape," in *The Philosophy of Sex: Contemporary Readings*, eds. Alan Soble and Nicholas Power (New York: Rowman and Littlefield, 2008), 328–330; Kleinig, "The Nature of Consent," 13.
33 Wertheimer, *Consent to Sexual Relations*, 223–236; Kleinig, "The Nature of Consent," 14.
34 Mappes, "Sexual Morality," 233–234; Laurence Thomas, "Sexual Desire, Moral Choice, and Human Ends," *Journal of Social Philosophy* 33, no. 2 (2002), 183; Wertheimer, *Consent to Sexual Relations*, 235–236; Teresa M. Downing-Matibag and Brandi Geisinger, "Hooking Up and Sexual Risk Taking Among College Students: A Health Belief Model Perspective," *Qualitative Health Research* 19, no. 9 (2009), 1196, 1203; Kleinig, "The Nature of Consent," 13–14.
35 Schulhofer, *Unwanted Sex*, 269; Alan Wertheimer, "Intoxicated Consent to Sexual Relations," *Law and Philosophy* 20, no. 4 (2001): 378–279; Wertheimer, *Consent to Sexual Relations*, 236–238; Kleinig, "The Nature of Consent," 13–14.
36 Robin West, "Submission, Choice, and Ethics: A Rejoinder to Judge Posner," *Harvard Law Review* 99, no. 7 (1986), 1449–1450.
37 Katz, "Choice, Consent, and Cycling," 628.

3

AGGRESSIVE HOOK UPS[1]

Now that we have established what is required for consent in Chapter Two, the next three chapters will discuss how the standard requirements for consent (freedom, information, and competence) are challenged by typical hook ups. I will argue that these challenges are significant enough that moral agents would wish to address them prior to hooking up, and so changes in current hook up practices will be necessary for ethical hook ups. In this chapter, we will examine the first requirement: for an agreement to be consensual, it must be freely made.

Most of the negative acts that undermine consent's freedom requirement will not be relevant to typical hook ups. If a coital hook up were to involve force, brainwashing, or frightening physical threats, then it unquestionably would be rape. Yet, one type of hook up that is well entrenched within socially accepted practices would, in certain circumstances, undermine the freedom required for consent. I am referring to the aggressive hook up, where one individual, usually a man, uses aggressive techniques either to obtain a hook up or during the hook up. Aggressive hook ups may place consent's freedom requirement at risk, and thus are worthy of careful attention.

I will begin this chapter by examining the aggressive hook up narrative, especially as feminist scholars analyze it. From these feminist critiques, we will see how aggressive hook ups endanger the freedom requirement by potentially instilling sufficient fear to produce false agreements for the sake of self-protection. Some scholars respond to this problem by noting that the aggressive narrative is so well-known that such problems will only come up rarely. In response, I will argue that since the risk involves a significantly grave harm (a hook up that would lack the freedom necessary for consent) and the amount of problematic incidents is not negligible, moral agents should do what is necessary to avoid this risk.

I will argue that moral agents who wish to engage in aggressive hook ups would follow the model provided by the BDSM community (BDSM is used to reference a variety of sexual activities, including bondage and discipline, dominance and submission, and sadism and masochism): they would have a sober, pre-hook up conversation where they discuss their intentions, limits, and opt-out options. This conversation, which will be further explored in the next chapter as well, may be quite difficult, especially as it initially works its way into social practice. Yet, if morality requires it, then moral agents will either only hook up after a pre-hook up conversation or will abstain from hooking up.

Hook Up Aggression

The aggressive man/passive woman sexual narrative, as typically found in romance novels, is well-known and various objections have been raised to it.[2] The narrative implies that it is romantic for a bold person – almost always a man – to overcome the resistance of a reluctant person – almost always a woman – to obtain sex. The bold man exhibits confidence that no one would intentionally refuse sex with him, and thus any resistance would have to be feigned. He proclaims his worth by seizing sex from a succumbing woman. While there may be potential moral problems with this narrative, many people, of both genders, enjoy enacting it. Hence, as we turn to critiquing the narrative, it is important to remember that quite often – maybe even most of the time – aggressive hook ups turn out to be enjoyable for both parties, which is worth preserving, if morally possible.[3]

Before getting to the specifics, it is important to note that various feminists have already cogently critiqued the aggression narrative. Legal theorist Lani Anne Remick notes the pervasiveness of the narrative when she says that, "our male-dominated society accepts a certain amount of coercion, aggression or violence against women as a normal, even desirable, part of sexual encounters."[4] Then she adds, "Thus, both men and women are socialized to accept coercive sexuality as the norm in sexual behavior. In many ways society sends the message that 'sexual violence is sexy.' As a result, men often see extreme forms of aggressive sexual behavior as seduction, rather than rape."[5] Remick not only sees this narrative as tying coerciveness into socially accepted seduction methods, but also understands the narrative as blurring the lines between seduction and rape by praising men for obtaining sex aggressively.

Philosopher Sally Haslanger argues that it is partially through adherence to this narrative that we define genders: "One is a man by virtue of standing in a position of eroticized dominance over others; one is a woman by virtue of standing in a position of eroticized submission to others."[6] And sociologist Lisa Wade agrees when she says, "If it's men's right to try for sexual contact, if it is the very definition of a real man, then the question isn't *whether* he should try to overcome her resistance, but *how*."[7] The power of the narrative is seen in how the social definition of being a man involves the aggressive sexual conquest of women – which, in turn, entails that a key norm for being a woman involves submission to masculine acts of aggression, conquest, and dominance. Just as aggressive sexual behavior is constitutive of being a good – or "real" – man, a mythical refusal to acquiesce becomes constitutive of being a good woman. It must remain mythical since women are expected to eventually submit. Female resistance is assumed to be feigned: women must pretend not to want the sex that men aggressively push upon them, but women also need to acquiesce insofar as the narrative requires that male aggression be rewarded.

This aggression narrative necessarily skews our social picture of sexual consent. One might think we should lower consent standards to account for a social narrative where men are expected to aggressively overcome women's supposedly feigned resistance. As philosopher Lois Pineau points out, "The reasoning that underlies the present criterion of consent is entangled in a number of mutually supportive mythologies which see sexual assault as masterful seduction, and silent submission as sexual enjoyment."[8] Pineau adds that this social view complicates consent since,

> if sexual aggression is a part of ordinary seduction, then it cannot be inconsistent with the legitimate consent of the person allegedly seduced by this means. And if it is normal for a woman to be reluctant, then this reluctance must be consistent with her consent as well.[9]

In this narrative, the usual indicators of dissent (including explicit refusal) can be reasonably ignored. The mere existence of the narrative leads to a dismissive attitude towards the requirements for consent. As legal theorist Karen Kramer says, "Believing that women tend to lie about their sexual desires and merely feign reluctance renders sexual aggression acceptable by making the woman's consent irrelevant."[10]

When hooking up with near strangers, aggressive sex techniques are problematic because they can cause fears that could lead someone to hook up unwillingly, even while they appear to be acting willingly. Just to be clear, when I say that someone is having sex unwillingly, I do not merely mean that they do not desire to have sex. As we will see, someone can choose to have sex of which they are not desirous: they willingly have sex for reasons other than sexual desire (they are doing it to have a baby, let's say). What it means to unwillingly have sex is that the person did not truly choose it, but was made to have sex anyway. Fears that lead to unwilling sex challenge consent's freedom requirement insofar as a person who is too afraid to say "no" is not freely saying "yes." Thus, our moral assessment must determine whether aggressive techniques lead to non-consensual hook ups. To make this determination, we will need to get clearer on aggression. We can do so by distinguishing it from similar techniques that also undermine consent's freedom requirement: force and coercion.

Let's say that someone uses force if she physically makes another person act against his will. A person is forced to hook up if he is physically made to engage in sexual activity against his will, such as through being held down or physically incapacitated. A forced hook up is rape. I will use "coercion," once again, to refer to the use of a threat to make another person choose to meet a demand.[11] A coercive hook up involves a person using threats to get another person to hook up out of fear. In the law, some threats are not considered sufficiently violent to warrant rape charges.[12] Moral condemnation, however, is warranted *whenever* someone uses a threat to make someone hook up against their will. Though some coercive hook ups may be legal, they are never morally permissible.[13]

To define "aggression," I will designate "aggressor" and "passive person" to be technical terms: the aggressor is whoever uses aggressive techniques and the passive person is whoever is on the receiving end of that aggression. These terms are consistent with a person being, at the same time, both aggressive and passive given different perspectives within a case of mutual aggression. I will also, for the sake of simplicity and because it represents the empirical trend, refer to the aggressor as male and the passive person as female.

Aggression consists neither in force nor coercion. Instead, aggression consists in an aggressor doing whatever he chooses based on an assumption that the passive person wishes for him to act in that fashion. The aggressor is not attempting to violate the passive person's perceived wishes, but he, instead, assumes that the passive person would independently choose to have the aggressor act as he does. Yet, the aggressor neither waits for nor seeks evidence that his assumption is accurate. He simply performs the acts he chooses regardless of whether the passive person indicates any willingness to go along with the aggressor's actions.

The aggressor can turn out to be wrong about his assumption, but, unlike a coercer, the aggressor will neither harm the passive person nor continue on if the passive person sufficiently establishes that she is not a willing partner. Ultimately, the aggressor desires, and even counts on, the passive person's voluntary participation. The fact that the aggressor does not check for voluntariness does not mean he does not wish for it – the failure to check, instead, is part of the aggression game. The aggressor is establishing his dominance: he is in charge and will act accordingly. But he is unlike forceful or coercive rapists because he hopes that the passive person wishes to be dominated. The aggressor's refuge is that if he truly does overstep his bounds, the passive person, at least in theory, will let him know. He gets evidence of the passive person's voluntariness from the lack of any serious attempt to stop him.

This last point, though, is tricky since the aggressor may feel that signals of unwillingness are feigned, and so should be ignored. Aggressors act on *their beliefs* that the passive person wants them to act. If the aggressor truly believes that the passive person is voluntarily going along, then the aggressor will continue regardless of contrary signals of reluctance. If the aggressor genuinely believes that the passive person is not willingly going along with him, then he will stop. The aggressor believes he is acting with an eager partner; he simply neither has nor seeks out sufficient evidence to warrant his belief.

For this chapter, I will use "non-aggressive hook up" to refer to a hook up where both parties seek out signals of consent prior to continuing. In such cases, when someone refuses to continue, the other person would either stop entirely or stop until overt signals clearly established that the prior refusal was feigned. Non-aggressive partners do not proceed based only on assumptions, but instead seek out clear evidence of their partner's willingness, which can include non-verbal communication provided that the non-verbal signals are overt and unquestionable. Each hook up partner can take his or her own clothes off without saying a word. Removing one's own clothes signals a willingness to be nude, and indicates some willingness to engage in nude sexual activity. A person could also move her partner's hands onto her body, thus signaling – without a word – that touching is allowed. Kissing can occur with both persons moving their heads and lips together. With each of these non-verbal signals, there is some vagueness in what is being communicated, but each party in a non-aggressive hook up waits for and receives fairly clear, overt signals prior to moving forward.

Aggressors do not wait for such signals of willingness. The aggressor would take off the passive person's clothes without waiting for any indication that she is willing to be nude. The aggressor would touch, kiss, and initiate sexual activity without prior signals that the other person wanted to touch, kiss, or engage in any sexual activity. Of course, the aggressor usually obtains signals after he acts – his partner smiles, helps with the removal of her clothes, or just generally shows engagement with and enjoyment of their hook up – but an aggressor never *waits* for such signals. The aggressor, as is fitting to his title, just does what he wishes based on the mere assumption that the other person wants him to do so.

As stated, the aggressor would also ignore refusals that he believes are feigned, and he will also likely believe that most refusals are feigned. Although research suggests that around 60% of women do not engage in token resistance, around 40% at least sometimes do.[14] This ratio (40/60) suggests that token resistance is real, but there is also a lot of room for dangerous confusion.[15] Political scientist Alan Wertheimer points out that the person who says "no" always means it at the moment at which it is said,[16] but some people do want their refusals to be overcome. Thus, a person who hears "no" may be uncertain whether it is a demand to stop or a request to keep trying.[17] Part of being aggressive includes ignoring initial refusals on the assumption that they are merely feigned.

We have seen, as a first type of aggression, that aggressors act aggressively when they initiate sexual activity. There are two other general types of aggression within hook ups. As a second type, aggressors can use aggression to overcome a refusal. The aggressor can aggressively respond to an initial refusal by sexually touching the passive person anyway, by insulting her for refusing, or by insisting that they continue regardless of what she says. These actions convey the impression that the aggressor does not take the refusal seriously.

As a third and final type, the aggressor can be aggressive within the sexual activity itself. The aggressor could do what he wants during the sexual activity without checking for signals of the other person's desires or limits. Since "let's hook up" is ambiguous over how far the sexual activity will go, this type of aggression includes pushing the sexual action further without being sure that the other person wants to go further. Therefore, there can be aggressive initiations, aggressive responses to attempts to alter or end the hook up, and aggressive sexual activity.

From the passive person's perspective it may be quite difficult, and sometimes impossible, to distinguish an aggressive hook up from a rape. Both the aggressor and the rapist take what they want without checking for willingness. The key difference between an aggressive hook up and a forcible rape may lie entirely within counterfactual facts that, unless challenged and revealed, only the aggressor knows. A counterfactual fact is a claim whose truth depends on the world being different than it is. If I say on a sunny day, "I would not be walking to the store if it were raining," my claim is counterfactual. Since it is not raining, the claim's truth depends on what would be the case if the world were different. What distinguishes the aggressor from the rapist is that the former counterfactually would stop if he were convinced that the passive person genuinely wanted him to. Of course, the fact of what the aggressor would do *given his appraisal* of the passive person's desires is counterfactual: the passive person cannot be sure what the aggressor would do if things were different, especially if the participants do not know each other well. It is completely reasonable for the passive person to be fearful because she is unsure whether she is in an aggressive hook up or a rape. She may, reasonably, acquiesce just to protect herself.

Accordingly, aggressive hook ups put the freedom requirement for consent at risk. The person who is physically forced into sex is not free to refuse, and so cannot consent. The person who is coerced into sex is not reasonably free to refuse due to the threat, and so cannot consent. The passive person in an aggressive hook up may similarly fear refusing. According to a study by social scientists Teresa Downing-Matibag and Brandi Geisinger, it is true in contemporary hook up practices that sometimes "young women find themselves alone with sexually aggressive men to whom they are afraid to refuse sex."[18] There are various ways that aggression can provoke such fear. Perhaps a young woman's initial refusals are ignored or overcome in aggressive manners that make her think that further refusals are futile. Perhaps the aggressor's actions are so substantially aggressive that she assumes from the beginning that there is no point to refuse. If, from the passive person's perspective, refusing does not seem to be a viable option, then she is not reasonably free to refuse and so cannot consent.

Even though the aggressor did not intend to engage in a non-consensual hook up, the aggressor may find it to be difficult, and sometimes impossible, to distinguish whether the passive person is acting out of fear. Aggressors act in ways that can make their partners unwilling to continue, and their passive partners may not provide clear signals of unwillingness. It is neither the passive person's responsibility to prove that she is frightened nor the aggressor's inclination to interpret the passive person's behavior as frightened. It cannot be the passive person's responsibility in part because she is the victim; it is morally on the person who may be committing a grave moral wrong to ensure that he does not do so. It is also not the passive person's responsibility because the burden is too high: since her refusals are not being taken seriously, it is not clear how she can ensure her refusal is accepted. It is perfectly reasonable for the passive person to send mixed or inaccurate signals that appear to be acquiescence, but that are intended to mask fear. It is fair both for the passive person to give up out of fear and for her to not want her attacker to know that she is afraid. The passive person does not have to establish her reluctance, especially given the high risk that the aggressor has unintentionally put her in. So, the aggressive person cannot be entirely sure what is going on. An epistemic problem (that the aggressor cannot always know whether the passive person is willing) turns into a grave moral problem (that the aggressor may engage in a non-consensual hook up due to unintentionally produced fear).

Even where both parties desire an aggressive hook up, the aggressor will have a difficult time being sure of that. When the aggressor acts, he cannot be certain that his action is morally permissible. But it cannot be morally acceptable to act if you cannot reasonably avoid gravely immoral deeds (such as making someone non-consensually have sex). Aggressive hook ups are morally problematic since aggressors act in ways that could undermine consent, and they do not do enough to safely avoid such a grave moral transgression. In fact, they cannot actively try to avoid the transgression while being aggressors since, by definition, they do not seek out clear signals of consent. Thus, this moral difficulty is inherent to the aggressive hook up practice.

The Social Argument for Aggressive Hook Up Permissibility

There are various responses to this problem: some theorists argue that aggressive techniques are morally permissible given social customs, while others accept the impermissibility of the techniques and either condemn them or try to find an alteration to allow for permissible aggressive techniques. In this section, I will consider and reject accounts where theorists argue that aggressive techniques are morally permissible in our society. Later, I will consider condemnations and attempts to alter the practice, with my own view offering a substantial alteration.

Alan Wertheimer provides an account where aggressive casual sex could be permissible. He argues that silence should suffice for consent if there is a social understanding that silence implies consent.[19] For silence to count as consent, the convention of intending to consent through silence would have to be well-known throughout society. In such a society, a person could assume that they are receiving silent consent provided that there are no contrary signals of dissent.

While Wertheimer understands that relying on silence may cause misunderstandings, for Wertheimer that problem is separate from whether someone acts permissibly in the face of silence.[20] If there is no sign of dissent, Wertheimer believes that the person acts permissibly even if the silence wasn't actually intended to convey consent. His argument is that it is not reasonable to expect aggressors to know what is in passive persons' minds, and they are acting on a well-established social custom (silent consent) that they reasonably believe applies. Therefore, aggressors, who read silence and the lack of signals of dissent as sufficient for consent, would act permissibly for Wertheimer as long as they are in a society, such as ours, where it is well-known that agents often consent through silence. Let's say that a pattern of behavior that is well enough known that you can typically assume that others know about it is a "social convention." A social convention does not mean you can demand others follow it, but that you expect that most people have heard about it. If the aggressor reads the silence incorrectly, he cannot be blamed according to Wertheimer since he followed a social convention (it would just be bad luck in cases where the silence does not convey what it usually does).

Let's look at a case. One night, Caitlin explicitly refuses when Dennis asks for sex. As the night continues, Dennis begins removing Caitlin's clothes. To use a token of consent that Wertheimer deems to be valid in our society, let's say that after her blouse is taken off, Caitlin smiles.[21] Dennis has acted aggressively both by continuing past Caitlin's explicit refusal and by taking Caitlin's clothes off without any prior signal that she desires to be nude in front of him. Yet, Dennis now has an affirmative sign – the smile – that indicates that his aggression is well received. Caitlin and Dennis live in a society where various sexual rituals are well-known, including that women sometimes feign resistance, it is sometimes considered romantic for men to overcome that resistance, and silence and smiles are tokens of consent.

Though the relevant studies indicate that only 40% of women feign resistance and only on occasion, we do not need the majority to engage in a practice for it to count as a social convention. Forty percent seems sufficient for most people to have heard of the convention. Given that there are rituals for token resistance as well as for smiles and silence counting as consent, Wertheimer's position would be that Dennis acts reasonably by assuming he has consent in this sort of situation. Since Caitlin, given her membership in the community of hook up participants, likely would know about these social conventions, she probably would know that a straightforward refusal would be insufficient to indicate that she does not want to hook up with Dennis. Given that Caitlin does not fully convince Dennis that she meant her refusal and she smiled as he acted, Wertheimer would conclude that Dennis acts reasonably, and his actions would be morally permissible.

Of course, for any given social ritual, there are exceptions: people who either do not know the ritual, cannot participate in it, or simply do not participate in it in a given instance (say they forgot about it). Caitlin may be frightened when

Dennis continues on after he receives a refusal. His act of taking off her clothes without permission may be terrifying. Smiles can be involuntary, and people behave unpredictably when forced to deal with scary people in close proximity. Wertheimer acknowledges that tokens of consent do not ensure actual consent: the person can appear to be consenting (their positive action is a token of consent) without necessarily meaning to do so (they lack the intention and so do not actually consent). Nonetheless, Wertheimer would think Dennis was still acting permissibly since the exception cases are so rare that Dennis could not be expected to work diligently to rule out their possibility. In Wertheimer's view, Dennis acts permissibly since he relies on a social convention that is so well-known that it would be very unlikely that Caitlin would be an exception to that convention.

In agreement with Wertheimer, philosophers Douglas Husak and George Thomas argue that social conventions provide guidance for what it is reasonable to infer from others' behavior.[22] We should base assessments of the reasonableness of aggressors' beliefs in part on whether their beliefs fit with standard operating procedures for casual sex in their society.[23] An aggressor who follows social conventions for an aggressive hook up, in their view, acts reasonably in proceeding as if he has consent.[24]

Husak and Thomas agree that agents can dismiss some evidence of dissent since, in our society, people both feign resistance and have undesired sex.[25] They support the latter point through empirical studies that indicate that people of both genders regularly have sex that is consensual but undesired for the sake of extrinsic reasons, such as to have a baby, make another person happy, make money, or fit in with peers.[26] Husak and Thomas argue that (especially when looking at it from the perspective of a juror – though the moral question has clear overlap) we should judge the reasonableness of inferring consent from the "totality of circumstances," and that we should not, "privilege or exclude *any* material evidence of consent."[27]

The Husak and Thomas approach overlooks key differences between aggressive hook ups and sex within committed relationships. The latter involves people who know each other sufficiently well to draw safe conclusions based on established non-verbal signals, including silence. Without knowing the other person, it is much harder to reasonably believe the other person is consenting when it is clear that sex is not desired. While there are plenty of reasons to have undesired sex in relationships, hook ups revolve around having fun. Sexual desire is fairly essential for hooking up. If a person sees signs that a potential hook up partner does not desire sex, it is not reasonable to assume that the hook up is consensual.

In spite of this initial worry, there is empirical evidence in favor of Wertheimer, Husak, and Thomas. Aggressive hook ups are common enough to establish social conventions. They probably work out fine for both parties in a significant number of cases. Their collective premise, that there is a social convention for aggressive casual sex, is true. The question is whether such a social convention justifies agents relying on it when such reliance entails risking harm to others.

For agents to justifiably rely on such a social convention, it would either need to have a very insignificant failure rate or primarily have failures that only involve minor harms. Since the failures in question involve people having non-consensual hook ups out of fear, the risk at stake is very serious. Permissibility then turns on the failure rate. To this end, it is important to look at the relevant literature that sheds light on the failure rate. The relevant studies will provide good empirical evidence that the rate of hook ups going poorly is significant enough that moral analysis cannot ignore the failure cases.

According to one study, 78% of "unwanted sexual intercourse" occurred during hook ups (the respondents did not wish to refer to these incidents as "rape" or "sexual assault").[28] In one survey, 90% of men who are patrons of drinking establishments admit to non-consensual activities, including rubbing up against women from behind, grabbing or groping women, or otherwise touching their bodies without consent.[29] According to another, 42% of women had terrible hook up experiences, which almost half described in terms of being pressured into going further than they were willing to go.[30] According to another study, 16% of people, male and female, had hook ups where they felt pressured.[31] About one out of every five or six individuals (about 21% by the first study or 16% by the second), at some time, has had a pressured hook up.

Rape studies further support this point. In one study, 27% of women who had been raped according to the legal definition, did not describe their sexual encounter as "rape."[32] In other studies, a disturbing 88% of men who had committed rape, according to the legal definition, insisted that they had not, and 47% of men who had committed rape said they would do so again in the future.[33] Unfortunately, the failure cases are much more frequent than is assumed.[34]

In our example, when Dennis wants to hook up with Caitlin, he has to make a judgment based on her words and non-verbal cues. Remember that she initially refused, but later smiled as he removed her clothes. Dennis knows that in many cases like this one in his society, the woman intends to give consent. But he also should know that there are other cases, albeit smaller in number, where women feel pressured, might respond out of fear, and might give in without consenting. If this case were one of those latter cases, which happen to one out of every five to six hook up participants, then Dennis would be about to commit a heinous moral transgression.

Even if Dennis did act on a social convention that represents the majority of cases, the probability that this particular hook up will likely work out fine does not suffice for moral permissibility. There is a non-negligible chance (one in five to six) that Dennis will one day partake in a pressured hook up. He is currently pressuring Caitlin without any explicit acknowledgement on her part that she consents. Further, many rapists also do not seem to recognize when they are engaging in rape.[35] Given these facts, there is a significant chance that if Dennis regularly acts as an aggressor, he will one day pressure his partner into a non-consensual hook up. While his odds that this particular hook up with Caitlin is consensual may be good, Dennis' overall chances of entirely avoiding a non-consensual hook up while regularly engaging in aggressive techniques are much lower, which should be very worrisome.

It is so incredibly worrisome that Dennis' aggressive techniques will eventually undermine the freedom required for consent because of the severity of the harms that he is risking. A failure entails that Caitlin is hooking up with Dennis against her will. Dennis would have violated Caitlin's right to sexual autonomy, forced her into a hook up through aggression, and may cause her serious harms, including physical and psychological harms. Dennis, after all, is making sexual decisions for Caitlin based on a generalization of what some other women would want in her situation. Even if it luckily works out, Dennis is disrespecting Caitlin's sexual autonomy by making substantial sexual decisions *for her* based on what *some other women* want. Since there is a significant chance of failure over Dennis' lifespan of aggressively hooking up, and the potential failure is quite serious (non-consensual sex), Dennis' aggressive techniques are not morally permissible.

Given the worry over failure cases, the moral agent would refrain from relying merely on social conventions to conclude that the person before him is just like the majority.[36] In this sense, the perspective from which we perform the moral appraisal matters quite a bit. I would still disagree with the claims made by Wertheimer, Husak, and Thomas when looking at the cases from an external, bystander perspective. Yet, their case is made more plausible from that external perspective since the odds suggest that Dennis will get lucky and his hook up partner will likely be willing. However, our question is what moral agents would do to ensure that their hook ups are permissible. Relying on generalizations and the probability that things will work out cannot represent the moral agent's perspective. Moral agents do not attempt to avoid grave moral transgressions by relying on probabilities or luck. Nor do moral agents think it is permissible to ignore a sexual partner's autonomy and treat them as a mere instance of a larger pattern. Thus, it is clear that moral agents cannot choose to act as Dennis does, but instead must either forego aggressive techniques or find a way around them.

We should reject any approach that argues that the failure cases are too insignificant to affect the moral appraisal of aggressive hook ups. Such an approach conflates the numbers needed to establish social conventions with the numbers needed to permissibly impose serious risks onto others. This position does not yet entail that we must morally condemn aggressive techniques. We must seek a preferable response to the moral problem posed by aggressive hook ups.

Slogans, Standards, and Inducements

One common response to the aggression narrative is to demand a change from the "'no' means no" slogan to a "'yes' means yes" slogan.[37] One problem with the no slogan is that it is useless when there is neither an explicit 'no' nor 'yes.' Some theorists object that the no slogan implies that silence counts as consent,[38] which is worrisome since a terrified person may be unable to express dissent. Therefore, a new slogan has been offered to replace the no slogan: "'yes' means yes." If a person waits for a verbal 'yes' prior to sexual activity, then chances are lower that the hook up will be non-consensual. If we want to minimize moral wrongs, requiring an explicit 'yes' makes some sense.[39]

This response appears to rule out aggressive hook ups almost by definition. An aggressor does not seek clear signals, much less an explicit 'yes'; he moves ahead on the assumption that the passive person is willing. It may be possible to be aggressive while following this slogan's requirement if the aggressor starts acting without signals of willingness, but he would not actually initiate sexual intercourse until he receives a verbal 'yes.' Of course, this would be an unusual aggressor, and, for the most part, accepting the moral necessity of an explicit 'yes' involves condemning aggressive hook ups. Since a total rejection of aggressive hook ups could be warranted, this concern is not yet an objection to this approach.

A more worrisome problem for the yes slogan approach is that it provides no help in cases where an intended 'no' changes to a fearful and non-consensual 'yes.' Aggression in sexual contexts with near strangers can cause people to become reasonably afraid. A frightened person can respond in many different ways to aggressive techniques, including silence, a forced smile, or even a forced 'yes.' We all respond to fear differently; it can be just as reasonable for terrified persons to go along with their apparent tormentors with verbal affirmations as it is for them to smile or remain silent. The yes slogan does not help when an aggressor makes someone so afraid that she says 'yes' just to be safe.

One way to improve upon the slogans would be to delineate permissible ways to turn a refusal into an acceptance. On this view, it would be preferable for a person, who is faced with a possibly feigned refusal, to have a method for permissibly changing that refusal into an acceptance. We need standards for judging acceptable methods for overcoming refusals. Legal scholar Stephen Schulhofer, discussing the problems of the no slogan, states, "But a 'no means no' rule does not help us sort out whether the things he does in response to her initial 'no' are legitimate or abusive. To separate appropriate emotional interaction from abusive pressure, we need substantive standards of permissible conduct."[40] Schulhofer, however, does not recommend what to do as much as he points out what is unacceptable. He argues that it is impermissible to turn a 'no' into a 'yes' through violence, physical coercion, or non-physical coercion, including coercion through implicit threats.[41] Clearly violence and physical coercion undermine the freedom required for consent. Schulhofer's response goes further by ruling out all coercion: physical, non-physical, and implicit. Schulhofer recognizes the practical difficulty of pinpointing implicit threats, which must be inferred from circumstances.[42] Schulhofer also notes that his answer is vague, and, given his focus on legal issues, he leaves precision up to the courts to decide.[43]

Leaving these issues up to the courts is unhelpful since the moral question precedes the legal question in two ways. First, aggressors must determine whether their actions are morally permissible even if they will not end up in court or do not know whether they will. Second, the moral question is fundamentally prior since we would not likely think that aggressive techniques should be illegal if they were morally permissible. Schulhofer's standards get us started, but they do not provide sufficient direction for permissibly changing someone's mind.

Lois Pineau starts with an empirically contentious presumption that initial refusals indicate lack of interest, but her points are still useful. Based on that assumption, she argues:

> Then it would be *prima facie* unreasonable for her to agree to have sex – unreasonable, that is, unless she were offered some payoff for her stoic endurance, money perhaps, or tickets to the opera. The reason is that in sexual matters agreement is closely connected to attraction. Thus, where the presumption is that she was not attracted, we should at the same time presume that she did not consent. Hence, the burden of proof should be on her alleged assailant to show that she had good reasons for consenting to an unattractive proposition.[44]

A positive method for changing someone's mind is usually preferable to aggression. We expect positive methods in almost every other area of life. When someone does not agree at first, the burden is on the offer maker to sweeten the deal. If the offer maker instead turns to aggression, then we will likely judge them poorly – or we would in any other area of life, at least.

We view negotiations this way even when initial rejections hide true interest. In any other context, if Dennis makes an offer and Caitlin refuses because she wants a better deal, we do not think Dennis has the right to become aggressive. Dennis can either refuse to give a second offer or he can augment his first one. It is a problematic oddity of sexual exchanges that, socially speaking, we think a proper response to an initial refusal involves ignoring the refusal and becoming more aggressive.

Although a positive approach is normal for other persuasion attempts, it may not work for hook ups. Pineau suggests offering money or opera tickets to change the woman's mind.[45] Given social realities, it can be offensive to offer money or concert tickets to someone who has refused to hook up. Positive incentives in a standard hook up could amount to implying someone is a type of person who is willing to sell sex, which brings to mind numerous social stigmas.

This positive approach, while it makes sense in other contexts, can come off as offensive, given current social mores, in sexual contexts.

Unfortunately, neither Schulholfer nor Pineau offer guidance on aggressive hook ups in particular. Even if we put force and coercion squarely on the side of illegal assault, that leaves out the morally troubling aggressive techniques discussed here. Schulhofer and Pineau do not offer enough practical guidance to tell us how to find a morally permissible way to turn an explicit refusal into an acceptance while maintaining a respect for the person's sexual autonomy. It will be useful, then, to seek out a method to retain aggressive hook ups while avoiding the problem posed by initial refusals.

Modeling Aggressive Hook Ups on BDSM Encounters

The moral problem of aggressive hook ups largely derives from an epistemic problem (that is, a problem concerning knowledge). Aggressive hook ups are immoral because the aggressor cannot know for sure that the passive person is willingly submitting. If this epistemic problem could be solved, aggressive hook ups could be morally permissible. After all, there are people who enjoy both the aggressive and passive roles. As long as people are well paired, both of their choices to hook up are consensual, and they each feel sufficiently free to retract their consent, an aggressive hook up can be enjoyable without a problem. Moral permissibility depends on solving the epistemic problem of ensuring that each partner has freely consented.

I will propose a solution that requires substantial changes in current practices, but that could allow permissible aggressive hook ups in an altered form. The solution involves treating aggressive hook ups similarly to contemporary BDSM practices (once again, BDSM is used to reference bondage and discipline, dominance and submission, and sadism and masochism). The suitability of this analogy lies in the fact that both aggressive hook ups and BDSM involve sexual activities that can be enjoyable if all participants consent, but that can also include troubling confusion over consent, which could endanger the freedom requirement and potentially lead to severe harms.

Heightened moral requirements are necessary to avoid unintentionally harming others due to consent misunderstandings. In BDSM, participants must have a prior conversation before the sexual activity begins: they discuss their intentions, limits, and plans on how to deal with any unintentional boundary crossing. This conversation ensures that agents not only go into the BDSM activity after having given meaningful consent, but also that, were they no longer willing to continue, they would have plans to effectively convey this reluctance – such as using safe words that indicate unwillingness to continue.[46]

Insofar as aggressive hook ups present similar moral problems as BDSM, there could be a similar solution. Prior to aggressively hooking up with a near or complete stranger, agents ought to have a sober discussion about their intentions, limits, and plans for dealing with any accidental boundary crossing. Aggressive hook up participants, like with BDSM participants, should make sure that they receive consent, along with having a method for withdrawing consent.[47] The conversation not only helps with the information requirement (an issue that I will expand upon in the next chapter), but also with the freedom requirement. The problem posed by aggressive techniques is that they could lead to someone being so afraid that they lack the freedom to refuse, and thus fail to retain the freedom required for consent. Were aggressive hook up participants to have this conversation, they could be aggressive during the hook up without unintentionally causing such fear. Therefore, the conversation helps ensure the consent is both informed and free.

That aggressors are obligated to have this conversation simply falls out of the fact that they cannot ensure that they have consent were they to act without the conversation. We are morally obligated to obtain consent whenever we are about to do something that would be morally wrong if we acted without consent. The strength of this obligation is determined by the likelihood that there would be harm in acting without consent, combined with the potential severity of the harm. It can be a grave harm to hook up with someone without consent, so that suggests the obligation is fairly strong. Since roughly one in five to six persons eventually has a hook up that goes too far, persons who regularly use aggressive techniques on near strangers face a significant chance of eventually hooking up with someone non-consensually. Since the chances of acting wrongly are not negligible and the consequences are potentially severe, there is a strong moral obligation to only hook up with someone if you are certain they are consenting, which requires making sure the person is informed and feels free to refuse. While in other circumstances, non-verbal and behavioral cues (including silence and the lack of resistance) may be sufficient to signal consent, in the face of a strong moral obligation to verify consent, the pre-hook up conversation is necessary for aggressive hook ups.

While the next chapter on the information requirement will further discuss pre-hook up conversations in general, it is important here to pinpoint a few matters that moral agents would have to discuss prior to a potentially aggressive hook up. During the discussion, they ought to proceed not just based on the social conventions that currently govern the hook up practice (which, for example, allow agents to already be inebriated and to communicate non-verbally), but on norms that govern obtaining consent in matters where doing so is necessary for avoiding grave moral wrongs. The moral agent must proceed in this fashion because their goal is not merely to hope to luckily avoid grave moral transgressions. Their goal, instead, is to ensure that they never engage in grave moral transgressions. Relying on a social conventional that *usually* works is clearly not a path to ensure one is *never* pressuring someone into non-consensual sex.

The discussion must include at least two main issues: the aggressor's intentions and the passive person's exit options. In terms of the former, the aggressor must give the passive person an adequate sense of his aggressive intentions so that the passive person can ensure she is going along willingly. Here, adequacy is determined by what the passive person needs to know to be able to consent. The conversation could be brief if the passive person says, "Do whatever you want; I'm ready." The participants could then just discuss opt-out options. The conversation could be much longer if the passive person has limits or fears. It is the passive person who is at risk, and so the prior discussion needs to go as long as necessary to ensure the passive person knows what she is getting into and feels comfortable with it.

The exit option, likewise, may involve something as simple as deciding on safe words, or something more complex if the passive person is worried that safe words may be insufficient. Maintaining consent is just as important here as obtaining consent. With both BDSM and aggressive hook ups, the activity can begin consensually, but a line could be unintentionally crossed where one person suddenly becomes afraid and, thereby, no longer feels free to withdraw consent. In that case, the moral problem is not that the activity did not have consent to begin with, but that consent was lost. It is just as wrong to continue sexual activity with someone who is no longer consenting, as it is to start sexual activity without consent. Thus, safe words and any other opt-out procedures must be established in the prior conversation to ensure that each participant knows what to do if the freedom required for consent is endangered.

This conversation will not be easy (talking about sex, especially while sober with near strangers, is never easy), but moral agents would not neglect to have a difficult conversation if having it could prevent them from committing serious moral transgressions. The conversation can simply begin with the aggressor asking, "Are you into aggressive hook ups?" If the other person says "no," then there is no need to continue and a possibly serious moral transgression has been avoided. If the person responds, "Yes, and I am down with whatever," then the conversation can briefly turn to safe words, and then they both can rest assured that they are avoiding a serious moral transgression. On the other hand, if the answer is, "Yes, but I have limits," then they can smoothly segue into discussing those limits. In each case, grave moral transgressions have been avoided by simply asking a straightforward question to another sober person. Hence, moral agents will definitely initiate this conversation rather than hoping to avoid grave moral wrongs simply through luck.

At this point, it is important to remember that we have been using gendered pronouns for the sake of simplicity, but the obligation to discuss the planned aggression will apply equally to aggressors of either gender. Some theorists object to giving men stronger obligations for casual sex since they claim that doing so treats women like they cannot protect themselves from their own choices.[48] These theorists, however, are the ones assuming that we ought to treat men and women differently by working from the implicit assumption that giving a moral obligation to aggressors entails giving an extra obligation only to men. The moral obligation argued for here is not on men merely because they are men. It is on aggressors, who in our society tend to be men. It is the same obligation on women whenever they act as aggressors. The obligation is not gendered. Its application happens to be mostly gendered due to real-life patterns.

All aggressors have a strong moral obligation to ensure they obtain and maintain consent through a prior conversation over intentions and exit procedures. The pre-aggressive hook up conversation may seem to alter the conditions of aggressive hooking up so much that it amounts to a different practice. My solution seems to run into the same problem as the yes slogan or Pineau's enticement standards: it seems to require too much change.

While modeling aggressive hook ups on BDSM requires substantial changes, in an important way, the practice can remain largely unchanged during the hook up itself. As we saw, during the prior conversation, the participants will need to discuss their limits and how to deal with boundaries being accidentally crossed. This prior conversation would certainly be a significant change to current aggressive hook up practices, but it is both fairly straightforward, as we just saw, and absolutely necessary to ensure that no grave moral transgression will occur. After the conversation, the participants would have given their consent to engage in a practice where one person (the aggressor) makes all the decisions and does not seek signs of willingness from the other person. Thus, after the conversation, they can engage in an aggressive hook up that is very similar to aggressive hook ups as they exist today. The conversation ensures the moral permissibility of the activity, but, like with BDSM, it allows the activity to occur within a fantasy where the agents can pretend that the conversation never happened.

One might object that the prior conversation prevents the aggression from occurring spontaneously and genuinely. After all, the aggressor cannot actually be aggressive, as if overpowered by passion, if the aggressor had to telegraph his general moves in a prior conversation. Further, his aggression is necessarily less genuine: aggression is defined in terms of not seeking out the other person's willingness, but the prior conversation establishes that very willingness. One might object that the prior conversation turns the aggressive hook up into a mere fantasy without genuine aggression.

These costs can be very real from the perspective of subjective sexual enjoyment, yet they are morally necessary losses since those aspects of the aggressive hook up are causally related to the central moral problem: it is when a hook up is so spontaneous and genuinely aggressive that the passive person cannot be certain that it is not a sexual assault. We could describe my position by saying that genuine aggressive hook ups with complete or near strangers are morally impermissible because they endanger the freedom required for consent, but fantasy aggressive hook ups with prior conversations can be acceptable, and may provide much of the same enjoyment. I would be willing to accept the view that my conclusion only established the permissibility of fantasy aggressive hook ups. In a way, this point may come down to semantics: we can either say that aggressive hook ups need not include genuine aggression, or say that only fantasy aggressive hook ups are permissible. Either way, I am arguing that moral agents would never risk genuinely aggressive hook ups that could pressure someone into non-consensual sex.

Importantly, BDSM – whether we ought to refer to it as "fantasy BDSM" – involves the same type of prior conversation and resulting lack of true genuineness. People regularly enjoy BDSM in spite of the fact that no one expects their BDSM encounters to occur spontaneously among strangers or to involve genuine desires to harm submissive persons. Instead, BDSM allows for prior conversations and an amount of fantasy, but individuals enjoy it as such.

To maintain the fantasy of aggressive hook ups while making the activity morally permissible, moral aggressors would just have to work much harder to ensure that they only interact with consenting passive persons. Just as there are BDSM clubs and websites, there could be methods for people interested in morally permissible aggressive hook ups to find like-minded individuals. It could be that they go to "aggression-friendly" bars and clubs, or they could go to standard bars and clubs and make sure to have a sober conversation about the aggressive hook up before starting. There could even be a cell phone app that signaled there was an aggressor/passive person nearby and that helped to establish safe words. The idea is that the fantasy can be maintained while participants are acting in ways that obtain and maintain meaningful consent.

Conclusion

There is, then, a part of the routine hook up practice that endangers the freedom requirement for consent. Aggressive techniques are regularly employed within a certain type of hook up, but those techniques can cause someone to become reasonably afraid. If a person is too afraid to refuse to hook up, then their verbal affirmation that they agree or any other positive signal that they agree is not made freely enough to count as consent. Thus, aggression challenges the freedom required for consensual hook ups.

As a response, I considered approaches that argued that this problem is overcome by social arrangements that ensure that almost all participants understand these aggressive techniques to be part of a sexual game. While there is sufficient empirical evidence for these practices to ground a reasonable assumption that your partner likely knows about them, we also saw that the amount of failure is not negligible. Aggressors who regularly hook up with near strangers will be blameworthy if they ignore the significant chance of eventually wronging someone in a possibly severe way.

One response to this problem requires that hook up participants seek an explicit "yes." Unfortunately, this response does not help with situations where participants say "yes" out of fear, such as in aggressive hook ups that go wrong. The yes slogan approach does not tell us how to acceptably turn a refusal into an acceptance. Hence, I next considered standards for turning refusals into acceptances. Yet, those attempts did not help sufficiently with the crucial cases where aggressive hook ups are almost indistinguishable from non-consensual hook ups.

Moral agents who wish to engage in aggressive hook ups would, instead, have a pre-hook up conversation to ensure that the passive person is consensually hooking up. While this pre-hook up conversation may make the aggression within the hook up exist as more of a fantasy, the moral agent would forego genuine aggression that generates significant risk for others. Thus, while this solution may only salvage a fantasy version of aggressive hook ups, moral agents would prefer the fantasy that includes much of the same fun, rather than a genuine aggressive hook up that risks grave moral transgressions.

Having established that a pre-aggressive hook up conversation is necessary to ensure the freedom requirement for consent is met, it will next be useful to look at the ways in which this same conversation can help meet the information requirement for consent. Thus, in Chapter Four, we will examine the various challenges to ensuring that hook up consent is adequately informed, and how a pre-hook up conversation can resolve many of those issues.

Notes

1 This chapter is based on the article: James Rocha, "Aggressive Hook Ups: Modeling Aggressive Casual Sex on BDSM for Moral Permissibility," *Res Publica* 22, no. 2 (2016), 173–192.

2 Onora O'Neill, "Between Consenting Adults," *Philosophy and Public Affairs* 14, no. 3 (1985), 254; Catherine A. MacKinnon, *Toward a Feminist Theory of the State* (Cambridge: Harvard University Press, 1989), 127–154, 171–183; Sally Haslanger, "On Being Objective and Being Objectified," in *A Mind of One's Own*, eds. Louise Anthony and Charlotte Witt (Boulder: Westview Press, 1993), 99; Lani Anne Remick, "Read Her Lips: An Argument For a Verbal Consent Standard in Rape," *University of Pennsylvania Law Review* 141, no. 3 (1993), 1104, 1144–1147; Karen Kramer, "Rule by Myth: The Social and Legal Dynamics Governing Alcohol-Related Acquaintance Rapes," *Stanford Law Review* 47, no. 1 (1994), 115–160, 118; Ayres A. Boswell and Joan Z. Spade, "Fraternities and Collegiate Rape Culture: Why Are Some Fraternities More Dangerous Places for Women?" *Gender and Society* 10, no. 2 (1996), 134; Lois Pineau, "Date Rape: A Feminist Analysis," in *Date Rape: Feminism, Philosophy, and the Law*, ed. Leslie Francis, 1–26 (University Park: The Pennsylvania State University Press, 1996), 6–17; Stephen J. Schulhofer, *Unwanted Sex: The Culture of Intimidation and the Failure of Law* (Cambridge: Harvard University Press, 1998), 47–51, 61–62; Michael W. Wiederman, "The Gendered Nature of Sexual Scripts," *The Family Journal: Counseling and Therapy for Couples and Families* 13, no. 4 (2005), 497–500; Rachel Kalish, "Masculinities and Hooking Up: Sexual Decision-Making at College," *Culture, Society & Masculinities* 5, no. 2 (2013), 158–161.

3 Rebecca Kukla similarly argues that it is important to allow for the sexual autonomy of people who wish to role-play non-consensual sexual activities. Her case would be an extreme version of the aggressive techniques that I will describe below. See Rebecca Kukla, "That's What She Said: The Language of Sexual Negotiation," *Ethics* 129 (2018), 21–23.

4 Remick, "Read Her Lips," 1104.

5 Ibid., 1145.

6 Haslanger, "On Being Objective and Being Objectified," 99.
7 Lisa Wade, *American Hookup: The New Culture of Sex on Campus* (New York: W. W. Norton & Company, 2017), 211.
8 Pineau, "Date Rape," 6.
9 Ibid., 9.
10 Kramer, "Rule by Myth," 118.
11 For theories of coercion, see: Robert Nozick, "Coercion," in *Philosophy, Science, and Method: Essays in Honor of Ernest Nagel*, eds. Sidney Morgenbesser, Patrick Suppes, and Morton White (New York: St. Martin's Press, 1969), 440–472; Joseph Raz, *Morality of Freedom* (Oxford: Oxford University Press, 1988), 148–149; Michael Gorr, "Toward a Theory of Coercion," *Canadian Journal of Philosophy* 16 (1986), 386; Martin Gunderson, "Threats and Coercion," *Canadian Journal of Philosophy* IX (1979), 253; Cheyney C. Ryan, "The Normative Concept of Coercion," *Mind* 89 (1980), 483; Onora O'Neill, "Which Are the Offers You Can't Refuse?" in *Bounds of Justice* (Cambridge: Cambridge University Press, 2005), 81; Tom L. Beauchamp, "Autonomy and Consent," in *The Ethics of Consent*, eds. Franklin G. Miller and Alan Wertheimer (New York: Oxford University Press, 2010), 69.
12 Schulhofer, *Unwanted Sex*, 114–136; Igor Primoratz, "Sexual Morality: Is Consent Enough?" *Ethical Theory and Moral Practice* 4, no. 3 (2001), 201–218, 211–212.
13 For a contrary position, see Primoratz, "Sexual Morality," 212.
14 Charlene Muehlenhard and Lisa Hollabaugh, "Do Women Sometimes Say No When They Mean Yes? The Prevalence and Correlates of Women's Token Resistance to Sex," *Journal of Personality and Social Psychology* 54, no. 5 (1988), 872–879; Susan Sprecher *et al.*, "Token Resistance to Sexual Intercourse and Consent to Unwanted Sexual Intercourse: College Students' Dating Experience in Three Counties," *The Journal of Sex Research* 31, no. 2 (1994), 125–126; Kramer, "Rule by Myth," 119; Douglas N. Husak and George C. Thomas III, "Rapes Without Rapists: Consent and Reasonable Mistake," *Philosophical Issues: Social, Political, and Legal Philosophy* 11 (2001), 96; Alan Wertheimer, *Consent to Sexual Relations* (Cambridge: Cambridge University Press, 2003), 158; Schulhofer, *Unwanted Sex*, 59–60, 64–5, 264.
15 Schulhofer, *Unwanted Sex*, 65; Husak and Thomas, "Rape Without Rapists," 95–97.
16 Wertheimer, *Consent to Sexual Relations*, 159.
17 Schulhofer, *Unwanted Sex*, 64.
18 Teresa M. Downing-Matibag and Brandi Geisinger, "Hooking Up and Sexual Risk Taking Among College Students: A Health Belief Model Perspective," *Qualitative Health Research* 19, no. 9 (2009), 1206, also see 1202–1203.
19 Wertheimer, *Consent to Sexual Relations*, 152–155.
20 Ibid., 153.
21 Ibid.
22 Husak and Thomas, "Rape Without Rapists," 88, 93–94, 98.
23 Ibid., 100–102.
24 Ibid., 92–4, 100–103.
25 Ibid., 102.
26 Husak and Thomas, "Rape Without Rapists," 97. Also see Sprecher *et al.*, "Token Resistance," 126; Lucia F. O'Sullivan and Elizabeth R. Allgeier, "Feigning Sexual Desire: Consenting to Unwanted Sexual Activity in Heterosexual Dating Relationships," *The Journal of Sex Research* 36, no. 3 (1998), 234–243; Robin West, "Sex, Law, and Consent," in *The Ethics of Consent*, eds. Franklin G. Miller and Alan Wertheimer (New York: Oxford University Press, 2010), 235–236; Kukla, "That's What She Said," 7, 15.
27 Husak and Thomas, "Rape Without Rapists," 102.
28 William F. Flack, Jr. *et al.*, "Risk Factors and Consequences of Unwanted Sex Among University Students: Hooking Up, Alcohol, and Stress Response," *Journal of Interpersonal Violence* 22, no. 2 (2007), esp. 150–152.

29 Wade, *American Hookup*, 206.
30 Tracy A. Lambert, Arnold S. Kahn, and Kevin J. Apple, "Pluralistic Ignorance and Hooking Up," *The Journal of Sex Research* 40, no. 2 (2003), 130.
31 Elizabeth Paul, Brian McManus, and Allison Hayes, "'Hookups': Characteristics and Correlates of College Students' Spontaneous and Anonymous Sexual Experiences," *The Journal of Sex Research* 37, no. 1 (2000), 81.
32 Robert Jensen, *Getting Off: Pornography and the End of Masculinity* (Cambridge: South End Press, 2007), 48–49.
33 Ibid., 49.
34 For more evidence for the correlation of hooking up with increased experiences of sexual violence, see: Robyn L. Fielder et al., "Sexual Hookups and Adverse Health Outcomes: A Longitudinal Study of First-Year College Women," *Journal of Sex Research* 51, no. 2 (2014), 140–141; Tara E. Sutton and Leslie Gordon Simons, "Sexual Assault Among College Students: Family of Origin Hostility, Attachment, and the Hook-Up Culture as Risk Factors," *Journal of Child and Family Studies* 24, no. 10 (2015); Kimberly A. Tyler, Rachel M. Schmitz, and Scott A. Adams, "Alcohol Expectancy, Drinking Behavior, and Sexual Victimization Among Female and Male College Students," *Journal of Interpersonal Violence* 37, no. 15 (2015), 2301 and 2314; Wendasha Jenkins Hall and Amanda E. Tanner, "US Black College Women's Sexual Health in Hookup Culture: Intersections of Race and Gender," *Culture, Health & Sexuality* 18, no. 11 (2016), 1265, 1268; Wade, *American Hookup*, 15, 20, 201–222, 243.
35 Jensen, *Getting Off*, 49.
36 For a similar position that we cannot rely on "background norms and presumed shared understandings," see Kukla, "That's What She Said," 4.
37 Remick, "Read Her Lips;" Rachel Kramer Bussel, "Beyond Yes and No: Consent as Sexual Process," in *Yes Means Yes: Visions of Female Sexual Power & a World Without Rape*, eds. Jaclyn Friedman and Jessica Valenti (Berkeley: Seal Press, 2008), 44–49; Hazel/Cedar Troost, "Reclaiming Touch: Rape Culture, Explicit Verbal Consent, and Body Sovereignty," in *Yes Means Yes: Visions of Female Sexual Power & a World Without Rape*, eds. Jaclyn Friedman and Jessica Valenti (Berkeley: Seal Press, 2008), 172–176.
38 Remick, "Read Her Lips," 1105–1106, 1110–1116; Thomas M. Millar, "Towards a Performance Model of Sex," in *Yes Means Yes: Visions of Female Sexual Power & a World Without Rape*, eds. Jaclyn Friedman and Jessica Valenti (Berkeley: Seal Press, 2008), 29.
39 David Archard argues for explicit consent for first sexual encounters. See David Archard, *Sexual Consent* (Boulder: Westview Press, 1998), 146.
40 Schulhofer, *Unwanted Sex*, 74.
41 Ibid., 74–76.
42 Ibid., 76–78.
43 Ibid., 78.
44 Pineau, "Date Rape," 8.
45 Ibid.
46 For another argument that safe words, such as those used in BDSM, should be normalized and used more generally, see Kukla, "That's What She Said," 18–21.
47 Rebecca Kukla argues that sexual consent would not be valid if there were not a way to clearly communicate the desire to withdraw consent (Kukla, "That's What She Said," 5–6).
48 Nadine Strossen, "A Feminist Critique of 'The' Feminist Critique of Pornography," *Virginia Law Review* 79, no. 5 (1993), 1147–1151; Katie Roiphe, *The Morning After: Sex, Fear, and Feminism on Campus* (Boston: Little, Brown, and Company, 1993), 53–54, 62, 67–69, 163.

4

ADEQUATELY INFORMED HOOK UPS

Since hook ups are regularly negotiated through non-verbal means,[1] it is contentious whether they could be adequately informed. Non-verbal communication appears to be a clear threat to consent's information requirement. The purpose of this chapter is to figure out what information moral hook up participants should convey to ensure that they obtain adequately informed hook up consent.

If consent is the method through which people create obligations for themselves, then it is absolutely necessary that they know what they are doing when they give their consent. You could not purposely create an obligation for yourself if you did not really know what you were agreeing to. Yet, it is not always a simple matter to know what one agrees to since consent occurs between at least two people who may have different ideas in their minds about what is going on. The standard solution, in every other context, is that the consenting parties must explain what is happening well enough so that everyone involved can come to a singular understanding about the main issues at stake. What counts as the main issues are whatever issues the parties need to know to decide if they want to take on the new obligations. That means we do not need to be fully informed: a good deal of information is superfluous. Yet, we try to tell people as much as we think they need to know so that they make an informed decision, which would allow them to give consent.

The problem is that lots of individuals would rather not have this conversation prior to a hook up.[2] Social norms make a long pre-hook up conversation count as "not sexy." In the previous section, we saw that a pre-hook up conversation was definitely necessary for aggressive hook ups. In this chapter, I will argue that such a conversation is necessary for all hook ups. We simply do not have any definitive moral basis for lowering, much less for removing, the information requirement for consent in sexual contexts. So here I will argue that we ought to maintain some level of adequate information requirement for hook ups. I will push for the view that moral agents can hook up, but only because I think it is plausible that they could have this pre-hook up conversation.

Non-verbal Hook Ups

As we have seen, hook ups generally involve gendered groups of friends going to a club, party, or bar, and then pairing off with people with whom they have some distant connection (they share a friend or a class). Often, women initiate the flirting through non-verbal means,[3] such as through flirtatious eye contact.[4] While there could then be some verbal conversation, it likely will neither be over the impending hook up nor anything else of substance since there is likely to be loud music and others talking loudly nearby.[5]

Although the exact non-verbal method of negotiating a hook up likely varies, it is useful to examine one particular method that uses dancing, specifically grinding, to signal the choice to initiate a hook up. Sociologist Lisa Wade describes the grinding process in detail.[6] Grinding typically involves a man dancing in an upright position while moving his groin area into a woman's buttocks. As one of Wade's student subjects describes it, "It is a bestial rubbing of genitals reminiscent of mating zebras."[7] Another student describes it as a "sneak attack" because the grinding is likely to begin without the woman having seen the man approach her from behind, and it continues with her back to him. As Wade explains: "Because men generally come up from behind, sometimes the identity of the man whose penis abuts their backside is a mystery."[8] This point is key because the woman signals her agreement to initiate a hook up (typically beginning with them making out then and there) merely by looking at the man grinding her behind. As Wade notes, "Once students are face to face, it's *on*" (emphasis in original).[9]

Not only is this entire method of negotiation occurring non-verbally through dancing, but the key moment of escalating into the hook up is made through the mere turning to see with whom one is dancing. For this reason, women must often use their friends (who will look at the grinder and signal back) to determine whether the person they are dancing with is sufficiently attractive for a hook up.[10] Far from being fully informed, grinding involves a decision to hook up in the absence of even knowing for sure what the other person looks like.

Prior to leaving the bar, club, or similar location where they met, the pair will determine where to go next, but they will make this decision without explicitly acknowledging that they are heading somewhere to hook up.[11] It may seem difficult to believe that going to a place with a near stranger will lead to anything other than sexual activity, but we should be careful with drawing such a hasty conclusion. Since they are likely having a hard time talking, it would be reasonable for one of them to infer that they are moving locations to better converse.

They may just think that it is time to change locations because both are tired or low on money, or a myriad other reasons. The mere fact that they are going to a new place together does not entail that either has yet consented to a coital hook up, or even to hooking up in any fashion.

Once they arrive at the new location, even their decision of how far to go sexually is determined non-verbally.[12] We can imagine how the pair non-verbally decides how far to go. One person (usually the woman in our society) gives non-verbal indications the moment after the other person (usually the man) goes a step too far. Women often play this gatekeeper role, not because they are less sexual than men, but because, in our society, men tend to respect women less the further they go, which women are quite cognizant of.[13] In one study, women indicated that they would not engage in serious sexual activities with men in whom they were interested since they didn't want to lose the respect of those men.[14] And since about half of people in hook ups never see each other again,[15] women can accept disrespect more when they expect they'll never see the person again (in Chapter Seven we will consider respect at greater length).

If initial indications of dissent did not work, then stronger indications would be necessary until both parties understood where their hook up was headed. If signs are completely missed or the person who is unwilling to go further gives up on trying to dissent out of fear or confusion, the hook up would be non-consensual, which, as we saw in the previous chapter, presents a significant moral problem. Non-verbal communication can easily lead to non-consensual hook ups. As scholars Lucia O'Sullivan and Elizabeth Allgeier, who have studied consent in unwanted sexual encounters, put it:

> The nonverbal nature of most sexual interactions may inhibit verbal expressions of reluctance, and the ever-increasing levels of physical contact and intimacy may obscure less overt physical attempts to resist. Further, some communications of nonconsent are unclear or may be viewed as 'token' attempts to resist … Thus, the issue of consent as a defining feature of sexually coercive interactions is fraught with difficulties.[16]

There is just too much happening in a hook up for non-verbal communication to overcome a potential consent problem. The physical contact makes a good number of non-verbal cues confusing: for example, placing your hands on someone to push them gently away is a good way to stop activity in non-sexual contexts, but may be considered a sexual action in a hook up and therefore may be ignored. Many non-verbal cues of dissent can even be taken the wrong way: fighting back could be accidentally (though probably not very reasonably) taken as a signal that the person wants the hook up to be rough. Then we add as a further complication that some signs of resistance will be taken as merely tokens of feigned resistance. Consequently, if two individuals are merely interpreting each other's signals, rather than openly and verbally communicating, then a signal indicating refusal can easily be mistaken for token resistance, and could, in some circumstances, even be mistaken for a sign that indicates consent to go further (and, in worst case scenarios, consent for a rougher hook up).

Non-verbal communication can create misunderstandings where a good deal – the difference between consensual and non-consensual sex – is at stake. Possible misunderstandings are not the only risks: any information necessary for someone to make up their mind about consenting to hook up would be lacking if that information is not, or cannot be, conveyed non-verbally. Consent's information requirement necessitates that agents have the information that they need prior to making their decisions. The non-verbal communication used to negotiate hook ups makes it highly unlikely that individuals have the necessary information for consenting.

Like with other issues, our focus here differs from most discussions on the sexual consent information requirement. I am focused on what moral agents would do to obtain consent to hook up ethically. It is more typical in the sexual ethics literature for philosophers writing on the information requirement to ask how much deceit is consistent with consent. These philosophers are usually providing a moral analysis that takes a step outside of the actual encounter (where we can judge with full knowledge of how deceitful the parties are being) and asks, as if from up above, "Is their sex consensual?" And often an affirmative answer is possible because the deceit ended up not mattering because neither party cared that someone was lying.

For example, suppose that we know, from a bystander viewpoint, that a couple is lying about their true feelings, as people often do when having sex with a near stranger (they may not wish to admit that they are not that much into their partner, they might want to omit that they settled when they could not obtain a hook up with someone better, they realize that they have no wish to see the other person ever again after this hook up, etc.). Some philosophers will argue that the participants are morally permitted to lie over their true feelings, specifically when it comes to sexual consent.[17] Others will argue that sexual deceit should be treated similarly to the deceit that undermines consent in almost any other domain (if the lie is significant enough that sharing it could undermine the deal, then it must be shared), and so significant lies can and do undermine sexual consent.[18] This disagreement is important, and although I agree with the latter viewpoint, it is not the focus of the discussion here.

Our primary question concerns what is necessary for a moral agent to ensure he or she obtains informed consent. Though it may be possible to obtain consent with a low level of normative strength while lying, moral agents would not lie since lying does nothing to help make an agreement consensual. Insofar as information is a vital part of consenting, lying hinders consent. Moral agents are not interested in how much deceit they can get away with. They are interested in providing the right amount of information: enough to ensure they obtain meaningful consent, but not too much since they do not want to overwhelm their potential partner with over-sharing. Neither deceit nor non-verbal communication accomplishes the task of providing the right amount of information to ensure your hook up partner is consenting. The moral agent would neither lie nor rely on non-verbal signals when communicating important matters. Moral agents try to communicate the information that they believe their partners may need. What we need to know, then, is what the standard should be for deciding how much information is required for a consensual hook up.

The Reasonable Causal Impact Standard

Moral agents would try to ensure that they are providing enough information to their potential hook up partners so that the resulting consent is adequately informed. The tricky part is figuring out how much information is required to meet that moral duty. We need a standard for how much information should be shared because it is highly impractical and maybe even impossible for an agreement to be fully informed.[19] Alan Wertheimer, for example, points out that we neither expect nor want doctors to explain everything; there is instead an acceptance that your doctor will surely know more about your procedure than you do.[20] It would then be useful to have standards to help determine what information ought to be conveyed.

Some theorists worry about making these standards too stringent. Philosopher Alan Soble, for example, believes in a right to withhold certain bits of personal information:

> But if I withhold the fact that I have an extraordinarily large or miniscule penis, and withholding that fact about my sexual anatomy plays a role in your eventually agreeing to engage in sex with me, it is not obviously true that my obtaining sex through this particular deception-by-omission is morally wrong … Does the other person have a *right* to know the size of my penis while deliberating whether to have sex with me?[21]

Soble is suggesting that the standard of disclosure should weigh privacy concerns against the supposed right to know. It may seem, at first, that Soble's example is poorly chosen, but it is in fact a good example to exhibit the intersection of privacy rights and necessary information for consent. After all, what could be more personal and private for a man than the size of his penis?[22]

On the other hand, penis size, as Soble is willing to admit here, is clearly relevant to the woman's likely deliberation: she may be unwilling to have sex with a man whose penis is too small for her enjoyment, just as she may be unwilling if the man's penis is so big that it may cause her pain. More importantly, if the man believes his potential hook up partner may need this information to consent, then he cannot act morally unless he shares the information.

After all, we can agree that an agreement would not be consensual if key information were withheld. The man has suspicion that his penis size could be that very kind of key information. He cannot morally justify withholding it since that very act of withholding could, for all he knows, make their sex act non-consensual. For if she would never consent to have sex with a man whose penis is too big or too small, and if she agreed without being given this information, then that particular agreement could not count as consent since she lacks the information that is crucial *for her*.

In such a situation, the man either has to give up his privacy right to ensure the woman consents to sex, or he could protect his privacy right and give up the sex.[23] Importantly, his privacy right does not in any way entail that he can demand others make uninformed agreements so that he can maintain that privacy – if he wishes to have an agreement where his privacy concerns a key issue that would need to be conveyed for the agreement to be consensual, then he has to waive privacy to be sure he obtains consent. There is, then, no real conflict here: by attempting to engage in the hook up, the man has knowingly created the conditions where he morally needs to waive his own relevant privacy rights. It is not that one person's rights to know overrule another's privacy rights. It is instead that the participants, in choosing to enter into a hopefully moral hook up, would choose to waive privacy rights so that they can ensure the hook up would be adequately informed and consensual.

This case leads us to the standard that we are looking for: a reasonable causal impact standard. The moral agent's goal is to ensure that their hook up is morally permissible, which requires that it is consensual and adequately informed. That means they must convey any information where the lack of information could reasonably cause an agreement to become non-consensual. Suppose Enid and Fredo are about to agree to hook up, and Enid is holding back one piece of information: let's say that she is pregnant and does not wish to share that private information. If there is a good chance that sharing that information would make Fredo refuse to have sex with her, then Enid has violated her moral duty to inform Fredo. Sharing the piece of information is necessary precisely because not sharing it could lead to the sex being non-consensual. The moral duty is to provide any information that has a reasonable chance of having a causal impact on the other person's agreement. If you think the information could reasonably change their mind, then you have to share it.

It is important to ask what "reasonable" tracks in the reasonable causal impact standard. I mean "reasonable" to be predictive (as in reasonably likely to change someone's mind) rather than normative (as in a reasonably good person could change their mind). Consent binds agents due to their own agreements. It is up to the agent whether they wish to consent, just as it is up to the agent to decide when they would like to withhold their consent. Suppose that we thought that were Fredo a reasonably good person, he would not care that Enid is pregnant. Yet, we also might think that most men would care. It is the latter fact that is more relevant for consent since it is up to each person to decide for themselves what they care about. That is especially true for sexual consent: if Fredo does not wish to hook up with pregnant women, then that is his choice. And if large numbers of men were similar to Fredo in this regard, then it is reasonable (in the predictive sense) for Enid to realize that she ought to share that information prior to hooking up with anyone.

For a similar view, it is useful to examine philosopher Tom Dougherty's deal breaker standard.[24] For Dougherty, consent is vitiated whenever someone is deceived about a matter that the person would actually consider to be a deal breaker – that is, they would not agree were they to know the truth.[25] Like the reasonable causal impact standard that I am arguing for here, it is essential for Dougherty's deal breaker standard that it is based on the individual's own determination of what is important.[26] Dougherty points out that such a view promotes the value of sexual pluralism where each person figures out what they value in their own sex lives, and no one forces a conception of "good sex" onto them.[27] So, in this way, our views are very similar.

The difference between my view and Dougherty's is that his view is based on the agents' actual intentions, where my view would start with actual intentions (which you could discover by asking about them) but then utilizes a reasonableness standard where actual intentions are not available (because you simply cannot ask about everything that could possibly matter). So, both my view and Dougherty's can use actual intentions wherever these are expressed: on both views, if a person says their consent depends on some factor, then any deception or withholding of information on that factor would undermine the consent.[28] Further, if deal breakers are already known, then both views can agree that deception about them would vitiate consent.[29]

The difficulty comes if the person does not express their deal breakers and these deal breakers are otherwise not known. On Dougherty's view, we then must go with the person's (unstated) intentions.[30] Suppose Fredo has not mentioned it, but he has an unstated rule that he does not hook up with vegetarians. It also turns out that Enid is a vegetarian, but there is no way for Fredo to know that, and Enid sees no reason to tell him. Surely such an anti-vegetarian hook up rule is rare. To cut off a clear objection to his view, Dougherty argues that in such a case a person could be excused for their justifiable ignorance when they ultimately act without consent.[31]

The problem with Dougherty's view is that it takes consent to be much more transparent than it can possibly be. As we saw in Chapter Two, philosophers Neil Manson and Onora O'Neill argue that consent is opaque in the sense that we cannot possibly see each other's exact intentions when we consent.[32] To be fair, Dougherty does acknowledge that deal breakers can be opaque even for the person herself,[33] but I would argue that this opaqueness leads to a different conclusion than the one that Dougherty draws. Consent's opaqueness implies both that attempts to consent can sometimes be undermined by unpredictable confusion and that even successful consent includes some amount of reasonable confusion. Two agents seeking to consent simply cannot cover everything. That means that sometimes deals should count as consensual even though something important was left out, provided that everything possible was done to try to cover the important factors that it seemed reasonable to go over. If two agents have a sober conversation about what their deal breakers are, and there is no purposeful attempt to manipulate or pressure the conversation, and they come up with an agreement, then I would argue that they have consented even if one of them left a key, but very unusual deal breaker out.

Enid's not telling Fredo that she is pregnant and a vegetarian are different in this respect. Enid can reasonably expect that her pregnancy might change Fredo's mind since it would change a lot of men's minds (regardless of whether that is reasonable or fair). Enid probably never met anyone who would not hook up with a vegetarian, and she may have never heard of such a rule. Since Enid cannot tell Fredo everything about herself, then it is reasonable for her not to include mention of her vegetarian lifestyle, along with millions of other details about herself that are not likely to change people's minds about hooking up. Since Fredo did not specifically ask, and Enid acted reasonably by not bringing it up, then Fredo should take responsibility for not mentioning his strange anti-vegetarian rule. In that case, since it is Fredo's responsibility to bring it up, then Fredo should still become morally obligated by what he agreed to do, and so their agreement should count as consent.

Consequently, such a deal should count as consent because the person who left their unusual deal breaker out should still be morally obligated by their agreement – after all, it is reasonable to assume that you have consent when you do the best job you can to try to adequately inform the other person. You did not attempt to lie or omit information to be deceitful. You simply could not cover every detail about your life, and you cannot always guess another person's unusual deal breaker. Thus, since both persons become morally obligated by this agreement, the agreement counts as consent by definition.

While I wish to hold stringent requirements for consent, the stringency is driven entirely by what it takes for an agreement to create new moral obligations. Some mistakes can be made that still allow such an agreement to create moral obligations even though the agreement is not perfectly negotiated. Yet, since no agreement can be perfectly negotiated, this result is simply realistic. In the end, this point is not a significant departure from Dougherty's view, but this refinement captures why I think the moral agent should be able to use a reasonableness standard. From that standard, they only have to discuss the things that reasonably could have a causal impact, and not everything that actually does create a causal impact, which would be practically unfeasible.

On the other side, some theorists are suspicious of any causal impact standard, which they argue is too high of a standard, at least for legal offenses.[34] And, legally speaking, there are reasons why we would not want to make all omissions and lies into criminal offenses. Perhaps a case could be made for allowing torts to proceed where key information is withheld, or lies are told that have causal impact on the sexual exchange,[35] but we should be wary of criminalizing information requirements. No one should go to jail for forgetting to mention something. Criminal law has to justify harsh penalties, and so numerous immoral activities should not be criminalized.

The moral case, however, is different. We are interested in what moral agents should seek to do as they seek moral hook ups. Moral agents would work hard, instead of relying on luck, to ensure that they provide adequate information prior to the hook up. That hard work is meant to ensure the other person is not missing any information that they need to make up their mind. Therefore, the moral agent would try to share any information that could reasonably have a causal impact on the other person's decision.

In a similar position, Thomas Mappes argues that withholding information prior to sex should count as using a person as a means:

> Suppose that Mr. A meets Ms. B in a singles bar. Mr. A realizes immediately that Ms. B is the sister of Ms. C, a woman that Mr. A has been sexually involved with for a long time. Mr. A, knowing that it is very unlikely that Ms. B will consent to sexual interaction if she becomes aware of Mr. A's involvement with her sister, decides not to disclose this information. If Ms. B eventually consents to sexual interaction, since her consent is the product of Mr. A's deception, it is rightly thought that she has been sexually used by him.[36]

In Mappes' case, it is quite clear that Mr. A is using Ms. B by withholding information that could change her mind. I would disagree with Mappes calling Ms. B's agreement "consent" since it is not clear that she could become morally obligated through an agreement that lacked the key piece of information that would have changed her mind. But, Mappes does establish the point that Mr. A acts wrongly by knowingly withholding the information that would change Ms. B's mind.

The case would be harder if Mr. A doesn't know whether the piece of information he has would change Ms. B's mind. Suppose instead that Ms. B and C are distant cousins, not sisters. Mr. A has no idea how Ms. B will react to the fact that he's hook up buddies (two people who regularly hook up with each other as mutual last resorts) with Ms. C. She might be appalled and refuse to hook up with Mr. A, but she also might not care since they are only cousins and he is not in a committed relationship with either woman – they are just hooking up. In this case, we can wonder whether withholding the information would be wrongful given a reasonable causal impact standard.

To determine whether the standard is met, we don't need to know what Ms. B in fact will do. We need to know whether it is reasonable to believe a person would likely change their mind based on this type of information. What Ms. B would actually do does not tell us how Mr. A should treat her unless he knows her well enough to have a good basis for believing that he knows what she would do. If he does know what she actually would do, then he should act based on that information. If he doesn't know her that well, he can only provide her with the information that other people in Ms. B's situation would likely require. Now, this piece of information is something that Mr. A suspects could be relevant to Ms. B, or else he wouldn't be asking the question of whether to convey it in the first place. And, if B and C were close relations, such as sisters, then Mr. A would know he has to share the information. Since their relation is more distant, and this is just hooking up, it is less clear what the standard requires. But surely if Mr. A is trying to ensure he is being ethical, and he wants to ensure that his hook up with Ms. B is consensual, then he should err on the side of giving more information, not less. After all, it could turn out that this piece of information could change her mind, in which case she would not be consenting without it. Since Mr. A would not want to risk unintentionally having a non-consensual hook up with Ms. B, he should err on the side of too much, rather than too little information.

Thus, the standard for conveying information in a matter where acting without consent is potentially serious is that agents should convey any information that could reasonably have causal impact, and, if they are unsure, they should err on the side of sharing information. If you know your partner well, then you are more likely to know the information they will need, and your act of informing them can be much more straightforward. If you are in a situation where it is not a serious matter to act without consent, then you also need not inform the person of everything that could be relevant. But if you do not know the other person well, and you have a strong moral obligation to be sure you only act with their consent, then you must share all information that could reasonably have a causal impact on the person's decision.

Required Hook Up Information

The causal impact standard requires the sharing of information that could reasonably change a person's mind. Since hook ups are typically between people who do not know each other well, there's a need to have a general sense of what kind of information should reasonably be shared between strangers or near strangers. Thus, we are looking for the general kinds of information that reasonable people would believe are: (a) often significant, (b) not easily known by potential hook up partners, and (c) could likely change people's minds about whether to hook up. This section interrogates potential types of information that moral agents would likely share prior to a hook up.

Legal theorist Lani Anne Remick provides one list of required information for informed sexual consent: "This information includes, for example, each partner's motive for participating in the encounter, information about sexually transmitted diseases, whether either partner is romantically involved with someone else, contraception, and discussion of sexual preferences."[37] Remick's list provides a good framework, but we should reexamine these topics in light of the reasonable causal impact standard. The division I will use, which is based on Remick's, focuses on: the participants' health statuses, their statuses and plans with respect to romantic relationships, their sexual preferences and proclivities, and their motivations for the hook up.

Health Status

It seems clear that moral agents would inform their partners about any sexually transmitted diseases (STDs), as Remick requires.[38] The problem is that such straightforward information is unlikely to suffice. These diseases can be life-threatening and life-altering (since even non-lethal STDs can have negative consequences for life), and their carriers do not always know they have them. Moral agents should be prepared to discuss STD indicators so that each potential partner can roughly judge STD probabilities. This requirement follows from there being so much at stake: the fact that someone has a high probability of giving you a STD could make a lot of people second guess the decision to hook up. Since this information can change minds, the moral agent would be ready to share it to ensure he or she receives adequately informed consent. Hence, a requirement for discussing STDs entails a requirement to discuss STD indicators, such as recent sexual history, drug use, and condom use.

This STD discussion is both essential and not nearly as difficult as one might imagine. Gerard simply says to Henri, "I don't share needles and I always use condoms. Further, I was tested two months ago and came out clean, what about you?" Perhaps the discussion would be more difficult were Henri to ask, "How much hooking up have you done in the last two months?" Surely, this conversation could become uncomfortable at this point, but since they are near strangers, their hook up frequency is unknown and so the significance of the timeframe requires some additional context: Gerard having hooked up once or twice in the last two months is quite different from him having hooked up 16 times in the same timeframe.

Of course, this requirement also entails that moral hook up participants would regularly get themselves tested; this additional requirement for testing though seems fairly obvious as a moral agent would have no desire to spread diseases. And, as the above discussion shows, how often the moral agent should get tested will depend a large deal on how often they hook up. Yet, clearly, since it is morally wrong to knowingly spread diseases, or to take the risk that you are spreading diseases, informing partners about STDs and testing seems like a clear moral requirement for sharing information.

Relationship Information

Perhaps it is also clear, though not universally practiced, that moral agents would share their relationship statuses with potential hook up partners. After all, a lot of people would think differently about hooking up with someone who is already in a committed relationship. Different people, though, may think differently about different types of relationships. Some people may be *more* willing to hook up with someone who is married than someone who is engaged, for example, because they may be more open to possibly contributing to the break up of a stale marriage. For the most part, it is likely that reluctance will be greater the stronger the other person's commitment is. Since this is a well-known reluctance, people who are cheating should let their adultery status be known.

In a way, this point may seem unnecessary since a moral agent would not cheat. That is correct, but it may be useful to put that issue aside so that we can isolate the morality of the hook up itself. The question of this book is not how a perfectly moral agent would hook up, but how would an agent proceed if they were looking to hook up in a morally permissible fashion. The agent may be doing something immoral outside of the hook up, but still endeavors to engage in the hook up morally. It can make sense to ask how an adulterer might hook up ethically.

It could even change people's minds about a hook up to find out that the other person has very recently left a relationship. Sometimes we are cautious when possibly hooking up with someone in an emotionally perilous state because the hook up may damage them. This judgment could be moral (you don't want to increase the person's emotional damage) or selfish (who wants an awkward hook up?). Other times, one might not want to hook up with someone recently estranged since it is thought that they could be on the rebound, seeking to attach quickly to someone new. Of course, many people may not care that their hook up partner recently broke up with someone. But we must remember that an agent cannot withhold information just because a good number of people wouldn't care. Instead, the moral agent reveals information that has a reasonable chance of changing the other person's mind. It is sufficient that a lot of people would care about a recent break up to make the moral agent obligated to reveal that information.

Although there may be some people who use the phrase "hooking up" in a way that they believe entails that there will be no future relationship, many people acknowledge that it is possible, even if unlikely, that a hook up could lead to a relationship. About 12% of people have hook ups turn into relationships, according to one study.[39] In part because people use the phrase differently and in part because there is room for relationships, moral agents should clarify their willingness to enter into relationships.

If an agent has already decided that he would never want to be in a relationship with his current hook up partner, he needs to let her know that fact in case it would change her mind. After all, she may only be consenting on the assumption that he is at least open to a relationship. For example, she may be hooking up in a hope of finding someone who is sexually compatible with her, and she wouldn't want to waste her time on someone who has decided in advance that he would never enter a relationship with her. To make sure their hook up isn't based on the type of misunderstanding that could undermine the information requirement for consent (since this piece of information could be causally key to the other person), either partner who decides in advance that there will be no relationship needs to tell the other partner.

There's some potential for awkwardness in this discussion. Let's suppose that Jacob and Inez are about to hook up, and Jacob intends for the hook up to be final, while Inez is open to it turning into a relationship. First, the burden is on Jacob: Inez is merely open to numerous possibilities. That openness seems fairly trivial, and should simply be assumed. It is the person who is closed off – in this case, Jacob – who should inform the other person that a decision has already been made. Yet, that decision could come off as offensive to Inez since Jacob is in fact saying that no matter how the hook up goes, he does not want to have a relationship with Inez.

In this case, there is a burden on Jacob not only to provide his position, but common decency would also require him to justify his decision in a non-offensive fashion (it would not be polite for him to simply say, "I would never be in a relationship with you; let's hook up now"). There are several potentially true claims that he could make: "I am about to move to a different city," "I just got out of a relationship and am not ready for a new one," "I'm only interested in hooking up at this juncture in my life," etc. Jacob's reasons are not meant to be derogatory to Inez's potential to make a good relationship partner. His reasons are general reasons that would make him unwilling to enter a relationship with anyone at this time.

It might be that Inez still takes offense – and that is her right. She can even change her mind and refuse to hook up with someone who has decided to foreclose any chance for a relationship with her. Thus, we can say that if Jacob has made this decision in advance, then he must share it with Inez, along with his reasoning. If that changes her mind, then that precisely shows that they would not have had a consensual hook up if Jacob had withheld the information.

The moral agent could have much to say about relationships prior to hooking up with a near stranger for the first time. The moral agent would not only give his or her relationship status as Remick requires,[40] but also may need to provide information on very recent break ups and perhaps thoughts about future relationship intentions. Hooking up revolves around sexual fun, and so the participants do not have to have relationship plans. It just has to be made clear to all the participants whether they've ruled them out in advance.

Hook Up Motives

Another area where information could be required is the motivation to hook up. There are many motives for hooking up that could change reasonable people's minds. Consider some of the following possibly illicit motives for hooking up: to cheat on a regular lover; to put women or men in their place through sexual conquests of them; to try out new sexual activities that frightened other lovers; to complete some bizarre sexual demographic game, such as by having sex with a person from every state, continent, or race; to prove one's own self-value by making someone fall in love through a heightened sexual experience; or simply to maximize the number of sexual conquests.

Many of these motives may be immoral in themselves. We can however put that issue aside since we are wondering whether motives ought to be communicated, and some of these motives could arguably be permissible. Let's take the sexual demographic game as an example. Let's say Gino decides he wants to hook up with a person from every state. Now, there may be something off-putting about Gino's motive since he will hook up with a person just because they were born in a certain state. Gino is not seeing his hook up partners as fully humanized persons whose distinct personalities, aspirations, hopes, and dreams are meaningful and inherently valuable. Gino is objectifying people by reducing them to mere representatives of their birth states. It is perhaps beyond doubt that a man or woman would be reasonable in rejecting Gino's request on the grounds that they do not want to be reduced to their state of birth. Although such a rejection would be reasonable, it is less clear that Gino's motive is significantly different than standard hook up motives. Hooking up with near strangers is objectifying almost by definition. Martha Nussbaum has argued that objectification is not always immoral,[41] and we will have to return to this issue when we examine moral questions that go beyond consent. For now, let's accept that most hook ups are motivated by lust and involve objectifying someone by reducing them to their physical body and its appearance. If hooking up can be moral, which we are assuming unless we cannot find a way to develop ethical hook ups in this book, then we cannot count objectifying hook ups as automatically immoral.

Gino reduces individuals to what state they are from, yet almost everyone who hooks up with near strangers reduces them to their body. If the latter could be permissible, Gino's actions are not necessarily immoral. In the end, if the demographic and physical reductions of others can be permissible, it would have to be because hooking up inherently involves taking sex less seriously than the value that our society currently places on sex. Absent some argument that we must agree with society on the value of sex, individual adults could decide not to take sex too seriously. What they cannot permissibly do is simply assume that other adults that they hook up with have the same view as them. Plenty of people, even within the hook up culture, continue to take sex seriously: some are new to the culture (studies suggest that first year college students are often confused about the practice, and are taken advantage of because of their confusion[42]), and some simply have different ideas on how hook ups should go. Accordingly, there should be a moral presumption that others may take sex seriously, even if you yourself do not take it seriously.

Since some people in the hook up culture do not take sex seriously, they may accept just about any motives that would be unacceptable for serious matters. Some people in the hook up culture may react favorably or indifferently to Gino's demographic game. That said, it is still reasonable to be turned off by his game. Since Gino cannot know near strangers well enough to know how they would react, and it is clearly reasonable for some to reject his motive, he would have to share the motive to ensure his hook up is consensual.

Thus, it is essential for moral agents to discuss any suspect motives that might turn off a good number of people (though more typical motives – such as hooking up for sexual fun – need not be mentioned at all). It is important to note that while saying some motives must be discussed, I am not arguing that there are certain motives required for hooking up. As has been pointed out in the literature numerous times, it is problematic to demand specific motives since people have a plethora of distinct motives, and they can always obtain consent from people who are perfectly fine with those motives.[43] The point here does not depend on what motives people have, but on the importance of conveying suspect motives so that the other person can judge for himself or herself. Since it is open that people may judge almost any motive as acceptable for themselves, this view need not rule out or require any specific motives. Nor does it require sharing standard or non-suspect motives.

Talking About Sex

Perhaps the most awkward category to discuss would be the sexual activity itself. In our society, discussing sexual activities with a near stranger may be much harder than engaging in sexual activity with one. Moral obligations cannot be overly burdensome, but it is hard to rule out an uncomfortable conversation about sex for agents about to engage in sex. If you are mature enough to hook up, you should be mature enough to talk about hooking up.

The sex discussion is necessary precisely because of the core ambiguity in the kind of sexual activity implied by "hooking up." Agents cannot consent to something if they don't understand what they are consenting to. In actual practice, it is common to determine the extent of the sexual activity non-verbally.[44] Yet, it is clearly dangerous to figure out how far agents will go sexually through a method (non-verbal communication) that lends itself to serious misunderstandings.[45] Since people may be unable to express their unwillingness to go further sexually, or non-verbal signals may become confused, there is a good chance that a hook up can start out as consensual but end up being non-consensual.

The moral agent would work to prevent non-consensual sex arising from any potential misunderstanding. That entails that the moral agent would seek to disambiguate the term "hooking up." They will discuss how far they wish the hook up to go so that someone does not become frightened by a confusion arising over what they agreed to do within the hook up. If the moral agent wishes the hook up to involve sexual intercourse, they will say so. If the other person does not wish for it to go that far, this simple communication will save them from a potential non-consensual hook up. Accordingly, the disambiguation of "hooking up" is morally required.

It may be necessary to share further sexual details for the sake of being respectful, but perhaps not for the sake of ensuring consent. Imagine Kelly and Leslie are about to hook up, and they have communicated that they both wish to have sexual intercourse. Unbeknownst to them, they have different sexual tastes. It would be respectful, as we will discuss in Chapter Seven, for them both to be interested in the other receiving sexual pleasure and to be aware of what it takes to do that. Yet, it is not clear to me that their consent entails any guarantee of mutual satisfaction. Consent is a method to come to an agreement where different priorities might have otherwise clashed. Hook up participants are, by definition, not in a relationship. They do not owe each other sexual gratification, and they are not likely to believe that the other person's consent was a guarantee to bring about satisfaction. It is instead an agreement to have sex, with each person at least hoping for their own satisfaction. Hence, they need not share details that ensure the hook up will be enjoyable; the real goal, for the reasonable causal impact standard, is to share details that would have causal impact on the decision. And if the decision is to have sex in a hook up, then I do not believe consent requires sharing too many sexual details.

Of course, the above point is undermined if the sexual details are such that a good number of people would likely change their minds. As we saw in the previous chapter, some people may turn aggressive as part of a sexual technique. And, as argued in that chapter, that sexual detail needs to be shared since it could likely change someone's mind.

Yet, most sexual details are not mind-changers in this sense, and so usually the most important thing to discuss prior to the hook up is how far the hook up is meant to go. This conversation topic seems quite clearly necessary, and anyone unwilling to have it is probably not well positioned to have morally permissible hook ups.

Conclusion

In an important way, all this chapter is calling for is a good, open conversation prior to hooking up. As hooking up is currently practiced, this demand may seem to be potentially burdensome. People often hook up with individuals with whom they will perhaps never have an extended conversation. This detail is one of the hallmarks of the change from dating to hooking up: even if individuals only dated to get sex, they were almost forced to communicate at some point prior to sexual activity by the nature of the dating practice. Dating required sitting down and talking about something. Hooking up has no such social norm that involves communicating, but the argument here is that communicating is still morally required.

And, here, the moral requirement is to have a conversation that meets a clear standard: any information should be shared that could reasonably have a causal impact on a person's decision to hook up. It is important here to note that this conversation is not very long for many people who are about to hook up. According to the arguments of this chapter, everyone must share their current health status, when they were last tested, and what they mean by "hooking up." For many hook up participants, that could likely be the entire conversation. For example, they could just say, "My health tested clean last week and I am hoping we will have sex." That could be the entire statement for many hook up participants.

For other participants, the reasonable causal impact standard requires a few more details only if the individuals have details that they know they morally should share. If they have potentially worrisome (from the other person's perspective) motives, if they have a relationship status that could affect the other person's decision, if they have very recently left a relationship, if they have decided to never enter into a relationship with this new potential partner, or if they plan to do something during sex, such as become aggressive, that could scare the other person, then they should also share those details.

The difficulty of the conversation then depends on each person. That opens up the possibility that there are issues that could be necessary to discuss that are not mentioned here because everyone is different. However, people will likely know what they need to share because they will have a good idea what specifically about them might change someone else's mind about the hook up. Therefore, the information requirement for consent will differ for different people.

The information requirement cannot be assumed away though. Consent is propositional, and so even a verbal agreement makes plausible a plethora of inferences of what each party had in mind for the agreement. A large number of these inferences will be reasonable. Since the verbal content will usually not suffice to explain what the agreement completely entails, both sides will have to rely on some of these reasonable inferences, and they may very well rely on conflicting ones. Thus, even verbal consent necessarily creates room for perfectly innocent and reasonable misunderstandings. Non-verbal attempts to come to an agreement about important matters are sure to fail the information requirement for consent.

Insofar as moral agents want to make sure that they receive adequately informed consent, they would do what they can to prevent potential misunderstandings. Since the room for conflicting inferences is infinite and morality cannot require what is either impossible (since "ought implies can" seems to be a perfectly reasonable rule) or overly burdensome, there are surely issues that the moral agent ought to bring up to prevent misunderstanding, and other issues that can be safely ignored. This chapter's list of topics provides a handful of important discussion points for most hook up participants. This list, however, is not meant to be exhaustive since a person may feel there is something that he or she ought to disclose that would not be relevant for others to disclose. The important point here is that there is certainly a moral requirement for at least a minimal conversation prior to every hook up, but the conversation can be tailored to an individual's own needs. We can now turn, in Chapter Five, to the competency requirement for consent.

Notes

1 Monica Moore, "Courtship Signaling and Adolescents: 'Girls Just Wanna Have Fun'?" *The Journal of Sex Research* 32, no. 4 (1995); Douglas N. Husak and George C. Thomas III, "Rapes Without Rapists: Consent and Reasonable Mistakes," *Philosophical Issues: Social, Political, and Legal Philosophy* 11 (2001), 88, 93–94, 98; Tracy A. Lambert, Arnold S. Kahn, and Kevin J. Apple, "Pluralistic Ignorance and Hooking Up," *The Journal of Sex Research* 40, no. 2 (2003), 129; Kathleen Bogle, *Hooking Up: Sex, Dating, and Relationships on Campus* (New York: New York University Press, 2008), 33–39.
2 Sociologist Lisa Wade discusses how difficult it is for people who hooked up in college to transition to dating after college, especially because honest and open communication would be expected. See Lisa Wade, *American Hookup: The New Culture of Sex on Campus* (New York: W. W. Norton & Company, 2017), 237.
3 Lucia F. O'Sullivan and Sandra Byers, "Eroding Stereotypes: College Women's Attempts to Influence Reluctant Male Partners," *The Journal of Sex Research* 30, no. 3 (1993), 270; Moore, "Courtship," 320.
4 Moore, "Courtship," 320; Bogle, *Hooking Up*, 33.
5 Bogle, *Hooking Up*, 33.
6 Wade, *American Hookup*, 31–39.
7 Ibid., 31.
8 Ibid., 33.
9 Ibid., 38.
10 Ibid., 33–37.
11 Bogle, *Hooking Up*, 34–36.
12 Ibid., 36–39.
13 Ibid., 38.
14 Ibid.
15 Elizabeth Paul, Brian McManus, and Allison Hayes, "'Hookups': Characteristics and Correlates of College Students' Spontaneous and Anonymous Sexual Experiences," *The Journal of Sex Research* 37, no. 1 (2000): 76–88, 81; Bogle, *Hooking Up*, 39.
16 Lucia F. O'Sullivan and Elizabeth R. Allgeier, "Feigning Sexual Desire: Consenting to Unwanted Sexual Activity in Heterosexual Dating Relationships," *The Journal of Sex Research* 36, no. 3 (1998), 234.
17 Steven J. Schulhofer, *Unwanted Sex: The Culture of Intimidation and the Failure of Law* (Cambridge: Harvard University Press, 1998), 84; Alan Wertheimer, *Consent to Sexual Relations* (Cambridge: Cambridge University Press, 2003), 198–199.
18 Jane E. Larson, "Women Understand So Little, They Call My Good Nature 'Deceit:' A Feminist Rethinking of Seduction," *Columbia Law Review* 93, no. 2 (1993); Thomas

A. Mappes, "Sexual Morality and the Concept of Using Another Person," in *The Philosophy of Sex: Contemporary Readings*, eds. Alan Soble and Nicholas Power (New York: Rowman and Littlefield, 2008), 234; Tom Dougherty, "Sex, Lies, and Consent," *Ethics* 123 (2013).

19 Wertheimer, *Consent to Sexual Relations*, 190; Neil Manson and Onora O'Neill, *Rethinking Informed Consent in Bioethics* (Cambridge: Cambridge University Press, 2007): 84–90.
20 Wertheimer, *Consent to Sexual Relations*, 190.
21 Alan Soble, "Sexual Use," in *The Philosophy of Sex: Contemporary Readings*, eds. Alan Soble and Nicholas Power (New York: Rowman and Littlefield, 2008), 270.
22 In a similar case, Raja Halwani argues that a man could lie about a deformity that he could hide while clothed, provided that the woman could easily leave once she learned of the deformity prior to sex. See Raja Halwani, "Are One Night Stands Morally Problematic?" *International Journal of Applied Philosophy* 10, no. 1 (1995): 63–64.
23 Tom Dougherty similarly accepts that privacy and honesty can conflict, but also argues that obtaining consent in a sexual context may simply require relinquishing some privacy. See Dougherty, "Sex, Lies, and Consent," 741 and footnote 52.
24 Dougherty, "Sex, Lies, and Consent."
25 Ibid., 719.
26 Ibid., 730.
27 Ibid.
28 Ibid., 732–734.
29 Ibid., 734.
30 Ibid., 734–739.
31 Ibid., 738.
32 Manson and O'Neill, *Rethinking Informed Consent*, 45.
33 Dougherty, "Sex, Lies, and Consent," 734.
34 Joel Feinberg, "Victims' Excuses: The Case of Fraudulently Procured Consent," *Ethics* 96, no. 2 (1986), 336, 339–40; Wertheimer, *Consent to Sexual Relations*, 195.
35 Larson, "So Little."
36 Mappes, "Sexual Morality," 235.
37 Lani Anne Remick, "Read Her Lips: An Argument for a Verbal Consent Standard in Rape," *University of Pennsylvania Law Review* 141, no. 3 (1993): 1103–1151, 1150.
38 Ibid.
39 Paul, *et al.*, "Hookups," 81. For more general information on hook ups leading to relationships, see Bogle, *Hooking Up*, 29; Wade, *American Hookup*, 46, 145–146, 235.
40 Remick, "Read Her Lips," 1150.
41 Martha Nussbaum, "Objectification," *Philosophy and Public Affairs* 24, no. 4 (1995), 250–251.
42 Bogle, *Hooking Up*, 39, 180; Norval Glenn and Elizabeth Marquardt, *Hooking Up, Hanging Out, and Hoping for Mister Right: College Women on Dating and Mating Today*, An Institute for American Values Report to the Independent Women's Forum (2001), 15; Wade, *American Hookup*, 20.
43 Alan H. Goldman, "Plain Sex," *Philosophy and Public Affairs* 6, no. 3 (1977), 268–279; Anthony Ellis, "Casual Sex," *International Journal of Moral and Social Studies* 1, no. 2 (1986), 160–165; Katie Roiphe, *The Morning After: Sex, Fear, and Feminism on Campus* (Boston: Little, Brown and Company, 1993), 60, 80; Halwani, "One Night Stands," 61–62; Catharine Pierce Wells, "Date Rape and the Law: Another Feminist View," in *Date Rape: Feminism, Philosophy, and the Law*, ed. Leslie Francis (University Park: The Pennsylvania State University Press, 1996), 46–48; Alan Soble, *Sexual Investigations* (New York: New York University Press, 1996), 1–58; David Archard,

Sexual Consent (Boulder: Westview Press, 1998), 78–80; Schulhofer, *Unwanted Sex*, 84–6; Igor Primoratz, *Ethics and Sex* (London: Routledge, 1999), 31–33, 173–175; Igor Primoratz, "Sexual Morality: Is Consent Enough?" *Ethical Theory and Moral Practice* 4, no. 3 (2001), 210–212; Wertheimer, *Consent to Sexual Relations*, 140–142.

44 Bogle, *Hooking Up*, 36–39.

45 O'Sullivan and Allgeier, "Feigning Sexual Desire," 234.

5

SUFFICIENTLY SOBER HOOK UPS

In looking at the competency condition for consent, one issue jumps out as requiring more attention for hook ups than any other: sobriety. Other competency issues would only arise in non-standard hook up cases. For example, while there are good discussions of why children cannot consent to sex,[1] sex with small children would not fit within the hook up paradigm. While our legal system varies on whether people under the age of consent (18, in many states) can consent to sex with similarly aged partners,[2] there is no reason to think that morality must be stringent when it comes to people who are close in age since there is little reason to think there is anything magical about the 18th birthday such that it would be wrong for 18 year olds to hook up with 17 year olds.[3] The largest competency issue for young hook up partners has to do with their large consumption of alcohol.

Most hook up participants drink quite a bit of alcohol prior to hooking up.[4] There is surely a level of intoxication where it is no longer possible for an agent to reason well, which means the agent would be in no position to purposely create new moral obligations. At that point the agent cannot consent.[5] There is then reason to think that hook up participants can become so intoxicated that their reasoning is too diminished for their hook ups to be consensual. For the rest of the chapter, unless stated otherwise, I will use "intoxicated" simply to refer to that level of intoxication where reason is diminished to this extent.

We have developed a standard for when intoxication undermines consent: if the agent is unable to reason well enough to take on new moral obligations, then they cannot consent. There is still quite a good bit of controversy over whether agents should have their intoxicated agreements count as consensual since most people prefer to hook up while intoxicated. Some theorists, such as Alan Wertheimer, argue that in this kind of case, we ought to count the agreements as consensual, even if intoxication would normally undermine consent, because most people would prefer a system where intoxicated agreements count as consensual.[6] This view can be interpreted in one of two ways. It could be a consequentialist view that we should develop consent rules that work best for a given group of people. That view, though, would violate the definition of "consent," which involves the creation of new moral obligations, and does not derive from what works out best. The view could also be a view based on *group advance consent*, which would involve a group deciding in advance that they would consent to a given intoxicated activity. Although such a view would fit closer to the definition of "consent," it would violate the idea that, for consent, individuals must be the sources of their own moral obligations; membership in a group that would generally prefer to have certain moral obligations will not be sufficient.

Instead, I will argue that we can obtain morally permissible intoxicated hook ups only where agents obtain *individual prior consent*, where agents individually give their consent, while sober, to activities that they later engage in while intoxicated. Through individual prior consent, we can continue to have intoxicated hook ups, but we would not be merely treating intoxicated agreements as consensual, which is impossible.

Alcohol in the Hook Up Practice

There are many reasons why it makes sense for alcohol to play a central role in the hook up practice. Hook ups involve near strangers using non-verbal communication to initiate sexual activity. Alcohol not only enables something (hooking up with near strangers) that individuals may struggle to do while sober, but it also gives them the courage to navigate such risky activity through non-verbal communication.[7] In an important way, alcohol can also initiate the interaction since many people believe that drinking signals hook up availability.[8] Sociologist Lisa Wade argues that students will drink and "get sloshed" prior to heading to parties, even – or especially – dry parties where there will be no alcohol.[9] According to one study, individuals also saw alcohol as, "as an anticipatory 'excuse function,' promoting uncharacteristic behavior that individuals believe they can't be held accountable for when they are drunk."[10] Finally, alcohol provides evidence that they did not mean anything to be serious or meaningful; insofar as both persons are drunk, their sexual activity becomes established as *just* a hook up.[11]

Not surprisingly, some studies indicate that alcohol produces problems in casual sex encounters. For example, as people lower their inhibitions, they also lower their abilities to respond effectively when boundaries are overstepped. According to one study, "effective evaluation and communication is thwarted upon intoxication, making attempts to stop short of sexual intercourse unlikely and ineffective."[12] In another study, it was pointed out that 75% of college men used alcohol to change women's minds about sex.[13] This study's results are very troubling. Suppose a woman doesn't want to hook up at t1. Then a man gives her alcohol at t2 and continues until she changes her mind at t3. If the alcohol is intended and expected to be a contributing factor to changing her mind, then the very point of the alcohol is to effect a change of mind through diminished rational capacity. The alcohol is being purposely used to undermine consent in the hopes of obtaining a normatively empty agreement. The fact that 75% of college men purposely try to undermine sexual autonomy in this fashion is very disturbing. In another disturbing study, men were more likely to receive erections while listening to tape recordings of rapes provided that they believed the victims were intoxicated.[14] As Karen Kramer puts it while summarizing these and similar studies: "As these studies indicate, some men intend to sexually conquer when they ply women with alcohol or seek out an obviously incapacitated woman."[15]

We can see alcohol as a problematic aspect of hook ups without having to think that intoxicated hook ups are necessarily immoral. In ideal circumstances, two agents could separately decide they each want to hook up with near strangers, each gets buzzed so they can pull it off, and then they fortunately meet each other and permissibly hook up with each other. Two issues must be kept clear here. First, this permissible hook up is fairly dependent on luck. The two individuals did not *know* that the other person wished to hook up with a near stranger while intoxicated. They happened to not violate each other's rights because they independently chose the same state of affairs, and simply got lucky because they found each other. Even if most people fall into this category, as long as some people do not, it is luck that the two people who got intoxicated while wishing to later have intoxicated hook ups ended up with each other.

The second issue is that the permissibility of this state of affairs is not best understood as deriving from consent. As discussed in Chapter Two, I am using the hybrid view of consent: consent consists of both a mental state, such as an intention to take on new moral obligations, and a performance, to indicate to the other person that one means to agree and take on those obligations. In a case where two people become intoxicated prior to deciding to hook up with each other, the requisite performance will be lacking. That is because any given performance in this situation will be an intoxicated one. The clear problem is that no one should take intoxicated signals as meaningful for consent. For instance, a car dealer should not accept any intoxicated signals associated with buying a car as meaningful – no matter how many such signals the person performs. The person can claim they are ready to buy a car, they can sign a contract, they can hand over a money order, they can demand the keys, etc. The car dealer would be wrong to accept any of these intoxicated signals to have the same meanings that they would were the person perfectly sober. And that is because intoxicated signals do not show that the person has rationally and calmly determined that they wish to take on new moral obligations. Intoxicated performances do not generate consent.

Nor can prior signals made when the person was sober count as meaningful since, given the way the scenario is drawn up, they are not performing those signals to the right person. We are describing a case where the person decides they want to have an intoxicated hook up, then gets intoxicated, and only then meets the person with whom they will have the intoxicated hook up – in that order. They may have performed their signal intentionally and while sober, but they did not perform it in the presence of their future hook up partner, and so that partner still lacks the performance needed to obtain consent. So, on either the hybrid view or the performance view, this situation cannot, even through luck, arrive at a consensual hook up.

It might be that the mental state view would allow for this kind of hook up to be consensual. After all, both persons intend to have intoxicated hook ups, and they luckily hook up with each other. They never have a sober performance with each other to indicate their consent, but the mental state view of consent does not require such a performance. The mental state view can explain the intuition that the intoxicated hook up participants have, through luck, consensually hooked up. They have the right mental state (an intention to have an intoxicated hook up with a near stranger), and they enact that mental state, and they are fortunate that their partner has the same mental state.

On the other hand, this is the very sort of situation that makes the mental state view appear to be implausible. If someone intends to give away their car, and they do not care who gets it, and I happen to steal the car, we may say that there is no harm, we may even say that my action fortunately turned out to be moral, but it is absurd to say that we consented for me to have the car. No consent took place because we did not work together to form consent. The situation may have no clear harm, but that does not mean we can work backwards and say that there was consent all along when no agreement was made.

Let's be clear that we are not talking about a situation where someone left a sign that said, "Free car." First, the perfectly analogous situation in a hook up would be unheard of and is not what we are here discussing. No one wears a sign that says, "I am intoxicated, but I am available for an intoxicated hook up." It is not even clear that too many people would even think of their original mental state in such an open fashion: even people who intend to hook up while intoxicated with a near stranger do not see themselves as intending to hook up with *just anyone*. Most people would be horrified by the idea of wearing such a sign. Second, any attempt to make a partially analogous situation will likely lead to offensively wrong claims. There is nothing that people do in getting intoxicated that can be assumed to count as advance consent to hook up with just anyone. The mere fact that somebody got intoxicated cannot reasonably be taken as a sign of advance consent to hook up. People get intoxicated for countless reasons, and no one should assume that someone's intoxicated state means they are open for hooking up with just anyone. Further, nothing an intoxicated person does should be assumed to mean they wish to hook up with just anyone, even if they yell out, "I am here to hook up with just anyone." The performance of a sober signal is absolutely necessary to ensure consent takes place: intoxicated signals are not meaningful simply because intoxicated people often do things they do not mean to do.

None of this is to say that people do not get lucky. It is to say that luckily hooking up with someone who wishes to hook up in the same fashion is not consent. It might be, as suggested earlier, that we could decide to count these lucky, intoxicated hook ups as morally permissible. Neither person wished to harm the other person, and neither person harmed the other person. Further, the luck in question is probable in a society where most people have intoxicated hook ups. That is, people relying on this kind of luck have good odds of receiving it because they live in a society where it luckily works out a large percentage of the time. So, since they have good odds, they are not trying to harm anyone, and they do not harm anyone in the situation under discussion, some people could say that their hook up is permissible in this situation. I am not, myself, weighing in on this question. I am willing to concede it since it is not the question I am after (so, I will, from here on, simply stipulate that the lucky situation can be permissible, though not consensual, for the sake of argument). I am, instead, arguing that such a situation just does not count as consensual since it lacks the required consent performance.

Importantly, I am also saying that moral agents would not rely on luck in this fashion, even if they have good odds. As a reminder, the question of this book is not "when do hook ups happen to turn out to be morally permissible?" I believe that question is the focus in the casual sex literature, and that question would require a definitive stance on whether these lucky scenarios are moral. Rather, my question is what moral agents would do to ensure their hook up will be moral. This latter question is what actual agents have to ask themselves: they do not want to know, as a philosopher might, whether a hook up happens to be moral from a God's eye perspective. They want to know, instead, if the hook up they are about to have will be moral. But moral agents who want to ensure their hook ups will be moral will not simply rely on luck, even if they are likely to get it. They instead will take steps to ensure that they have the required performance to have a consensual hook up. So, I will be arguing that moral agents will not become intoxicated first and then hope they hook up with someone who also wished for an intoxicated hook up with a near stranger. One main reason for this view will be that even if they are likely to get lucky, the circumstances where bad luck ensues would be horrible. And, further, the lucky case and the horrible case will be quite difficult to distinguish.

Let's examine three hook up cases that are almost externally indistinguishable. These cases do not exhaust all logical options, but are simply meant to show how similar intoxication cases can look in spite of clear normative differences. The first case, which was just described, involves two near strangers, who both would like to have permissible, intoxicated hook ups, successfully finding each other and fulfilling their goals. Let's say, for the sake of argument, that this pair has a permissible, intoxicated hook up.

The second case involves two near strangers, who both would like to have permissible, intoxicated hook ups, successfully finding each other, but then developing a misunderstanding due to a joint inability to reason and communicate well because of their intoxication. We will concentrate on the version of the second case where the misunderstanding is severe enough to lead to one person wishing to end the hook up. Let's further suppose, in this version, that the person who wishes to end the hook up is simply too intoxicated, confused, and now frightened, to express this wish. So, the hook up continues, against one person's wishes, because they are both too drunk to stop the impermissible hook up. In this case, the person who overlooks the misunderstanding and continues is blameworthy for having impermissible sex since they both could have understood the situation better, communicated better, and likely prevented the impermissible behavior had they been sober. This leads to a significant amount of blame since a hook up ended up being impermissible due to intoxication. This intoxicated hook up began as permissible, but it ended up as impermissible and the intoxication undermined the ability to see this morally significant change.

The third case involves two near strangers getting intoxicated, but for different reasons. One person is hoping to later have an intoxicated hook up, while the other person does not wish to have a hook up at all. Nonetheless, when both are intoxicated, both signal a desire for an intoxicated hook up. One of them is doing this signaling according to their sober plans, while the other will regret the signals they made only because they were intoxicated. It is possible that their signals are being sent purposely but only due to the intoxication (as in, they would not do this while sober). It is also possible that the intoxication is leading them to signal in accidental fashions: such as an intoxicated person trying to signal negatively, but their intoxication leads them to accidentally signal positively (they nod yes when they meant to indicate dissent). Either way, they would not choose to provide these signals were they sober, and when they chose to become intoxicated, they had no desire to end up having a hook up. In this third scenario, the intoxicated person who wanted to hook up is blameworthy because they are pushing an intoxicated person into a hook up that the person would not choose while sober. This is a significant amount of blame since someone is being made to hook up against their will due to intoxication. In this case, the intoxication prevented the awareness that someone else's intoxicated signaling neither entails consent nor even a sober willingness.

Although these cases are normatively very different, it may be incredibly difficult for individuals to distinguish between them because of their structural similarity: two individuals begin drinking separately and then, after they are intoxicated, they hook up with neither person complaining nor dissenting in a sufficiently clear fashion. The external façade can be deceptive because intoxicated agreements are being taken for consent. As I have argued, none of these three cases involve consent because intoxicated agreements cannot amount to consent. Further, in the second and third cases, the individuals do not luckily and unproblematically hook up with someone who wished to complete an intoxicated hook up. Yet, the individuals in those first type of cases do not know that they are neither in the second nor third case types. Intoxicated individuals may struggle to exhibit clear signs of dissent – they may even have trouble knowing whether they in fact dissent. In addition, intoxication makes it hard to see and correctly interrupt signals. So, the person who is trying to hook up may not know which of these three kinds of cases they are in. This determination, though, is morally very significant since only the first type of case has a chance for moral permissibility.

One intoxicated person may think their intoxicated partner consents even if a misunderstanding undermines their agreement, or even if the partner never intended to agree to intoxicated sex. This person may be too intoxicated to realize that the hook up is going wrong, just as his partner may to be too intoxicated to signal that it is. An intoxicated hook up could be impermissible without the person who is blameworthy (it is important to note that both could be blameworthy) even realizing it. Thus, the moral agent cannot allow themselves to be in this situation, and so they must avoid these kinds of intoxicated hook ups since misunderstandings may become unavoidable in such cases. Moral agents would not become intoxicated first and then try to obtain an intoxicated agreement to hook up.

Moral agents have to be aware that alcohol has this power to lower competency. It is essential for moral agents to be aware of the fact that alcohol could lead to impermissible hook ups. They must also realize that intoxication, for themselves or their partners, entails relinquishing control over whether the resulting hook up will be permissible. These three intoxication cases, where only one of the three involves permissible hook ups, can be quite difficult to distinguish for the people in them. That means that moral agents should be concerned about the use of alcohol in hook ups, and they must avoid becoming intoxicated prior to the agreement to hook up.

It might seem that a moral agent should simply avoid alcohol when hooking up. And, there are general contexts, such as in medicine and business, where we do think, morally and legally speaking, that the consensual activity should necessarily be sober. Yet, socially speaking, we tend to think that in certain contexts, such as gambling and hooking up, there can be intoxicated activity that is nonetheless consensual. The next step then is to consider the view that treats hooking up as analogous to gambling: some theorists consider each one to be consensual even if they are likely performed while intoxicated.

A Contextualized Sobriety Requirement

There appear to be some contexts where society allows intoxicated agreements to be permissible (which other theorists might consider to be "intoxicated consent," though I disagree that this phrase is sensible), and others that we think require sobriety. For example, no one would think that a person could give permission for a medical procedure while drinking alcohol.[16] Similarly, when it comes to contract law, an intoxicated person's contract is voidable if the other person could reasonably tell that intoxication led to the making of the contract.[17] Further, several jurisdictions have laws against giving tattoos to drunk people.[18] It is socially accepted that you cannot consent to surgery, contracts, or tattoos while intoxicated. Yet, our society has completely different standards when it comes to gambling and casual sex. The question then is whether this differential treatment based on context can be justified, or whether our society is just wrong when it comes to gambling and/or sex.

Intoxicated Gambling

Where casinos are legal in the United States, they routinely sell alcohol to gamblers. Some casinos will even give away free alcohol. There is a cynical explanation for this difference: where gambling is legalized, casinos hold a good deal of political power, and people who run casinos would prefer the legalization of intoxicated gambling. If that was all it was, then we wouldn't be able to use gambling as a context where intoxicated agreements were permissible.

In contrast to this cynical approach, Alan Wertheimer offers an alternative perspective on the permissibility of a system that allows intoxicated gambling. Wertheimer argues that whether intoxicated agreements should count as consensual for a given activity depends on whether the active agents in that activity would choose, when sober, to have their intoxicated agreements count as consensual.[19] Wertheimer believes, reasonably, that gamblers would choose to have intoxicated agreements to gamble count as consensual since they would prefer to gamble while drinking (especially when casinos give away free alcohol).[20] As Wertheimer puts it:

> Suppose that potential gamblers were given a choice between a rule that treats gambling losses incurred while intoxicated as recoverable and a rule that treats them as nonrecoverable and that the consequences of adopting both rules were well understood. What would they choose? I suspect that most would choose the 'nonrecoverable' rule, for unless their losses were nonrecoverable, casinos would be reluctant to allow them to both drink and gamble.[21]

Since people would choose to gamble under a rule where drunken losses were not recoverable, and since they openly choose while in the casinos to drink and gamble, Wertheimer argues that we should accept intoxicated consent for gambling.

Wertheimer's argument can be interpreted in two ways. At times, it seems that he is making a utilitarian or consequentialist argument that a gambling system that allowed intoxicated consent would make people happier than one that didn't. At other times, Wertheimer seems to be arguing for a group advance consent view where a group of people are all situated so that it makes sense to see them as all giving advance consent to do something later when they will be unable to consent, say because they will be too intoxicated.

On the first, consequentialist interpretation, it doesn't seem that Wertheimer's view gets consent right. If we were merely looking at which rule would make people happier within a given practice, then we would have a good reason to allow intoxicated gambling. Perhaps we should adopt that intoxicated gambling rule even if we thought that much of the gambling would be non-consensual – we might, that is, allow non-consensual gambling for greater utilitarian considerations. However, these utilitarian considerations do not make intoxicated gambling *consensual*. Consent requires agents to purposely create their own obligations. The fact that a rule would make people happier has nothing to do with whether people intentionally give their consent to follow that rule. Even if utilitarianism were true, it would only follow that everyone would be obligated to accept this rule *because it maximizes happiness*. It wouldn't follow that anyone was obligated *through consent* to accept the rule. Arguing that it would make people happier if we counted certain intoxicated agreements as "consensual" in a certain context does not imply that there is intoxicated consent in that context – one point is irrelevant to the other, and so this argument has no traction to the conceptual issue of what counts as consent.

Perhaps a more plausible interpretation is that Wertheimer is arguing for a group advance consent view. It is surely possible for agents to give their consent in advance. An agent might say that she wants to get drunk and then do some action, X, while intoxicated. The agent then has a problem: she only wants to do X while intoxicated, but X requires her consent, which she cannot give while intoxicated. So, the agent gives her sober consent for X in advance of drinking and performing X. Thus, she can engage in X in the intoxicated manner that she prefers by giving her advance consent.

Wertheimer would likely apply this notion of advance consent to a group, such as gamblers, who would generally prefer to drink and gamble. Gamblers as a group are giving their advance consent to accept the moral consequences for their intoxicated betting. On this interpretation, Wertheimer would be asking us to imagine that gamblers, as a group, think of their agreements to drink and gamble in this fashion, and so it makes sense to count them as giving *group advance consent* to intoxicated gambling.

This group advance consent position runs into concerns. The consent is meant to apply generally to all people who gamble while drunk, even though only some subset of them – even if it is a very large subset – would hypothetically consent, while sober, to accept intoxicated losses later on. After all, many people get more intoxicated than intended, gamble more than intended, and are reasonably upset that they must accept heavy losses that were incurred while intoxicated. It is relevant that they would be upset because the moral transformation created by consent is meant to be purposely chosen. If these agents can honestly say they never would have chosen to drink or gamble *that much*, then they didn't consent to do so. It could have been consent if agents merely changed their minds after they saw their losses (as in, "Now that I saw I lost that much, I wish I hadn't consented" – but this is only a statement of regret, which proves that they did in fact consent in the first place). Yet, we can suppose that some gamblers would make different initial choices while sober, before finding out what the results would be. The alcohol, in such cases, is leading to them gambling beyond the state of affairs they would accept while sober. Surely there are some intoxicated gambling losers who can honestly say they didn't purposely choose their fate. It isn't clear why those people should be covered by the group advance consent of others who would accept whatever fate will befall them as long as they can gamble while intoxicated.

Wertheimer responds to this point in a footnote where he suggests the possibility of dry casinos for people who would prefer to gamble while sober.[22] If there were separate dry and wet casinos, people entering the alcohol serving ones would seem to be giving advance consent to intoxicated gambling. Conversely, this practical suggestion ignores a possibly large group of individuals who would prefer to drink in moderation while gambling, but who unintentionally find themselves over-gambling after becoming intoxicated more than they intended. Again, the question is not one of personal responsibility; we aren't interested in whether these individuals who drink more than they intended should be held responsible for their intoxicated gambling. The question is whether these individuals are morally obligated to pay their intoxicated losses *specifically because* they consented in advance to accept the responsibility for those losses. For those individuals who do not intend to gamble after alcohol has impaired their reasoning, they have not given advance consent even while gambling in wet casinos. These individuals may have personal responsibility for their losses, but, if so, it is not because they consented to accept that responsibility. They may have consented to drink and gamble, but when the alcohol leads to things getting out of control, then they have arrived at a set of circumstances that they did not foresee. That is a rather trivial point: insofar as things got out of control, they did not specifically intend that outcome and so, it seems, they could not have consented to that specific set of circumstances.

One could argue that they hold responsibility for an initial choice to drink that allowed things to get out of control. Consent is a purposeful agreement to accept consequences a person is informed about, but casinos could have signs that inform patrons that drinking and gambling could lead to large losses of money. So, these people who are attempting to be moderate drinking gamblers could be said to be consenting to an open-ended state of affairs: while they may not wish to agree to get so intoxicated that they lose large sums of money, they are consenting to be open to that possibility.

That response seems correct for a good number of these moderately drinking gambling cases, but there still seem to be cases where it is doubtful. The type of case where this response works is one where a person thinks to themselves, "I would like to only drink moderately while gambling, but I realize I am taking a chance that my drinking will get out of control, and so if I incur large losses, it would be my fault. I accept this potential problem, and choose to moderately drink and gamble." Such a person would seem to consent, even if they end up losing big. Imagine another type of person, however, who thinks to themselves, "I will only drink moderately while gambling, and so these warning signs about serious drinking do not apply to me." Let's add to this latter person type that they do end up becoming overly intoxicated, incur large losses, and it was reasonable for them to begin with the belief that these results would not occur. The last point is clearly contentious, but we can imagine a few ways to make it work. Suppose they are simply unused to casino alcohol, which ends up being much more intoxicating. Suppose the mixing of gambling and alcohol causes psychological effects that one would not encounter doing each activity separately. Suppose the casino has other factors in play that facilitate either of the first two suppositions: the person is not used to drinking while surrounded by smoke, the lack of clocks has an additional, unexpected psychological effect, being offered free alcohol is psychologically different from being offered more drinks at a cost, étc. The point is that there could be situations where someone is reasonably surprised to discover that they are becoming intoxicated while reasonably planning to only drink moderately.

There are a few things one might want to say about such situations. Foremost, I think objectors would want to respond that these unexpected causes are not the casino's fault. Although casinos may purposely create these situations with a hope for these unintended effects, let's set that aside and stipulate that the casinos are not at fault. I believe this response again conflates obligations purposely created by consent and obligations that derive from elsewhere. As a society, we may expect individuals who gamble while drinking at all to take personal responsibility for doing so. That sense of personal responsibility may be applicable in all of these situations that I've described here. Yet, that is different from saying that the person consented to what would happen when they became intoxicated even if they reasonably did not think they would become intoxicated.

Thus, even if we had Wertheimer's ideal system with dry and wet casinos, we would still have individuals who engaged in intoxicated gambling at the wet casinos who would not have given their advance consent to gamble at a high level of intoxication. It might be that these individuals are few in number: even many moderate drinkers may be consenting to incur whatever losses happen when they drink too much. The number, provided it is one or greater, is irrelevant. The problem is that group advance consent is misleading at best. For consent to morally obligate any given individual, that individual must give it herself. We could suppose we have group advance consent if we have every single member of the group consenting, which includes each individual having the right intention and making a relevant consent-sealing performance while sober. However, as long as there are some individuals who do not consent, they are not in any way morally obligated by what other members of the group, even the vast majority of the group, consent to. Intoxicated gambling is only consensually done by individuals who choose in advance, for themselves, to engage in it.

Wertheimer could still be correct that society ought to expect intoxicated gamblers to accept their losses. We may have reasons, other than consent, for holding gamblers responsible for their intoxicated losses. I am not here saying I support such a position, but I have said nothing to rule it out. The point here is that there is no group advance consent for intoxicated gambling. This point undermines the argument from analogy that if we allow group advance consent for intoxicated gambling, then we should allow group advance consent for intoxicated hook ups. I will still look at the other side, though it turns out that the case for group advance consent for intoxicated hook ups is even worse off than it is for gambling.

Group Intoxicated Hook Up Consent

Even if we reject Wertheimer's arguments with respect to gambling, we should look at his arguments that he believes provide an even clearer case that intoxicated consent can be given in advance both for individual sex cases,[23] and as a general rule for the casual sex culture[24] (or the hook up culture, though Wertheimer doesn't use the "hook up" phrase).

Wertheimer's first argument begins by admitting that there are three key differences between gambling and casual sex that suggest, contrary to his view, that there is less room for advance consent for the latter. First, non-consensual sex involves emotional and physical harms that are much more severe than non-consensual gambling.[25] Second, there is a practical difference in that a casino must make a uniform decision whether to allow intoxicated gambling for everyone or no one – it is not feasible for casinos to monitor individual drinking habits.[26] Third, when gamblers start drinking, they usually expect and intend to engage in intoxicated gambling later on.[27] People who drink at a bar or club do not necessarily intend to hook up, and even if they hope to hook up, they may not intend to hook up with just anyone (whereas gamblers may not care what slot machine or table they may end up gambling at after they are intoxicated). As Wertheimer says:

> Whereas people who enter a casino and then become intoxicated intend to gamble all along (although perhaps not as much), women who become

intoxicated and then token consent to sex do not necessarily intend to have sex all along, although there is evidence that women are more likely to drink when they are willing to have sex.[28]

Casual sex is definitely distinct from gambling in that it is wrong to assume someone has an intention to hook up just because they are drinking at a club or a bar.

In spite of these three disanalogies, Wertheimer believes the case for allowing intoxicated consent in sexual exchanges is even *stronger* than it is for gambling. Wertheimer believes that with sex, unlike gambling, the results are almost always positive: "Indeed, whereas most gamblers lose on a given day (intoxicated or sober) and almost all gamblers lose over the long run, many intoxicated sexual relationships are pleasurable and do not typically involve significant physical or psychological harms."[29] In fact, Wertheimer warns us that, "our moral and legal rules should not be driven by the cases that go badly."[30] Since Wertheimer thinks the negative outcomes from intoxicated sex occur very rarely, he supports adopting a general rule that accepts intoxicated sexual agreements as consensual.

We can object to Wertheimer's first argument in two ways: first by questioning his consequentialist position with empirical evidence, and second by questioning whether his position makes conceptual sense of consent. Like with gambling, Wertheimer's initial argument seems overly consequentialist. After noting the disanalogies that work against his view, Wertheimer makes heavy use of the empirical disanalogy that he believes helps him: the idea that more people win with casual sex than with gambling. Nonetheless, we have already seen reasons to think that hook up failures are more common than is often assumed: based on various studies, we can tell that about 42% of women have terrible hook ups,[31] around 16% of men and women feel pressured during hook ups,[32] and 27% of women have been raped according to the legal definition, but do not describe their experiences as "rape."[33] These studies do not specifically reference alcohol, but the prevalence of alcohol within hook ups suggests that many bad hook ups would likely involve alcohol. These numbers also do not represent the percentage of bad hook ups, but how many people eventually have bad hook ups. But with so many people eventually having gravely problematic hook up experiences, we cannot completely discount the cases that go badly when making our moral rules – especially since Wertheimer acknowledges that the bad experiences can be very psychologically, emotionally, and sometimes physically damaging.[34]

Further, when people are intoxicated, it may be quite difficult for individuals to tell whether they are actually in the failure cases. Often, an intoxicated person may miss key signs from another intoxicated person that things are going poorly. An intoxicated person may even fail to give those signs because of the general confusion and difficulty to think straight that alcohol can induce. Thus, we can expect that the failure cases are not only more numerous than Wertheimer might assume, but also that they are harder to spot, making them even more important to be wary of.

Let's also note that there is another disanalogy with gambling here. When someone is exceptionally intoxicated while gambling, they are engaged with a dealer, a pit boss, and other casino employees who are sober. If someone is so intoxicated that they cannot signal their true desires while gambling, the casino employees will likely stop them from continuing. In the hook up, both persons are probably intoxicated, and one's inability to think or communicate effectively is greatly worsened by the other's similar inabilities.

Turning to the conceptual point, the large patterns of pleased persons do not resolve the issue of whether their intoxicated agreements count as consent. If people are unable to give intoxicated consent for a given activity, it is irrelevant how much they enjoy that activity while intoxicated. Hence, this first, more consequentialist argument is less relevant than an argument that establishes the possibility of the kind of moral transformation that constitutes consent. Fortunately, Wertheimer has another argument.

Wertheimer's second argument, which moves away from this consequentialist thinking, is worth quoting at length:

> Moreover, it is not just that some women may wish to engage in sex and drinking simultaneously. Rather, drinking to the point of at least moderate intoxication may be crucial to what some regard as a desirable sexual and social experience … some women deliberately become intoxicated so that they can engage in sexual relations without experiencing guilt or to excuse themselves *ex post*. Given that a decision to regard intoxicated consent as invalid would limit the positive autonomy of women to engage in sexual relations while intoxicated, we cannot say that something like the Brown University policy enhances women's autonomy, all things considered.[35]

According to Wertheimer, the Brown University policy, "does not allow sexual relations when one student is aware or should be aware that the other student is incapacitated by some substance such as alcohol."[36] This second argument supplements Wertheimer's group advance consent argument for intoxicated gambling. Wertheimer explicitly moves away from the consequentialist considerations when he says in the first sentence that the issue does not come down to what people merely wish would happen. Instead, the second argument is that respect for people's sexual autonomy requires allowing them to act in ways that they see as crucial to their current, autonomously chosen goals.

Let's pause for a moment to examine autonomy. "Autonomy" literally means self-legislating, and we can say an agent meets the ideal of autonomy when she does what she can to ensure that her actions meet up with standards that she has set for herself based on her reasoning over what's important to her.[37] In other words, an autonomous agent holds herself up to standards, but they are standards that she chose when reasoning over her values. Autonomy does not require that individuals must select standards all on their own, that they must be selfish, or that they must be overly individualistic.[38] Autonomy only requires that individuals do not accept or act from standards that are forced upon them, but that they instead reason over their values, which can come from multiple sources, and develop standards, which they will act according to, based on their own determinations of what matters in their lives.

People could reason about their values and decide that it is important for them to seek out intoxicated sexual encounters with near strangers. These people would autonomously choose intoxicated hook ups. The point is not merely that intoxicated sex makes these people happy – it is that they could autonomously choose intoxicated sex as key to their chosen life goals. Since these individuals would, upon reasoned deliberation, agree in advance to having intoxicated sex with near strangers, Wertheimer argues that it would be a violation of their autonomy to not count their intoxicated sexual agreements as consensual.[39]

There is definitely something right about Wertheimer's point. Individuals could have deep-seated preferences to hook up while intoxicated. They may autonomously choose to hook up like that, preferring it greatly over either sober hook ups or intoxicated sex within relationships. Since it is part of these individuals' autonomy to have intoxicated hook ups with near strangers, we could grant that it could be permissible for those near strangers to hook up with them while they are intoxicated.

Although that point is correct, it doesn't translate well into a general policy. We can split people who go out to get intoxicated into three groups. The first, Wertheimer's group, gets intoxicated because they autonomously choose to have intoxicated hook ups, and they are willing to give blanket advance agreements for those hook ups. The second group, which Wertheimer acknowledges exists,[40] goes out to get intoxicated without any intention of having sex with anyone. The third group, which may very well be the most populous of these groups, goes out to get intoxicated with a hope to hook up with someone, but it is important to them to be selective about their hook up partners. This final group is analogous to gamblers who wish to gamble while drinking, but they do not wish to become so intoxicated that they gamble large sums erratically, nor do they believe that such intoxication is likely to happen to them. Members of this final group would not agree in advance because they do not want to hook up with just anyone, but wish to retain the power to decide with whom they will hook up. Further, they do not believe (perhaps they are wrong) that they will become so intoxicated that they will be unable to deliberately make this choice. Since members of the two latter groups would not agree in advance, we cannot adopt a general policy that treats everyone like they are in the first group.

Wertheimer concentrates on the autonomy loss for members of that first group.[41] Without a policy that counts intoxicated hook ups as consensual, autonomous choices certainly could be diminished for that group, but it isn't clear why that point should be decisive. After all, a social rule that said you can treat another person's intoxicated agreement to have sex as consent leaves people vulnerable who wish to get intoxicated but do not wish to have sex or who wish to have sex selectively. Such persons would have to be careful about autonomously choosing to get intoxicated simply because they do not know what would result when others take intoxicated agreements to always be consensual. Such a policy endangers the ability to make autonomous choices to get intoxicated without wishing to hook up with just anyone. Thus, members of the second group, who may autonomously prize their virginity or who may autonomously prize their right to not hook up on certain nights, are opened up to life-altering intoxicated mistakes by a general rule that counts their intoxicated agreements as consensual. Members of the third group may wish to autonomously choose to hook up only with people they prefer, but they too could, due to either manipulation or mistakes, end up hooking up with the wrong people because of a general rule that counted their intoxicated (and, thereby, confused or easily manipulated) agreements as consensual. Whatever rule we adopt, there would be hindrances of autonomy. It is not clear why the first group's autonomy should be the one that wins out.

Therefore, autonomy alone does not settle this issue. As mentioned, I would wager that the second and third groups would far outnumber the first group that Wertheimer concentrates on. I do not have empirical data to back that up, but I feel confident that most people who go out drinking are not hoping to awaken to find out that they have hooked up with just anyone. Since that claim is empirical and I cannot back it up, I will argue that the more important point is that the autonomy violation is much more serious with the second and third groups. Yes, with a general policy that says intoxicated agreements to hook up are not consent, the first group will have a harder time autonomously having intoxicated sex with near strangers without moral blame. Yet, with a general policy that treats intoxicated hook up agreements as consensual, people who like to get intoxicated for fun will have to be extremely careful. They probably will have to give up that fun since the worry of being taken advantage of sexually will be very serious. In short, all intoxicated activities, except for the choice to have sex with just anyone, would have to be given up for their own safety. That is a much more sweeping autonomy hindrance.

We should also return to the conceptual issue. We should not be interested in the best general policy, but whether a certain way of looking at these situations makes sense of the consent concept. Just like with gambling, no general policy will work since each individual is different and may or may not agree in advance to intoxicated hook ups. Further, given what consent means, you just cannot consent while intoxicated and you cannot consent in advance of meeting the person with whom you are consenting since you must give a sober performance of consent.

Contrary to any intuitions to the contrary, this position is exactly how we should think of sexual consent. First, intoxication-related mistakes are especially worrisome when it comes to sex – the sex that someone agrees to while intoxicated should never just be assumed to be what they really wish to be doing. Intoxicated persons do not fully know what they are doing, and it is clearly morally blameworthy to hold someone accountable to an intoxicated agreement to have sex. You cannot insist that someone must hold to what they said while intoxicated, and that just shows that we do not really think of their intoxicated agreements as consensual. There is just no telling, from an intoxicated agreement, whether the person really means to consent to sex. So, we morally should never accept an intoxicated agreement to sex since we do not know if the person would be a willing sexual partner were they sober.

Second, sex is very much an activity where people should have every right to be selective. The idea of advance consent to sex with just anyone is a possible decision someone could make, but not likely a common decision that lots of people make. We all have the right to be selective about our sexual partners, and we cannot fully enact that selectivity while intoxicated. So, to truly consent to sex, a person has to both be sober and actually be directly interacting with the person with whom they are consenting to have sex.

As we turn to what moral agents should do when faced with intoxicated hook up partners, we have seen that they cannot choose a blanket policy that ignored the many people who would not agree in advance to hook up with just anyone. Rather, the moral agent has to approach this problem with the knowledge that the hook up failure cases are real, and that they must ensure they have consent, which surely goes beyond assuming all intoxicated agreements count as such. In other words, the moral agent would ensure they have sober consent with the specific person they hope to hook up with.

Sober Individual Prior Consent

A moral agent would not adopt a general policy that treated all intoxicated agreements to hook up as consensual. It is the moral agent's job to ensure that he or she only hooks up with people who have clearly given consent. That means that it is not sufficient to rely on luck that the person who you are hooking up with wishes to hook up while intoxicated with you. Instead, the moral agent recognizes that you cannot obtain intoxicated consent from near strangers. The moral agent must ensure that consent is received from sober persons.

As we saw, this position leads to a potential worry that moral agents then could not have intoxicated hook ups. One answer is to bite the bullet and say that moral agents must avoid intoxicated sex until they are in a relationship with someone who they know also enjoys intoxicated sex. In such cases, the people who know each other well can ensure that they only have intoxicated sex when both consent to it in advance while sober. That position still allows that intoxicated agreements to sex do not count as consent, but the couple who already knows how to negotiate sex with each other is in a much easier position to ensure they have sober consent prior to any intoxicated sex.

Another answer is that the moral agent has to obtain *individual prior consent* from a particular near stranger before he or she becomes intoxicated. In the two previous chapters, we saw several reasons why agents ought to have a good conversation prior to hooking up. That conversation clearly must happen prior to alcohol diminishing either person's ability to reason well since it would not count as providing adequate information to a person if they received the information when they could no longer reason well about it. Thus, in this chapter, we add to that conversation a requirement that if the agents want to have an intoxicated hook up, they must discuss and negotiate that desire prior to becoming intoxicated. That way, they can get consent both for the hook up and for becoming intoxicated first.

It is worth pausing to note that most of this discussion has occurred as if one were either sober or intoxicated, where in truth there is a continuum between them. Where exactly would moral agents seek to have their discussion? Well, there can be no exact answer to this question, but it is clear that they would not have the discussion at the level of intoxication where they cannot reason well. Further, the moral agent would seek to err on the side of being more sober rather than less: they wish to ensure they are obtaining consent, which cannot be obtained if intoxication has undermined the ability to reason or communicate well. Further, if they do not know their hook up participants well, then they do not know, with any level of certainty, what the other person's signs are for being too intoxicated. So, the moral agent will seek to have a discussion where individuals are clearly sober enough to consent.

In this way, people can pursue their autonomous choices to have intoxicated hook ups with near strangers. And, were everyone to act from this method of solving the problem, all three above mentioned groups could satisfy their autonomy, theoretically. The group that wants to have intoxicated hook ups with anyone only need to find each other and have this discussion prior to becoming intoxicated. The group that doesn't want to accidentally hook up after they purposely become intoxicated are better off since moral agents would seek hook up partners who would explicitly choose to hook up while sober. Finally, the group that would like to be selective about who they hook up with can be selective while sober, and then get intoxicated with their chosen partner.

This methodology, however, will not work for people who use alcohol to create excuses for their choices. Since the heavier drinking comes after the hook up decisions, they will be responsible, both morally and prudentially, for their choices. Many people will not be pleased with this result, but that won't affect what's at stake here. Moral agents cannot permissibly choose to use a substance to take away the control necessary for them to responsibly make choices. Moral agents, by definition, take responsibility for their choices. For moral agents who autonomously choose to have intoxicated hook ups, they will accept that a sober or mostly sober discussion is necessary to obtain individual prior consent.

In an earlier case in this chapter, we considered a situation where two individuals both wanted to have an intoxicated hook up, but one changed their mind and found it quite difficult to express this change. Accordingly, the final problem to consider is that even the individual prior consent view allows for a type of consent for intoxicated hook ups that seems to be closer to advance consent than contemporaneous consent. As we saw, hook up consent should be contemporaneous consent, not advance consent, because each person should always be able to withdraw their consent.

The first response is a simple one: like with aggressive hook ups, intoxicated hook ups would require safe words. All hook ups, including intoxicated hook ups, always involve contemporaneous consent, and not advance consent. In any hook up, the consent is contemporaneous because it can be withdrawn without any moral wrongdoing (which differs from advance consent where it is morally wrong to withdraw one's consent since one consented in advance).

Unfortunately, from a practical perspective, intoxicated hook ups do not always allow for consent to be easily withdrawn. For example, it is too easy for either intoxicated party to forget the safe word. While intoxicated consent to hook up is necessarily contemporaneous consent, in some intoxicated hook ups it will simply not work as such. That does not mean that withdrawing consent would be morally wrong, but that attempts to withdraw consent may fail because the hook up partners are intoxicated. This means that intoxicated hook ups involve risk that cannot be fully removed by having a pre-hook up conversation.

There is nonetheless a difference between this case and the ones previously discussed, such as genuine aggressive hook ups and intoxicated hook ups without pre-hook up conversations. In those previous cases, the aggressor and the intoxicated person were placing the risk onto the other person. The aggressor uses methods that put the passive person into a risky situation. The person who gets intoxicated first but who wishes to have an intoxicated hook up places the risk onto the person they meet who may not wish to have an intoxicated hook up. However, this scenario, where there is a pre-hook up sober conversation and where a safe word is established, involves two people choosing to accept risk for themselves. They so much want to have intoxicated hook ups that they are willing to accept the risk that they could change their mind and forget the safe word. Since the risks are self-incurred, then they could consent to accepting those risks because they feel that having intoxicated hook ups are worth that much risk. Therefore, the pre-hook up conversation both lowers the risk (by allowing the individuals to choose their partners while sober and by setting up safe words), and also allows the individuals, while sober, to decide if the remaining risk is worth it. So, their sober and informed agreement in such a situation would be consensual.

Conclusion

It does seem that intoxication undermines consent, but that does not mean that individuals cannot engage in intoxicated hook ups. They simply have to gain individual prior consent in conversations before they become intoxicated. When it comes to the sexual arena in general, or the hook up practice more specifically, moral agents could have intoxicated hook ups with near strangers by having a sober conversation where both individuals confirm that they do indeed give their consent to later become intoxicated and hook up, even if their later intoxicated choices may have consequences that they would not normally like.

These last three chapters have looked at three different requirements for consent (free, informed, and competent), but came up with a good strategy for moral agents to follow. To ensure that no one is too intoxicated or too aggressive, and to similarly ensure that everyone is adequately informed, hook up participants will engage in a sober conversation about their goals and intentions. This conversation only needs to be as complicated as the two hook up participants want it to be. If they have almost no limits and are happy with their hook up partner, then they can have a short conversation for a relatively straightforward hook up. If at least one person's hook up plans were more complicated (for instance, they want to hook up with aggression and/or while intoxicated), or at least one person has more limits, then the conversation would have to be a bit longer. And this additional discussion simply is a necessary requirement for avoiding morally severe problems. Since moral agents want to ensure they have consent and ensure they avoid morally severe problems, they would definitely have this hook up conversation prior to hooking up.

We have thus seen that the requirements for consent are best met through a pre-hook up conversation that is sober. Some theorists, who believe that consent is sufficient for hooking up morally, would think this would be the end of the matter. Yet, as we will see in the next chapter, there is reason to believe that consent is not yet sufficient for moral agents looking to have permissible hook ups.

Notes

1 David Archard, *Sexual Consent* (Boulder: Westview Press, 1998), 116–129; Alan Wertheimer, *Consent to Sexual Relations* (Cambridge: Cambridge University Press, 2003), 216–222.
2 Wertheimer, *Consent to Sexual Relations*, 216.
3 Ibid., 216–218; Archard, *Sexual Consent*, 126–129.

4 Elizabeth Paul, Brian McManus, and Allison Hayes, "'Hookups:' Characteristics and Correlates of College Students' Spontaneous and Anonymous Sexual Experiences," *The Journal of Sex Research* 37, no.1 (2000), 77, 83–5; Norval Glenn and Elizabeth Marquardt, *Hooking Up, Hanging Out, and Hoping for Mr. Right: College Women on Dating and Mating Today*, An Institute for American Values Report to the Independent Women's Forum (2001): 15–16; Tracy A. Lambert, Arnold S. Kahn, and Kevin J. Apple, "Pluralistic Ignorance and Hooking Up," *The Journal of Sex Research* 40, no.2 (2003), 129; Joan McGregor, *Is it Rape? On Acquaintance Rape and Taking Women's Consent Seriously* (Burlington: Ashgate, 2005), 147; Kathleen A. Bogle, *Hooking Up: Sex, Dating, and Relationships on Campus* (New York: New York University Press, 2008), 30, 47, 63–64, 166–168; Gary Gute and Elaine M. Eshbaugh, "Personality as a Predictor of Hooking Up Among College Students," *Journal of Community Health Nursing* 25 (2008), 27–28, 35–36; Michael Kimmel, *Guyland: The Perilous World Where Boys Become Men* (New York: Harper Collins, 2008), 199; Teresa M. Downing-Matibag and Brandi Geisinger, "Hooking Up and Sexual Risk Taking Among College Students: A Health Belief Model Perspective," *Qualitative Health Research* 19, no.9 (2009), 1196, 1203; Lisa Menegatos, Linda C. Lederman, and Aaron Hess, "Friends Don't Let Jane Hook Up Drunk: A Qualitative Analysis of Participation in a Simulation of College Drinking-Related Decisions," *Communication Education* 59, no. 3 (2010); Jesse J. Owen *et al.*, "'Hooking Up' Among College Students: Demographic and Psychosocial Correlates," *Archives of Sexual Behavior* 39 (2010), 658–659; Rachel Kalish and Michael Kimmel, "Hooking Up: Hot Hetero Sex or the New Numb Normative?" *Australian Feminist Studies* 26, no. 67 (2011), 143; Jesse Owen and Frank D. Fincham, "Young Adults' Emotional Reactions after Hooking Up Encounters," *Archives of Sexual Behavior* 40 (2011), 328; Jesse Owen , Frank D. Fincham, and Jon Moore, "Short-Term Prospective Study of Hooking Up Among College Students," *Archives of Sexual Behavior* 40 (2011), 337, 338–339; Julie A. Reid, Sinikka Elliott, and Gretchen R. Webber, "Casual Hookups to Formal Dates: Refining the Boundaries of the Sexual Double Standard," *Gender & Society* 25, no.5 (2011), 556; Melina M. Bersamin *et al.*, "Young Adults and Casual Sex: The Relevance of College Drinking Settings," *Journal of Sex Research* 49, no. 2–3 (2012); Melissa A. Lewis et al., "What is Hooking Up? Examining Definitions of Hooking Up in Relation to Behavior and Normative Perceptions," *Journal of Sex Research* 50, no.8 (2013), 764–765; Allyson L. Dir, Melissa A. Cyders, and Ayca Coskunpinar, "From the Bar to the Bed via Mobile Phone: A First Test of the Role of Problematic Alcohol Use, Sexting, and Impulsivity-Related Traits in Sexual Hookups," *Computers in Human Behavior* 29 (2013); Molly K. Bachtel, "Do Hookups Hurt? Exploring College Students' Experiences and Perceptions," *Journal of Midwifery & Women's Health* 58, no. 1 (2013), 42; Megan Manthos, Jesse Owen, and Frank D. Fincham, "A New Perspective on Hooking Up Among College Students: Sexual Behavior as a Function of Distinct Groups," *Journal of Social and Personal Relationships* 31, no.6 (2014), 824–825; Spencer B. Olmstead *et al.*, "Hooking Up and Risk Behaviors Among First Semester College Men: What is the Role of Precollege Experience?" *The Journal of Sex Research* 52, no. 2 (2015), 188; Patricia N. E. Roberson, Spencer B. Olmstead, and Frank D. Fincham, "Hooking Up During the College Years: Is There a Pattern?" *Culture, Health & Sexuality* 17, no. 5 (2015), 578, 586, 587; Tara E. Sutton and Leslie Gordon Simons, "Sexual Assault Among College Students: Family of Origin Hostility, Attachment, and the Hook-Up Culture as Risk Factors," *Journal of Child and Family Studies* 24, no.10 (2015); Lisa Wade, *American Hookup: The New Culture of Sex on Campus* (New York: W. W. Norton & Company, 2017), 28–31, 43–45, 70–91.

5 Steven J. Schulhofer, *Unwanted Sex: The Culture of Intimidation and the Failure of Law* (Cambridge: Harvard University Press, 1998), 269; Alan Wertheimer, "Intoxicated Consent to Sexual Relations," *Law and Philosophy* 20, no.4 (2001),

378–379; Wertheimer, *Consent to Sexual Relations*, 236–238; Dir *et al.*, "Bar to the Bed," 1668.
6 Wertheimer, "Intoxicated Consent," 378–379; Wertheimer, *Consent to Sexual Relations*, 236–238.
7 Paul *et al.*, "Hookups," 77, 83–85; Glenn and Marquardt, *Hanging Out*, 15–16; McGregor, *Is it Rape?*, 147–149; Bogle, *Hooking Up*, 30, 47, 63–64, 166–168; Kimmel, *Guyland*, 199; Carolyn Bradshaw, Arnold S. Kahn, and Bryan K. Saville, "To Hook Up or Date: Which Gender Benefits?" *Sex Roles* 62 (2010), 663; Kalish and Kimmel, "Hot Hetero Sex or the New Numb Normative?," 143; Reid *et al.*, "Casual Hookups," 556; Olmstead *et al.*, "Hooking Up and Risk Behaviors," 1881; Roberson *et al.*, "Is there a Pattern?," 578.
8 Emily Finch and Vanessa E. Munro, "The Demon Drink and the Demonized Woman: Socio-Sexual Stereotypes and Responsibility Attribution in Rape Trials Involving Intoxicants," *Social Legal Studies* 16 (2007), 594; Reid *et al.*, "Casual Hookups," 556.
9 Wade, *American Hookup*, 29.
10 Paul *et al.*, "Hookups," 77. Also see Wade, *American Hookup*, 44–45.
11 Wade, *American Hookup*, 43–45.
12 Paul *et al.*, "Hookups," 85.
13 Karen M. Kramer, "Rule by Myth: The Social and Legal Dynamics Governing Alcohol-Related Acquaintance Rapes," *Stanford Law Review* 47, no. 1 (1994): 122–123.
14 Ibid., 119.
15 Ibid., 123.
16 Wertheimer, "Intoxicated Consent," 389; Wertheimer, *Consent to Sexual Relations*, 245–246.
17 Wertheimer, "Intoxicated Consent," 392; Wertheimer, *Consent to Sexual Relations*, 248.
18 Wertheimer, *Consent to Sexual Relations*, 249.
19 Ibid., 245–253.
20 Ibid., 250.
21 Ibid.
22 Ibid., 250, fn. 41.
23 Wertheimer, "Intoxicated Consent," 377–380, 395–7; Wertheimer, *Consent to Sexual Relations*, 251–253.
24 Wertheimer, *Consent to Sexual Relations*, 245–253.
25 Ibid., 250.
26 Ibid.
27 Ibid.
28 Ibid.
29 Ibid., 250–251.
30 Ibid., 251.
31 Lambert *et al.*, "Pluralistic Ignorance," 130.
32 Paul *et al.*, "Hookups," 81.
33 Robert Jensen, *Getting Off: Pornography and the End of Masculinity* (Cambridge: South End Press, 2007), 48–49.
34 Wertheimer, *Consent to Sexual Relations*, 250–251.
35 Ibid., 251.
36 Ibid., 234–235.
37 For a selection of autonomy views, see Ellen F. Paul and Fred D. Miller, Jr., eds., *Autonomy* (Cambridge: Cambridge University Press, 2003); and James Stacey Taylor, ed., *Personal Autonomy: New Essays on Personal Autonomy and Its Role in Contemporary Moral Philosophy* (Cambridge: Cambridge University Press, 2005).

38 For a selection of essays on this topic, see: Catriona Mackenzie and Natalie Stoljar, eds., *Relational Autonomy: Feminist Perspectives on Autonomy, Agency, and the Social Self* (Oxford: Oxford University Press, 2000).
39 Wertheimer, *Consent to Sexual Relations*, 251.
40 Ibid., 250.
41 Ibid., 251.

6

THE INSUFFICIENCY OF CONSENT

The point, until now, has been to argue that even if we accepted the centrality of consent, hooking up ethically has challenges that are often overlooked. In this chapter, I switch to challenging the view that consent is sufficient for hook up permissibility. The issue is whether consent alone is sufficient for the hook up to be morally permissible, or whether there are further moral questions that need to be asked beyond consent.

Surely respect – which includes a manner of treating others as important and valuable, a way of thinking of them in those same ways, and an earnest attempt to make others feel that they are important and valuable, all without overstepping personal boundaries – is necessary for moral permissibility in general. Respect is not a substantial requirement that is added onto hook ups, but is instead an ever-present moral requirement that cannot be justifiably omitted from hooking up. Respect is just part of ordinary, everyday moral interactions. Thus, we do not require something extra in saying that respect is necessary for moral hook ups; in treating hooking up like any other human behavior, we necessarily demand respect.

The goal of this chapter will not be to argue for the view that moral hook ups require respect or anything else in particular beyond consent. I will provide that argument in the next chapter. In this chapter, I will consider and respond to arguments that consent is all we need for morally permissible hook ups. When those arguments come up short, I will then use Chapter Seven to seek out what else is necessary for hooking up permissibly.

Consent Sufficiency

Although many scholars believe that more is required for moral permissibility in sexual contexts than consent,[1] many others believe that consent is sufficient, or at least close to sufficient, for the moral permissibility of a sexual encounter.[2] There are at least three view types for this sufficiency of consent position. The first view, which I will refer to as "the strict libertarian view," holds that consent is morally foundational in such a way that it wouldn't make sense to ask further moral questions after consent is obtained. The next view, the "non-harmful consent view," holds that consent is almost sufficient, with the only other requirement being that no third party is harmed. The final view comes from scholars who hold that you can derive the moral sufficiency of consent from Kant's formula of humanity – let's call it, "the formula of humanity view."

Strict Libertarian View

One view that would consider consent to be sufficient for hook ups to be morally permissible would be libertarianism. And just to be clear, different people use "libertarianism" to describe different theories. In political philosophy in the United States, libertarianism is largely considered to be a right-wing view, and that is the view I will be referring to. In other countries, libertarianism is considered to be a more left-wing view where liberty is only prioritized if doing so is consistent with promoting everyone's liberty. Such a view will likely involve several moral values and will not likely consider consent to be morally sufficient. We will see that the libertarianism that I'm describing allows consent to have a much more powerful role in moral appraisal.

Libertarianism is a political and moral theory that places primary moral value on liberty. For the libertarian, one of the key ways in which agents are free is through consensual exchanges: through their own consent people rightfully choose to limit their liberty in one way to gain more liberty in another way. Libertarianism makes consent morally foundational and leaves little, if any, room for other moral values to trump consent. Yet, we will see that this view makes consent too easy to come by, which limits the moral value we should place on consent. The issue is that the libertarian's moral theory has very few core values, of which consent is one. Thus, the libertarian trivially sees consent as sufficient for permissibility. I will argue that a non-libertarian, whose core moral values are likely much more numerous and in competition with each other, will not be persuaded by the libertarian's dominating view of consent. I will therefore be arguing in a fashion that is not meant to convince the libertarian, whose core principles will prevent them from agreeing with my points. I instead hope to show why the rest of us should not adopt the libertarian view of consent for the moral questions at stake here.

On the strict version of libertarianism, which I will term "strict libertarianism,"[3] morality is reducible to three main tenets. First, humans have self-ownership, meaning that they have a fundamental moral right to do as they please with their own bodies.[4] Second, humans can gain ownership over objects by acquiring them in justified transactions.[5] Third, humans can exchange their rights with each other through consensual exchanges.[6] Thus, humans have liberty rights over their bodies, their objects, and whatever they gain through consensual exchanges. The strict libertarian limits morality to these three tenets, and allows that any results that are consistent with these tenets are thereby morally acceptable.[7]

On the strict libertarian view, it is fairly trivial that consent will be sufficient for moral permissibility. In a consensual exchange, there is not a lot of room for the three core libertarian values to be in conflict. If Tabitha and Teresa make a consensual exchange, then they have each decided that they wish to limit their liberty in exchange for whatever they are receiving from the other person. Though they may limit either their self-ownership or property-ownership liberties, it is through their own personal choices. And this is the very point of consent: it is the way in which people limit one of their liberties to gain something they want more. So, there is not a lot of room for either the moral values of self-ownership or property to outweigh consent here. If Tabitha and Teresa receive each other's consent, then that is almost surely the end of the matter, morally speaking, for the libertarian.

This same point would clearly apply to sexual contexts as well. For the libertarian, consent is sufficient to make sex morally permissible because no third party would have any right to intrude on two competent adults who have freely and with adequate information decided to have sex. As libertarian Igor Primoratz says, "Those who hold consent to be morally decisive see the line between right and wrong in sex as that between consensual and non-consensual sex, and understand rape as a particularly grave type of the latter. Consensuality is the norm, while nonconsensual sex acts are sporadic cases of deviation."[8] Thus, for Primoratz, as with other libertarians, there is a bright line: if it is consensual, then it is permissible, and if it isn't permissible, it must be non-consensual.

There are a good number of arguments against this strict libertarian view. Some scholars believe that consent is not morally foundational, and we instead must have an argument for its moral importance.[9] While I agree with that stance, the point here is to show that the libertarian does not give us a view where it seems consent would be sufficient for moral permissibility. To establish this point, I will point to the sort of competing moral values that could interfere with an agreement counting as consent. On the libertarian view, these values likely would not undermine consent since they would not recognize these values as fundamental. Thus, my problems will not likely worry the strictest of libertarians. Yet, I believe that the rest of us will see that strict libertarian consent does not do the normative work that libertarians think it does.

To show this point, it will be worthwhile to look at a few agreements that the libertarian would likely consider to be consensual, in spite of competing moral values. First, consider any case where an agreement is made to do something immoral. I will lie for you if you pay me $100. Someone agrees to commit adultery with a lover. Someone else agrees to sell lakeside property to a factory owner who plans to pollute the lake. Consent is defined as an agreement that generates a moral obligation. Nevertheless, in each of these cases, someone has agreed to do something immoral. That creates tension, at the least, and maybe a contradiction: you become morally obligated to do something (lie, assist with adultery, allow harmful pollution) that you are morally obligated not to do. The simple resolution of this conflict is to simply not count these cases as consent (they are mere agreements), which is the view that I would endorse.[10] In doing so, that would be to accept that these other moral values (honesty, marital commitment, protecting the environment) prevent the free, informed, and competent adult from being able to consent. However, the libertarian is unlikely to allow such a trumping from other moral values, and so they would likely count these cases as consent.

Let's consider another, more specific example. In the above cases, agents were attempting to consent to immoral behavior, which caused the problem. Let's consider now the use of immoral behavior to obtain the agreement. For instance, suppose one person, Pauline, exploits another person's bad situation: suppose Roberto has fallen down a well and cannot get out without help. Let's say that Pauline asks Roberto to hand over the deed to his house in exchange for letting him out of the well. It seems plausible to say that when Roberto agrees to hand over his house, he does not consent to do so because this scenario cannot create a moral obligation: Roberto does not become morally obligated to give over his house because that would be a moral travesty for him to become homeless just because Pauline was willing to exploit his difficult situation. So, I would argue there is no consent in this scenario.

A strict libertarian could not make this argument since it uses moral notions to develop a more comprehensive understanding of consent. In developing this case, I am relying on the wrong of exploitation and a moral intuition that Pauline is demanding too much. And I hope non-libertarians share my intuitions here. Nonetheless, I am using other moral notions to limit what counts as consent, and such an approach is unavailable for the libertarian. The libertarian would instead note that Roberto is making the decision that works best for him in his given circumstances, and Pauline is doing the same thing. Each is expressing their liberty by making a deal that helps them best given the situations they are in. Pauline did not put Roberto in that situation, and so she is not violating his self-ownership or property rights. She is simply taking advantage of his problem to enlarge her own property. So, the strict libertarian would have to say that Roberto consents to give his house to Pauline.

The strict libertarian is likely to count a lot of agreements as consensual even when competing moral values make that declaration contentious. Thus, the libertarian will have a rather inclusive view of consent because they will include so many cases that the rest of us might otherwise wish to exclude. The problem with such an inclusive view of consent is that it will no longer be plausible to count every instance of consent as morally sufficient. When we see people agreeing to immoral behavior or agreeing only due to the immoral behavior of others, we have reason to believe the agreements should be limited. The libertarian has to say that Roberto consents to give up his house because he has to after falling into that well. Society, though, may want to exclude agreements as consensual where they involve severely exploiting people since such agreements are inherently unfair and result from immoral behavior. Thus, the libertarian calls this agreement consent, but society has reason to worry that the agreement should not be upheld. Even if you do not agree that society should preclude the agreement, if you just agree that it is worth thinking about and/or discussing, then you agree that libertarian consent is not the end of the matter. In these types of cases where various moral factors conflict, libertarian consent is not sufficient because the other moral factors need to be weighed in our determination of whether to uphold the case. In other words, the libertarian has made consent so inclusive that there would be cases of consent where we should consider other moral factors. Hence, consent cannot be presumed to be sufficient given these types of cases.

The strict libertarian would respond that those other moral factors simply should not be considered and consent is always sufficient. I must acknowledge this point, and I accept that I am not likely convincing the strict libertarian of anything here. I am instead aiming the argument towards anyone who at least believes that these other moral factors that conflict in these cases must at least be weighed in our ultimate decision. For people who agree to weigh these other factors, at least, libertarian consent is not sufficient.

Consequently, if we used the strict libertarian's view of consent in our moral analysis of hooking up, we would not have reason to believe that consent was sufficient. If when we said two people hooked up consensually, we meant in an inclusive, libertarian view of consent, then we would still have to ask if the hook up was morally permissible based on other potential moral factors. However, the view of consent that I pursued in Chapter Two is much less inclusive than the libertarian view since I believe an agreement can only become consent if it morally obligates, and numerous moral factors are relevant in determining whether agents become morally obligated by their agreements. Even though the libertarian view does not show that non-libertarians should take consent to be morally sufficient, it is worth asking if another view might do that work instead.

Non-Harmful View

On the non-harmful view, consent itself is almost sufficient – there is just one additional stipulation required: no third party will be harmed. If two adults agree, and they are competent, free, adequately informed, and are not harming anyone else, then it seems wrong to constrain their activity. Thus, on this view, consent is not entirely sufficient, but the final addition is not too significant: since we accept that we should not harm third parties who are not party to an agreement, consent is sufficient if there is no such third party harm.

We see this view in philosopher David Archard's work when he lays out the two principles of what he takes to be the common view of consent, which he also adopts as his own view.[11] I will give both principles, though we will concentrate on the first. Archard's first principle is the principle of consensuality, which states, "a practice, P, is morally permissible if all those who are parties to P are competent to consent, give their valid consent, and the interests of no other parties are significantly harmed."[12] His second principle, the principle of non-consensuality, states, "a practice, P, is morally impermissible if at least one of those who are parties to P, and who are competent to consent, does not give their valid consent, even if the interests of no other parties are significantly harmed."[13] Archard's first principle states that if two persons give valid consent and no third person's interests are harmed, then their action is morally permissible, regardless of any other moral factors. Archard's second principle states that an action is morally impermissible if one party does not consent, even if no third parties are harmed. Thus, the second principle clarifies that you need not harm any third party for an action to be impermissible: it can be impermissible if one of the parties to the action does not consent. The second principle is fairly straightforward then: if you are performing an action that requires someone's consent and you do not receive their consent, then your action is impermissible, even if you are not harming anyone else.

By his first principle, Archard's view goes beyond consent but only in the least controversial way by requiring no significant harm to third party interests. Harms to the parties to the agreement are irrelevant, morally speaking, since their consent entails their acceptance of any harms accrued to them. As long as the only persons being harmed are the ones who have freely accepted the risks, Archard believes there is no basis for objecting to a consensual agreement.

This view is problematic for two main reasons. First, "harm" is so vague that this view would unintentionally exclude many cases where consent ought to be acceptable, though a re-wording may solve this problem. Second, it is not clearly morally acceptable to allow violations of the two consenting agents just because they consented. Such a theory would allow treating someone poorly just because he or she made an unwise agreement. I will argue, through this second problem, that this view doesn't actually show that consent plus no third party harm is morally sufficient.

To begin with the first point, it is often morally acceptable to harm others. Let's examine three problems that derive from using "harm" with vagueness. The first is that harms can be part of an overall positive outcome: the doctor, for instance, harms you when she gives you a shot, which causes pain, but shots are clearly not morally problematic. Suppose Bill and Jane are each trying to buy Al's gun. Al and Jane consent to the gun exchange. Bill is harmed since he was unable to buy the gun, but ultimately this situation benefits Bill since he was going to use the gun in a bank robbery, and their exchange saved Bill from a life of crime.

Second, harms can be unintentional, which would alter their moral relevance. People making consensual agreements can accidentally harm the interests of third parties in ways that they could not have predicted even if they took reasonable care to avoid such harms. Jane buys Al's gun for self-defense, but decades later, her grandson accidentally shoots his foot with it. Were the gun sold to Bill, maybe this would not have happened. Yet, the harm also couldn't be predicted and happened decades later. These agents are not morally responsible for accidental harms, and so their consent is not problematic in spite of third party harms.

Finally, there can be intended, negative harms to third party interests that are not morally problematic because they are byproducts of a morally permissible agreement. For example, any competitive exchange may harm the third parties who lose out. Suppose I am selling my car, and Beatrice and Candice make separate and equal offers, but I do not like Beatrice. I do not owe my car to Beatrice. So, I sell it to Candice with the intention of making sure Beatrice does not get my car. My consensual deal with Candice intentionally harms Beatrice's interests in a negative way. Since I do not owe anything to Beatrice, there is nothing wrong with our consensual deal.

Still, perhaps we could get around all of these problems by rephrasing Archard's principles and making the wording more precise. As such, an alternative approach would be that consent is morally sufficient provided that the consent doesn't violate the rights of third parties. With this principle, we would not have to worry about a rights violation being positive overall because a rights violation is inherently wrongful. We also think rights violations are so serious that they are usually intentional or negligent. That is because due care is required when others' rights are at stake. If you violate someone's rights accidentally, you probably were not being careful enough to avoid violating their rights. Finally, if you wish to violate someone's rights as a byproduct of an exchange, you are still acting wrongfully even though this is not your direct goal. This re-wording then seems to largely help with the problem of the vagueness of "harm" in the non-harmful view. There may be remaining cases that wouldn't be fully covered, such as morally problematic harms that aren't quite rights violations. However, that could just be a problem of working out the precise wording of the view, and we can leave those details to someone who supports this view.

The second problem with Archard's view is that moral agents would not intentionally harm others just because those others have made an unwise agreement that met the requirements for consent. It makes sense that unwise agreements could count as consensual since consent is not defined in terms of prudential wisdom. Suppose Sabrina and Tyrone are about to consent to something. If Sabrina meets all the requirements for giving consent but is not thinking clearly – for reasons that Tyrone did not cause – then Tyrone will gain permissions to do to Sabrina anything that is consistent with her consent. It undermines consent to take advantage of someone during the process of securing consent, but it cannot affect the status of the consent to take advantage of someone after they have consented to an unwise deal. In other words, for consent, you cannot manipulate someone into making an unwise agreement. Yet, someone can, on their own, make an unwise agreement that meets the requirements for consent (it is freely and competently made with adequate information). It would then be consistent with their unwise consent to take advantage of them. Far from guaranteeing morally permissible action, consent appears to license immoral mistreatment as long as the deal is made according to the rules for consent. However, I hold that taking advantage of people is not morally permissible just because they unwisely consented.

Let's develop a case. Once Tyrone has secured Sabrina's consent, then he can do anything to or with Sabrina that is sanctioned by that consent without violating that consent. That is a trivial point: consent cannot cover anything beyond what is consented to. It is much more contentious how we should morally look at Tyrone's consent-sanctioned actions. Suppose Tyrone is a research psychologist, and Sabrina consents to be experimented on in a way that could lead to serious psychological harms. Sabrina doesn't fully appreciate the deeper psychological repercussions of the experiment, even though Tyrone explicitly covered them and Sabrina listened to Tyrone's explanation. She even understood the ramifications, but simply dismissed them as she did not think they would happen to her. Given that Tyrone did his part in adequately informing her, and given that Sabrina is competent and did freely consent, Tyrone would not violate the terms of their consent by running an experiment that threatened to create deep psychological scars for Sabrina.

I should quickly note that this case is distinct from the previous exploitation case. When Roberto fell down the well, Pauline exploited his bad situation to take his house from him. I said that case was not consensual because Pauline manipulated Roberto's situation to force him into an agreement. In this case, Tyrone had nothing to do with Sabrina's mistake. He adequately informed her, and she understood the information but merely made a judgment error that the risk of psychological harm would not apply to her. Thus, their agreement is well formed and should count as consent. Tyrone is taking advantage of Sabrina after the fact of consent, whereas Pauline took advantage of Roberto as part of the process to get Roberto to agree. Hence, the Tyrone/Sabrina case involves possibly bad behavior after consent (and so does not undermine the consent that already exists), whereas the Pauline/Roberto case involves bad behavior leading up to the agreement (and so it undermines the consent).

In this sort of case, there is a clear question of whether Tyrone acts morally in threatening Sabrina's psychological well-being. If consent plus not harming third parties were sufficient, then Tyrone would act morally simply because no third party is harmed and he acts within the confines of Sabrina's consent – her consent *entails* that Tyrone acts morally on views like Archard's. On my view, there is much more to morality than consent, and Tyrone acts immorally in spite of the fact that he's obtained consent. While I have yet to argue that Tyrone acts immorally, it is important to point out that Archard's non-harmful view cannot give any reason to think Tyrone acts immorally. The non-harmful view doesn't explain why we are tempted to think Tyrone morally should not run the experiment even though Sabrina consented. It simply asserts that once consent is established, moral questions need only concern harms to third parties and not to parties to the consent. Yet, this example sets up a tough question where this view cannot explain why the question shouldn't feel easy.

On one side of this question, we have the view that consent is sufficient, which would entail that the parties who consent must accept whatever harms result from their own consent. The idea is that two agents who agreed according to consent's requirements should not have their agreement overturned. And if we were talking about consent from a legal point of view, that might make for a good argument. But there is no attempt to use external power to overturn agreements in the moral discussion – we are merely questioning whether these agreements can morally license mistreatment. We can surely declare that an agreement is morally troubling without, from a legal perspective, believing that the government should use its coercive powers to overturn the agreement. We certainly shouldn't be moved to a conceptual normative conclusion (that a person can do no wrong to a person who consented) based on a practical fear that too many agreements would be legally overturned if we say that there is more, morally speaking, than consent.

A proponent of these views might argue that we have no justification for calling actions that follow from consensual agreements immoral since both parties agreed while competent, informed, and free. But surely that isn't right. Surely we can judge people who take advantage of others' unwise agreements. There is no good reason why we must put our moral judgments aside just because two people made an agreement, even if that agreement fit strict standards. We are imagining a case where Sabrina agrees to Tyrone's experiment due to Sabrina's mistake of assuming that the experiment will not harm her. The fact that Tyrone did not cause Sabrina to make an unwise agreement does not mean that Tyrone can do as he pleases, within the confines of her agreement. Such a view encourages people to feel morally warranted in taking advantage of people who have made unwise deals. In other words, a view that says that there are no moral problems once another person consents encourages the idea that you can do anything to another person as long as you can get them to consent first. That isn't necessarily an extremely low standard: you cannot do anything that would undermine their agreement being free, informed, and competent. But it isn't a very high standard either: it would mean morality becomes silent just in case someone makes a free, informed, and competent agreement. Instead, it is much more plausible that morality requires being respectful and taking due care for others even after they have consented to a deal. Morality does not allow just any treatment to become permissible just because it fits within someone's (possibly unwise) consent.

Morality involves much more than people keeping their agreements. You could do everything necessary to get someone's consent while hoping they mess up so that you can take advantage after that fact. Morality includes treating people well after the exchange. It is wrong to mistreat the other party after they have consented, even if their consent allows the mistreatment. Consent creates new obligations and permissions, and consent alone sanctions acting accordingly. Consent, though, cannot create a blanket sanction of any mistreatment between parties; consent does not otherwise silence morality. Accounts that are only interested in harms to third parties would have to give good reason to think that consent should end our moral questions about harms to the consenting parties. I do not believe there are any such arguments available because morality extends to numerous issues beyond just consent. Thus, we need an alternative view that motivates why we should think it is ok to mistreat someone as long as they give their consent. The next view attempts to add to the non-harmful view by giving just such a motivation: it derives consent's sufficiency from Immanuel Kant's formula of humanity.

Formula of Humanity Basis for Consent Sufficiency

The formula of humanity view holds that consent is sufficient for moral permissibility because obtaining a person's consent ensures that you treat her as an end, and, therefore, you don't have to be concerned that any post-consent mistreatment would count as treating her as a mere means. If acting from Kant's formula of humanity – "So act that you use humanity, whether in your own person or in the person of any other, always at the same time as an end, never merely as a means"[14] – provided a good basis for ensuring your actions are moral, and if gaining consent were sufficient for meeting the formula, then consent would likely be sufficient for ensuring your hook up is morally permissible.

On this view, you can be sure you treat someone as an end, and not as a mere means, as long as you receive consent first. Alan Wertheimer states the view in the following manner:

> Consensual minimalism does not involve a minimalist account of consent. It maintains that a suitably but not excessively robust consent is sufficient to legitimize sexual relations. One may treat others ungenerously or be indifferent to their experience or interests, but one does not treat them *merely* as a means as long as we do and should regard them as the appropriate judges of what will serve their ends and they give consent that is consistent with PVC [principles of valid consent].[15]

On Wertheimer's view, if we build enough into consent, and two agents do consent, then it follows that their sexual relations are legitimized. On this view, you could not treat someone as a mere means if you recognize their right to deliberate over their choice and to decide what's best for themselves. By seeking their consent prior to acting, you are giving them the power to deliberate and decide for themselves. The more robust consent is, the more plausible this view is: you give them the information they need, you only interact with them when they are competent, and you are not using coercion, exploitation, or aggression to manipulate their choices – so it would seem you are treating them morally when they consent. It seems that all of this treatment suggests that you think of the person as an end in herself who should make the choices that she deems are good for her.

Another proponent of basing the sufficiency of consent on the formula of humanity is philosopher Thomas Mappes, who says, "I would suggest that the morally significant sense of 'using another person' is best understood by reference to the notion of *voluntary informed consent*."[16] Mappes builds a good deal into consent's requirements. He requires not only the avoidance of coercion, but also coercive offers (which, in the way he thinks of coercive offers, I would refer to as "exploitation").[17] For Mappes, an offer is coercive and undermines consent, when it involves "taking advantage of [someone's] desperate situation,"[18] because the person "is in circumstances of genuine need, and acceptance of the offer seems to present the only realistic possibility for alleviating the need."[19] Mappes excludes agreements that derive from coercive offers because they use the other person as a mere means to gain what is desired from the exchange. The other person may end up agreeing, but only because they are desperate. Using people's desperation to get their agreement cannot count as treating them as ends in themselves. Since Wertheimer would allow exploitation (or coercive offers in Mappes' sense) to be consistent with consent,[20] Mappes' more stringent notion of consent seems even more fitting with the formula of humanity.

There are a few different objections to the formula of humanity basis for consent sufficiency.[21] In one such objection, David Archard argues that it is possible for two people to obtain each other's consent to sexual relations and then to enter the sexual exchange only concerned for their own ends.[22] Thus, the agents do not intend to treat each other as ends after they have received the consent. One has to wonder how consent could be sufficient for a Kantian when it doesn't require continuing to think of the other person as an end after consent is obtained. Kantians would not think it is morally acceptable to stop thinking of others as ends just because they have consented to something. Instead, Kantians are primarily interested with intentions and how you view the people you are interacting with. Therefore, this view of consent sufficiency, which makes mention neither of what you must intend nor of how you must think about the people with whom you are consenting, does not seem to be a good interpretation of Kant's formula of humanity.

Of course, in the previous section, we saw that Archard was a proponent of the view that consent is sufficient as long as third parties are not harmed. Archard, then, doesn't think that one must think of the other person as an end after consent is obtained. In a sexual exchange, Archard believes that agents would only have to treat each other as ends if that was either consented to in advance or was assumed as a part of an existing relationship.[23] Archard would probably view hook ups, for example, as situations where it is understood by both parties that you do not have to treat the other person as an end: each person merely uses the other for sexual gratification. Hook up consent, for Archard, implies an understanding of mutual sexual using.

Still, it is worrisome to think the default for any activity is using people, such that the burden would be on the person who would prefer respectful treatment. It is perhaps more, not less, worrisome to think of sexual activity in this way. Archard seems to ascribe to a worldview where people who do not wish to be used as sexual objects must make their feelings known, or else using people sexually is *assumed* to be permissible. Archard seems to be aware of the worrisome nature of this view, and he admits he cannot adequately respond to it in his book.[24]

As a larger counter-argument to the idea that the formula of humanity establishes that consent is sufficient, I will next argue for the contrary position that the formula of humanity actually shows that consent cannot be sufficient for moral permissibility. On this alternative view, consent is not sufficient for satisfying the formula of humanity, and satisfying the formula of humanity is necessary to be morally permitted to act. If this alternative view is correct, then consent cannot be sufficient for moral permissibility. One Kantian philosopher who agrees that the formula of humanity captures a key part of being moral, but who doesn't think that consent is sufficient for meeting the formula of humanity, is Onora O'Neill.

O'Neill gives the main thesis for her "Between Consenting Adults," by saying, "I shall argue that an adequate understanding of what it is to treat others as persons must view them not abstractly as possibly consenting adults, but as particular men and women with limited and determinate capacities to understand or to consent to proposals for action."[25] In other words, O'Neill challenges the reduction of persons that occurs when we think we can fulfill our moral duties with respect to them simply by confirming their consent. There is much more to a person than whether they have consented. Our moral interactions must reflect how we deal with the complexity of the person we interact with (which variously includes their projects, ideals, limitations, needs, vulnerabilities, and feelings), and this complexity cannot be sidestepped just because the person gave consent.

O'Neill argues that treating others as persons requires a dual, and somewhat conflicting, approach, which she characterizes through the ideas of respect and love.[26] Respect, as O'Neill thinks of it here, involves recognizing that others need their space, which includes avoiding anything that might prevent them from acting for their ends.[27] Love is the other side, and it involves giving others the help they need to fulfill their ends by providing them with sympathy, generosity, and assistance.[28]

The tension lies in the fact that respect involves proper distance and space, while love involves maintaining enough proximity to readily give assistance.[29] Respect requires giving others space so that they can choose and develop their own ends as independent persons. Love requires helping people with their independently chosen ends. Managing this tension in real life can be quite difficult, and will depend a great deal on each agent's particular circumstances (thus, philosophers should be wary of thinking they can provide practical guidance on such tricky issues while working on them in the abstract[30]).

The formula of humanity requires seeing the person as a whole person who needs distance (requiring respect), and is vulnerable in ways that may depend on assistance (requiring love). It is by seeing the person in such a complete fashion that we respect that they are an end in themselves, and not someone whom we can make into our means by getting them to do something (consent) that would purportedly legitimize treating them however we like (within the confines provided by their consent).

Treating consent as the end of the matter can endanger both aspects from O'Neill's view. Respect can be endangered by an agent using consent to invade the other person's private space, which would include their physical personal space, private activities, and emotional boundaries. After all, once you have consent, then you will likely have more access to their private space since they let you in. But it would be contrary to respect to try to change a person in ways that happen to fit within their consent but that they would not autonomously endorse. Suppose an undergraduate student asks a professor for help in choosing a career. The professor lets the student know that she has strong opinions and can be entirely persuasive when discussing such matters, but the student, perhaps doubting the professor's power of persuasion, consents anyway. Then, she uses the student's consent to push him into becoming a professional philosopher – knowing that she can really sell that profession, while also knowing that he wouldn't choose it for himself without the professor's pushing. Here, the professor has not violated their consensual agreement, but she has surely invaded this student's private space by pushing a certain career instead of just laying out the various advantages and disadvantages of many careers.

For O'Neill's other component, if you see someone will be harmed through a consensual deal in ways that they don't foresee, love may require helping them avoid those harms. For example, if two people hook up, and then afterwards one of them is crying and clearly depressed, love would certainly require seeing what's wrong and what can be done to help. Notice though that their original consent is very unlikely to entail a duty to provide that help. But, just by hooking up, even if they are near strangers, they have produced a relationship where it would make sense that someone's becoming depressed and crying would produce a duty of love (in O'Neill's sense – not to be confused with romantic love) to find out what's wrong and at least genuinely offer to help.

Consent is not sufficient to ensure that an agent is respected or loved in these ways, and that is especially clear in sexual contexts. O'Neill believes that a sexual encounter automatically raises issues of intimacy. Contrary to certain objections made against O'Neill,[31] she does not argue that sexual encounters require intimacy to be permissible. Sexual encounters simply raise issues of intimacy.[32] We are all different. Some people feel at least somewhat intimate with everyone they hook up with. Other people will at least wonder whether the hook up could lead to greater intimacy. There are surely some people who completely divorce feelings of intimacy from hook ups. We need not say that intimacy is required or always at stake to say that issues of intimacy are at least relevant when two people hook up. Hence, a hook up would raise issues of intimacy, especially when two people are near strangers and cannot know which of these groups the other person fits into.

Whenever issues of intimacy are at play, respect and love become more salient because a person feeling like they have an intimate connection with someone is more vulnerable to interference with their independence and is more likely to have needs arise where assistance is necessary.[33] Such a person within a sexual situation may have more difficulty expressing important limits or asking for assistance. It is then quite easy to fail to respect such a person because their limits are not clear, or to fail to show love because signs of discomfort are similarly unclear.

These issues need not apply to every hook up for them to be important. The claim is not that everyone feels vulnerable or intimate in a hook up. But when hook ups are with near strangers, it is unclear who would take a hook up to be intimate or would feel vulnerable. Thus, failures of respect and love can be quite difficult to notice in these situations – and nearly impossible to notice for a person who assumes consent is sufficient. So, the moral agent has to think a lot more about the partner that they hook up with. As O'Neill says: "Intimate bodies cannot easily have separate lives."[34]

O'Neill shows that the standard picture of consent cannot assure us that we are meeting the formula of humanity. Instead, we must respect and love other humans because they are vulnerable and fragile, but yet also independent and potentially autonomous. Only through respect and love are we truly seeing these persons as ends in themselves. The idea that we can use someone after we have obtained their consent implies that it is sufficient to have seen them as ends early in the process (while obtaining consent), but that we can then treat them as mere means after consent is received. Instead, O'Neill offers a picture, using respect and love, where treating people as ends, and not mere means, is an ongoing process, which would be much more in keeping with Kant's formula of humanity.

Another philosopher, Howard Klepper, makes similar points as O'Neill, about the insufficiency of consent, when he says:

> Our moral obligations to our sexual partners surely do not end with their voluntary informed consent. Closer to the truth is that they begin there. We

> have an ongoing obligation to be respectful and considerate of our sexual partners' needs. Like voluntary informed consent, this is not an obligation unique to sexual relationships. It applies to all our relationships with others, but the requirements imposed by this obligation increase with the intimacy of the relationship. The obligation applies with particular force to sexual relationship, because the intimacy of those relationships involve relinquishing defenses, which leaves people particularly vulnerable to feeling used.[35]

Klepper then agrees that consent is not sufficient for moral permissibility in sexual relations just as it is not sufficient in other matters. But, since sex raises heightened issues of intimacy, Klepper, like O'Neill, thinks that we gain stronger, not weaker, requirements to go beyond consent to ensure that we do not harm people when they are feeling vulnerable and could easily be used.

In other words, it cannot be morally permissible to take advantage of someone's vulnerabilities just because the person has consented in a way that allows you to take advantage of them – sex is a clear case for this point, instead of being a counter-example. A person can easily take advantage of a hook up partner because hook up partners have somewhat uniquely (especially for near strangers) strong abilities to make each other feel crappy about who they are as sexual bodies and persons. Since those vulnerabilities have been opened up, the fact that the partners have not consented to look out for each other does not get them beyond the standard moral requirement to look out for people around you.

Let's consider an example. It would not be contrary to consent, in almost all ordinary cases, for a hook up partner to tell the other partner how he or she was performing sexually. Suppose they agreed that it was ok to talk during sex, and so when the man is performing quite poorly, the woman chooses to tell him. She further adds that it has much to do with his inability to compensate for his inadequate penis. She has neither violated the terms of their consent nor is she being dishonest. Because of the implied intimacy in a sexual exchange that is quite difficult to get around, these words are likely to hurt quite intensely. And it is reasonable to assume the woman would know her words would dig into a vulnerability that is augmented by their hook up. She has not violated their consent, but she has done something morally wrong by not seeing and respecting the man's likely personal limits. Consent then does not seem sufficient for moral permissibility.

Thus, instead of the formula of humanity showing us that consent is sufficient, we obtain a picture of moral permissibility that derives from the formula of humanity and extends beyond the mere requirements of consent. Consent serves as a necessary condition that cannot be sufficient for moral permissibility since limits can be overstepped and human vulnerabilities can be exposed within the confines of the consensual agreement. Since the moral agent does not seek to take advantage of someone just because the person consented, the moral agent would not think consent is the end of the moral story.

Conclusion

We saw three attempts to argue for the moral sufficiency of consent, and none provided us with a good reason to think that there can't be further moral questions after consent has been obtained. The strict libertarian view provides a notion of consent that would be normatively weak, but it is hard to see a normatively weak view as sufficient for moral permissibility.

The non-harmful view fails to give a good reason to think consent ought to be thought of as morally sufficient. That view seems to rely on an intuitive, but unfulfilling, notion that consent should be enough as long as the only people harmed are the people who make the agreement. But insisting on this point of view does not tell us why it is *morally* acceptable to harm the people who consent.

Finally, we saw two opposing formula of humanity views. On one view, the formula of humanity is met by consent alone since securing someone's consent shows that you are treating them as an end. On the other view, consent cannot be sufficient for treating someone as an end since there is so much more to a person than whether they agree to something. People have needs, vulnerabilities, and personal limits. Treating the person as an end requires seeing them holistically and treating them as such. Thus, consent is merely the start of treating someone as an end, and is not sufficient for the formula of humanity. And this latter view seems to better represent the formula of humanity, which would imply that Kantian ethics would not condone treating consent as morally sufficient.

The reason these arguments fail to show consent is sufficient for moral permissibility is because there are other moral problems that consent doesn't seem to solve. I will group these problems, which we have looked at in various ways already, into three potentially overlapping groups: hooking up leaves people vulnerable and needy, hooking up necessarily involves sexually objectifying people, and hooking up as a practice is currently constituted in sexist ways. In the next chapter, we will examine why these problems require that moral agents do more than just obtain consent, and we will identify what else is required for hook ups to be morally permissible.

Notes

1 Onora O'Neill, "Between Consenting Adults," *Philosophy and Public Affairs* 14, no. 3 (1985), 252–277; Roger Scruton, *Sexual Desire* (London: Continuum, 1986), 337–345; Raymond A. Belliotti, *Good Sex* (Lawrence: University Press of Kansas, 1993), 86–227; Lois Pineau, "Date Rape: A Feminist Analysis," in *Date Rape: Feminism, Philosophy, and the Law*, ed. Leslie Francis (University Park: The Pennsylvania State University Press, 1996), 1–26; Patricia Marino, "The Ethics of Sexual Objectification," *Inquiry* 51, no. 4 (2008), 358–359; Howard Klepper, "Sexual Exploitation and the Value of Persons" in *The Philosophy of Sex: Contemporary Readings*, eds. Alan Soble and Nicholas Power (New York: Rowman and Littlefield, 2008), 251–256; Robin West, "Sex, Law, and Consent," in *The Ethics of Consent*, eds. Franklin G. Miller and Alan

Wertheimer (New York: Oxford University Press, 2010); Timothy Hsiao, "Consenting Adults, Sex, and Natural Law Theory," *Philosophia* 44 (2016); Rebecca Kukla, "That's What She Said: The Language of Sexual Negotiation," *Ethics* 129 (2018), 7.

2 Alan H. Goldman, "Plain Sex," *Philosophy and Public Affairs* 6, no. 3 (1977); David Archard, *Sexual Consent* (Boulder: Westview Press, 1998), see esp. 2; Thomas A. Mappes, "Sexual Morality and the Concept of Using Another Person," in *Philosophy of Sex: Contemporary Readings*, eds. Alan Soble and Nicholas Power (New York: Rowman and Littlefield, 2008), 229–249; Alan Soble, *Sexual Investigations* (New York: New York University Press, 1996), 27–28, 33–43; Igor Primoratz, *Ethics and Sex* (London: Routledge, 1999); Igor Primoratz, "Sexual Morality: Is Consent Enough?," *Ethical Theory & Moral Practice* 4, no. 2 (2001), 201–218; Laurence Thomas, "Sexual Desire, Moral Choice, and Human Ends," *Journal of Social Philosophy* 33, no. 2 (2002), 181–182; Alan Wertheimer, *Consent to Sexual Relations* (Cambridge: Cambridge University Press, 2003), see esp. 140.

3 I mean strict libertarianism to abstract away from any particular additions and nuances that come along with particular libertarian views from individual libertarian theorists. In other words, strict libertarianism is not the view of one specific libertarian, but it brings forth the core components of libertarian views in general.

4 See David D. Friedman, *The Machinery of Freedom: Guide to a Radical Capitalism* (Chu Hartley LLC, 2014), Kindle Edition, Introduction, Loc. 206. Also see Introduction, Loc. 287–289; Jan Narveson, *The Libertarian Idea* (Ontario: Broadview Press, 2001), 66–68.

5 F. A. Hayek, *The Constitution of Liberty* (Chicago: University of Chicago Press, 1960), 207–209; Robert Nozick, *Anarchy, State, and Utopia* (New York: Basic Books, 1974), 171–182; Friedman, *Machinery of Freedom*, Introduction, Loc. 300.

6 Nozick, *Anarchy*, 58.

7 Narveson, *The Libertarian Idea*, 110–184, esp. 165.

8 Primoratz, "Is Consent Enough?," 208.

9 Wertheimer, *Consent to Sexual Relations*, 124; Neil Manson and Onora O'Neill, *Rethinking Informed Consent in Bioethics* (Cambridge: Cambridge University Press, 2007), 72–84; Hsiao, "Consenting Adults," 512–513.

10 For other theorists who believe you cannot consent to something that is unquestionably immoral, see Robin West, "Submission, Choice, and Ethics: A Rejoinder to Judge Posner," *Harvard Law Review* 99, no. 7 (1986), 1449–1450; Leo Katz, "Choice, Consent, and Cycling: The Hidden Limitations of Consent," *Michigan Law Review* 104, no. 4 (2006), 628.

11 Archard, *Sexual Consent*, 2.

12 Ibid.

13 Ibid.

14 Immanuel Kant, *Groundwork*, in *Practical Philosophy*, ed. and trans. Mary J. Gregor (Cambridge: Cambridge University Press, 1996), 80.

15 Wertheimer, *Consent to Sexual Relations*, 140.

16 Mappes, "Sexual Morality," 231.

17 Ibid., 242–245. Let's quickly clarify these terms (coercion, exploitation, and coercive offer). Coercion involves using a threat to make someone give into a demand. Exploitation involves using someone's bad situation, which you did not create, to make them give into a demand. A coercive offer involves making someone an offer that implicitly includes a threat. A coercive offer is closer to coercion than exploitation because in both coercion and coercive offers, the person making the proposal is creating the bad situation. The coercer uses a threat where the coercive offer maker implies a threat through the offer to do the same work. "I found you in a well. I will help you out if you give me your house," is exploitation. "I will push you into the well if you don't give me your house," is coercion. "I have a deal for you: you give

me your house and you don't get pushed into that well," is a coercive offer. Mappes is describing exploitation when he says "coercive offer."

18 Ibid., 245.
19 Ibid., 243.
20 Wertheimer, *Consent to Sexual Relations*, 190–191, 219–20.
21 O'Neill, "Between Consenting Adults"; Klepper, "Sexual Exploitation," 249–259; Belliotti, *Good Sex*, 98–105; Archard, *Sexual Consent*, 40–42, 78–80; Alan Soble, "Sexual Use," in *The Philosophy of Sex: Contemporary Readings*, eds. Alan Soble and Nicholas Power (New York: Rowman and Littlefield, 2008), 262.
22 Archard, *Sexual Consent*, 41.
23 Ibid., 78.
24 Ibid., 83.
25 O'Neill, "Between Consenting Adults," 253.
26 Ibid., 263–266.
27 Ibid., 265.
28 Ibid.
29 Ibid., 265–266.
30 Ibid., 266–268.
31 Soble, *Sexual Investigations*, 42.
32 O'Neill, "Between Consenting Adults," 269–270.
33 Ibid., 270.
34 Ibid.
35 Klepper, "Sexual Exploitation," 251.

7

RESPECTFUL, BENEFICENT, AND TRUSTWORTHY HOOK UPS

As we have seen in the previous chapter, consent is not morally sufficient while hooking up because significant moral problems come up where consent alone cannot provide the solution. These problems include the fact that any sexual situation will raise heightened vulnerability, which would call for a moral response, even if prior consent does not necessitate such a response. Second, hooking up necessarily involves objectifying others, which raises moral issues that are distinct from what consent covers. Finally, we have seen ways in which the hook up practice is sexist, and even though an agent may not have to be responsive to that sexism to fulfill a consensual agreement, morality would not allow an agent to ignore his own contribution to a sexist practice.

In this chapter, I will argue that moral agents would respond to these sorts of moral problems in respectful ways. I will use "respect" to refer to a broad range of ways to treat a person. Respect includes some ways of acting towards people that are almost always necessary: being polite, being sensitive especially to other people's problems, and not being cruel or uncaring. In terms of hooking up in particular, I will argue that respect will include additional manners of acting, such as being beneficent when called for and finding ways to provide others with a basis for trust.

Hooking up opens up a wide range of vulnerabilities that any moral agent would have to be sensitive to. Many of these vulnerabilities arise because agents are being objectified and treated differently because of the sexism within the practice. In response to these vulnerabilities, moral agents would look to act respectfully and with beneficence, even where these responses aren't necessary to meet the terms of a consensual agreement.

Some of these vulnerabilities, however, may come up after the hook up is over, which will also largely be outside the domain of the consensual agreement.

For this reason, it may also be necessary for agents to provide a basis for trust so that future vulnerabilities are not exposed, such as when individuals brag about hook ups and endanger their former hook up partners' reputations. By giving their partners a basis for trust, moral agents can help their hook up partners not feel vulnerable after the fact.

The goal of this chapter is to examine the main problems that lead us to conclude that consent is not sufficient for moral permissibility. Once we see how those problems take the morality of hooking up beyond consent, we can examine how moral agents would add respect, beneficence, and a basis for trust on top of obtaining consent to ensure that their hook ups are morally permissible.

Problems Beyond Consent

Three issues suggest that hook up morality extends beyond whether agents have consented: vulnerabilities and needs that come up during or after a hook up, the inherent objectifying nature of hooking up, and the pervasive sexism throughout hook up culture. Each of these issues is likely to come up in typical hook ups, is unlikely to be covered by consent, and is relevant to any overall moral evaluation of how an agent acts. Let's look at these issues, and then turn to how moral agents would respond to them.

Unexpected Vulnerability

A standard hook up can raise unexpected vulnerabilities that call for moral responses. The problem, put simply, is that no matter how much participants try to act as if a hook up entails meaningless sex, we, as human beings, probably cannot completely separate our emotions from sex acts.[1] That is not to say that there can't be a person out there who always has emotionless sex, but such a person is likely to be rare, and many people have feelings arise in typical hook ups, and almost everyone can have feelings arise in at least some hook up scenarios. It is nearly impossible to completely avoid emotions while hooking up. Since emotions cannot be avoided and things might go wrong, we all have vulnerabilities that might become exposed in a hook up.

A few examples will suffice to show how standard hook ups can expose vulnerabilities, but this issue references a larger set of possible problems that we cannot expect to exhaust here. We can imagine someone accidentally saying something hurtful (say about their partner's nude body), someone becoming physically injured during the sex act, someone coming to regret their decision to hook up (and the other person may agree to stop, since sexual consent is contemporaneous, but there could still be questions of how to deal with a person who is suddenly confused and upset), someone becoming embarrassed by some involuntary biological function that isn't meant to happen and certainly isn't sexy (passing gas, burping, early ejaculation, etc.), and/or someone performing poorly in the hook up in an obvious way (being a bad kisser, inability to achieve an erection, accidentally falling asleep, etc.). All of these cases involve vulnerabilities that bring with them moral obligations that are neither included within consent nor unrelated to the hook up. The latter point is important because there may be moral issues that could come up in a hook up that have nothing to do with the hook up. If, for example, you are hooking up in a near stranger's room and you discover their plans to rob a bank, then you will suddenly have a new moral obligation thrust upon you. Yet, that moral obligation is only tangentially connected to the hook up. Each of the examples I've mentioned would fit securely as parts of the hook up, and moral agents need to respond well if any of these things, or something similar, comes up.

These cases are unlikely to fit into the consensual agreement as they are unexpected and lie at the boundary of the sex act. People consent to arrangements that they expect to happen: I lend you my lawn mower, and we discuss details that we believe are likely to come up. We probably will not discuss what happens if my lawn mower unexpectedly blows up when you plug it in; our consent would not cover what we morally owe to each other in such an unpredictable mishap that we never discussed. Unexpected mishaps that expose vulnerabilities raise noteworthy moral questions because consent is often silent on how agents should respond. In real life, things come up that are related to the terms of the consent (they lie at the boundary of the agreement), but that are not covered by what was consented to since you cannot cover every possible boundary issue.

Sociologist Lisa Wade shows that the common pattern among hook up participants is to try to become more emotionally distant from their partners.[2] Hook up participants face a few problems that lead to this trend. First, they do not wish to mislead the other person into thinking that the hook up means something serious, and being caring, kind, or even respectful can give the wrong impression.[3] Second, they may face peer pressure to establish the social worth of their hook ups. Much of this social worth derives from having one's friends finding one's hook up partner to be sexy. Yet, where a person's friends are unlikely to deem the hook up to have social worth (the partner is not deemed to be sexy), the person will feel pressured to diminish the importance of the hook up by showing how little they care about or even respect the person who their friends do not find attractive.[4] As Wade says, "The preemptive strike when hooking up with a 'bad girl' is to treat her badly."[5] Third, hook up participants may compete with their partner to show that they care even less than the other person, so as to prove that they did not become emotionally invested and are instead sexually liberated.[6]

Wade argues that these motivations to appear emotionally distant lead to an active effort to disrespect one's hook up partners. She explains: "It's one thing, after all, to have causal sexual encounters with someone with whom you are not in love, but it's entirely another to do so with someone who may have no positive regard for you at all."[7] Wade adds that "men's disrespect of women is the bargaining chip," insofar as they show their social worth to other men by showing how little they think of the women they are hooking up with.[8] Hook up participants engage in a practice that can definitely expose vulnerabilities, but the social conventions of the practice demand a coldness to each other's vulnerabilities that is disrespectful and potentially capable of causing significant psychological pain.

Thus, we see that it is likely that hook ups will involve unpredicted problems at the boundaries that raise new moral issues. The possibility of such issues arising in itself shows that consent cannot be morally sufficient: consent cannot answer all moral questions that can come up within a consensual transaction, and so additional moral tools are needed. So, while there may be numerous actual cases where consent is actually sufficient, it cannot be assumed to always be morally sufficient because there are surely some actual cases where vulnerabilities are exposed by something outside of consent's scope. In such cases, it is trivial – yet hugely important – that morality requires something – responding to the exposed vulnerabilities of others – that goes beyond obtaining consent.

Hook Up Objectification

As we saw previously, hook ups are certainly objectifying.[9] When discussing possibly illicit motives in Chapter Four, I acknowledged that hooking up with someone just because they are physically attractive cannot be considered illicit if this practice is at all justifiable. It is a defining norm of the practice that individuals are primarily, and often solely, motivated by lust. It is also a standard norm of the practice that individuals are unlikely to know their partners well. Thus, if they aren't motivated by lust, then their motives are likely to be more illicit, not less. Since hook up partners act from lust, their interaction is directed towards each other's bodies. Hook up partners have no interest in each other's minds or personalities. Hooking up is inherently objectifying.

Martha Nussbaum, in her landmark piece "Objectification," argues that objectification is not necessarily immoral.[10] I will first explain her view and then return to why and when she thinks that objectification can be permissible. Nussbaum explains objectification by saying, "I suggest in all cases of objectification what is at issue is a question of treating one thing as another: One is treating as an object what is really not an object, what is, in fact, a human being."[11] She then follows this definition by giving seven notions that make up objectification in various cases, with these notions providing the normativity that allows us to pinpoint when a case of objectification is morally wrong.[12] The first notion is instrumentality, which involves treating a person as a tool for the objectifier's ends. The second, the denial of autonomy, amounts to denying that the other person ought to be able to choose and pursue the actions that are best according to her own standards. Third, an objectifier treats someone as inert if she denies the other person is an agent who can choose and act at all. The fourth notion, fungibility, involves treating a person as interchangeable with other persons or with objects. Fifth, violability, involves treating someone like it is acceptable to violate his or her boundaries and purposely injure or harm him or her. The sixth notion is ownership, which means the objectifier acts like he or she owns the objectified person. Finally, the seventh notion, denial of subjectivity, denies there is any value or worth in the experiences or feelings of the objectified person.

As we turn to hook ups, we can divide these seven notions into four groups. In the first group, we can place the notions that are covered by consent. Denial of autonomy would likely be covered by consent. If hook up partners are obtaining consent in a robust sense, then they are communicating, while sober, and ensuring that each person is freely deciding what is best for themselves. This effort shows some respect for the other person's autonomy. So, we can set this notion aside since it is covered by consent.

In the second group, we can put the notions that violate consent and so are not necessary for our discussion. We can therefore set aside inertness and violability as they would violate consent. An agent who treats his partner as inert – not caring if the partner is stiff or even passed out – is likely raping his partner, and so such a hook up is never consensual. If an agent is treating his partner as violable where this is not explicitly agreed upon, then they are physically harming the partner, and, again, this is probably a rape and not a consensual hook up. Hence, these notions will also not be worth further exploration.

That leaves two other groups, which will need further discussion. The third group includes ownership and denial of subjectivity. I will argue that these are not necessarily common, but are morally problematic when they arise. The fourth group, which includes instrumentality and fungibility, are parts of typical hook ups, and it will be much more contentious whether they raise moral issues.

Let's then turn to ownership and denial of subjectivity. There is a sense of ownership in the fairly common idea of seeing hook up partners as objects to be acquired, with their acquisition later being celebrated through bragging. Anyone who brings a conquering attitude to a hook up treats his or her partner as an owned object. After all, such a person treats their hook up partner not as a mutual partner such that joint pleasure is being sought, but as an embodied representation of their own prowess – as a conquered trophy. If morally suspect motives are communicated (as I argued for in Chapter Four), then this conquering attitude may be consented to, but that doesn't remove the large amount of disrespect this objectification notion brings into standard hook ups. After all, treating a person as a conquered thing amounts to acting like you are superior to the other person. Insofar as morality requires an important acceptance of our moral equality as persons, this ownership claim is in itself morally troubling, even if consented to.

Anyone who doesn't care about the sexual pleasure of his or her hook up partners engages in denial of subjectivity. Though we can imagine hook ups where there is a mutual agreement to care about each other's feelings, two people could also agree that they will each concentrate entirely on their own pleasure. Where such a selfish agreement is made, denying the subjectivity of the other person would not interfere with consent. Yet, it is normally thought to be morally problematic to deny someone's feelings and emotions, especially while engaging in sexual activity with that person. After all, we show people that they matter to us by caring about their feelings. To not care about a person's feelings is a definite step towards not caring about the person in a way that morality cannot sanction. To this extent, we would think that denying subjectivity raises moral issues even when it does not interfere with consent.

Let's turn to the final group, the most common notions among typical hook ups: instrumentality and fungibility. That instrumentality and fungibility are involved in typical hook ups is almost trivial in that it may be difficult to make sense of hook ups without those two notions. Since hook up partners likely have no solid knowledge of each other – and may not be interested in acquiring such knowledge – they are almost certainly using each other as tools for their own sexual gratification. And so instrumentality is quite common. Further, hook up partners are chosen primarily for their physical appeal, and so they are certainly fungible in that they could always be traded for a better looking person. Robust consent would not diminish the instrumentality or fungibility of hook ups since agents are knowingly consenting to precisely those kinds of hook ups.

In spite of being consented to, issues of instrumentality and fungibility are not necessarily morally benign. We tend to think that it is morally problematic to treat someone as a tool or as interchangeable with anyone or anything else. Although Nussbaum thinks objectification, when limited to notions such as these, might be morally acceptable, she thinks their moral acceptability depends on their occurrence within relationships that are themselves characterized by mutual respect.[13] Relationships of mutual respect may be difficult to establish within hook up culture. Thus, if Nussbaum were right, we would need another way to make hook up objectification permissible.

One philosopher, Patricia Marino, doesn't think Nussbaum is right that even a respectful relationship can sanctify objectification. Marino argues that it is not clear that you can justify objectifying someone in one context by the fact that you do not objectify them in other contexts.[14] After all, we don't normally think that it is okay to mistreat your spouse or friend in some specific situation just because you otherwise have a relationship of mutual respect.

However, this is not the right way to think of Nussbaum's argument. It is not that the positive parts of the relationship *make* the negative parts bearable or acceptable. Instead, Nussbaum's point is better understood as seeing the positive parts of the relationship as giving good epistemic evidence that objectifying treatment that is normally disrespectful is not meant as such. Both agents understand perfectly well what is happening within the moment of objectification because they can draw on their shared positive experiences. While objectifying someone normally indicates a lack of respect, that indication can be defeated by sufficient epistemic evidence that there is continued respect in spite of the objectification.

But it is precisely this evidence that is missing in the typical hook up with near strangers. Near strangers do not know that their objectification is consistent with the other person's respect. Thus, objectification raises particular moral problems when the hook up is between near strangers, and consent is not responsive to these moral problems.

Contrary to this position that consent is not responsive, Marino argues that we should replace Nussbaum's understanding of permissible objectification with an idea that agents should be seen as separately consenting to their own objectification.[15] In her example, if a woman puts pornographic pictures of herself on the internet with the intention for others to see them, then she is giving her consent to have others objectify her.[16] Marino admits, however, that this consent to be objectified cannot be genuine in an atmosphere of sexism and inequality, where people may feel pressured to objectify themselves.[17]

Though Marino's exceptions (atmosphere of sexism and inequality) apply to the actual hook up culture, her alternative view nevertheless presents a problem for the position being presented here. Objectification, on her view, could be handled directly through consent. On this view, since a hook up is almost surely inclusive of instrumentality and fungibility objectification, then one would think that consent to hook up entails consent to be objectified at least in these senses.

The problem with this response lies in the need to distinguish the type of action that consent entails with the moral permissibility of the manner in which one performs that action. That is, if persons A and B consent to action X, and X entails action Y, then we can say that A and B have consented to Y. In the hook up, X will be the hook up and Y will be the entailed objectification. But suppose that Y can be done either respectfully or disrespectfully, but A and B neither foresaw nor discussed this difference. Their consent then left open how Y should be performed, but morality does not leave that issue open: the action should be performed respectfully.

Let's use a quick medical example that will parallel a hook up case in terms of exposed vulnerabilities. A patient consents for a skin doctor to give a full-body mole inspection. The patient's consent entails that they will remove all their clothes in front of the clothed doctor. There is no agreement of whether the doctor would make illicit, sexual comments about the patient's nude body. Yet, it would be ludicrous to think that the doctor is licensed by their consent's silence on this issue to make such comments. Even though their consent entails there will be nudity, other moral obligations ensure respectful treatment of that nudity regardless of whether that kind of treatment was discussed when they consented.

In the hook up case, if two people consent to hook up, they have, thereby, consented to be objectified. Yet, there can be permissible objectification where no disrespect is intended by the objectification or impermissible and disrespectful objectification. In terms of the latter, someone can go too far in making the other person feel like they are a tool for sexual gratification or that they are completely fungible. For instance, they could make explicit statements to these effects: they could, that is, say out loud that they are using the other person as a sex toy or that they are only hooking up with them because there wasn't a more attractive person available. So, the fact that consent licenses objectification does not in itself entail which kind of objectification is licensed (respectful or disrespectful). The two hook up partners' consent will not entail what kind of objectification exactly they agreed to since they are unlikely to discuss the idea, which comes from Marino, that their hook up consent entails consent to be objectified. Thus, they are unlikely to explicitly consent to a certain kind of objectification.

The fact that they have consented to objectification, in the sense that Marino lays out, does not entail that the moral issues with their objectification have been worked out. Most likely, as Marino argues, their consent to hook up entails that they have consented to be objectified, but they could still feel they are being treated disrespectfully within the objectifying hook up. Of course, since Marino laid out exceptions (not occurring within an atmosphere of sexism and inequality), this point is less likely to be salient in the kind of society she is imagining. That is, were we to live in a society with less sexism, then people are less likely to objectify each other in disrespectful manners. But that just shows that there are other moral issues besides consent at work here, including whether the society is sexist and unequal.

Also in support of this view of consent's limitation, Howard Klepper argues that, "consent to being abused or degraded does not render the abuse or degradation moral. (Although, with some limitations, it may make it legal)."[18] Klepper's view, combined with Marino's caveat, brings out the point that it is not clear that the moral problem goes away just because someone consents to an action that entails their objectification, especially in a society where sexism is rampant. Hence, in the hook up society that we currently inhabit, the idea that consent to hook up entails consent to be objectified would still not settle the moral questions at stake with respect to how that objectification is done.

It seems that we cannot set aside the objectification problem so easily. Thus, we will want to see how moral agents would deal with the moral issues raised by objectification, but first I will return to the reason why Marino's caveat does apply: the contemporary hook up culture is sufficiently sexist to make objectification even more worrisome.

Sexist Culture

The third problem, which has come up a few times already, revolves around the sexism that is rampant throughout hook up culture. We have seen, back in Chapter One, that the hook up practice has a sexist structure in that it is much more likely to satisfy the goals of men, while the norms place harsh judgments almost entirely on women. Further, the aggressive narrative that so often makes up typical hook ups, as we discussed in Chapter Three, usually places men into the aggressive role while demanding that women adhere to passive roles. Since it is easier for men to meet their goals and women will receive greater social disapproval, the practice is quite sexist.

Given the various ways that the hook up culture favors men in a sexist fashion, men face a unique moral problem. Even if these men are not sexist, they contribute to a sexist practice by doing nothing about their prevalent male privilege. That is, men need not be sexist to have male privilege socially thrust upon them, but that same privilege creates a moral difficulty: these men, by doing nothing, become morally complicit in the sexism of hook up culture.

Notice, importantly, that the consent of women does nothing to erase the moral obligation of men to deal with their male privilege. There are a few reasons for this point. First, the women are consenting to hook up – they are not consenting to mitigate or remove the privilege of the men they are with. Second, it is not clear that a single consenting woman could somehow ease a man's male privilege even if she explicitly consented to that. The moral problem of accepting privilege in a sexist practice is not located in individual interactions, but in systemic ubiquities. Accepting privilege is a general problem that cannot be erased just because one woman agrees that one man should not let his privilege bother him. Finally, consent cannot possibly remove the privilege since it occurs within the context of that privilege. It is a part of the man's privilege that he can put a woman in a situation where she is more likely to consent to what he wants because the sexist arrangement of the practice provides him with a superior bargaining position.

Sexism then raises moral problems, especially for men, that can neither be solved by consent nor are really relevant to consent. Since moral men would want to do what they can to avoid acting immorally while hooking up, they would want to do something about this sexism, if they can. None of these moral problems (exposed vulnerabilities, objectification, and sexism) provide definitive moral conclusions. Just because hook up partners will quite often expose vulnerabilities, objectify each other, and further sexist practices, does not mean that hook ups are immoral, or even that consent doesn't often provide enough tools to settle the morality of individual hook ups. The point being made here is simply that these issues are present throughout much of hook up culture, and there will be occasions where they raise moral questions that consent is insufficient for answering. So, we need more moral tools to ensure that hook ups are consistently morally permissible.

Morally Hooking Up, Post-Consent

We spent so much time discussing consent because it is clearly a necessary condition for moral hook ups. We have now seen that consent is not morally sufficient since there are moral problems in hooking up that consent alone cannot solve. It is clear both that moral agents looking to hook up should seek to be certain that they have consent prior to proceeding, and that consent is not the end of the moral matter. The next step is to look at how respect, beneficence, and trust can provide more solutions for the moral agent who wants to overcome these additional moral difficulties in hooking up.

Respectful Hook Ups

In morally requiring respect for hook ups, I am suggesting that we treat hook ups the same as, and not different from, any other human interaction, where moral demands of respect are assumed – though they may apply differently. And they apply differently because different situations require more or less signals of respect. I will argue that respect applies quite clearly to hook up situations since dealing with the previously mentioned three moral problems – vulnerabilities, objectification, and sexism – requires clear signals of respect.

There are a few different things that we can mean by "respect." I will mention three aspects of respect. Each aspect ties into recognizing and appreciating the unique worth or value of a person. We can think of the first aspect of respect as the way in which we recognize any person's value through treating them in a decent and considerate manner that is appropriate to being human. This aspect of respect applies to almost all human interaction, and can be exemplified by our regular interactions with people in service industries, such as clerks, wait staff, and even telemarketers (a moral challenge for many of us). A second aspect of respect requires not doing anything to indicate a discounting of a person's worth. It is disrespectful to discount a person's importance, to say things that undercut that importance, or to treat them in any fashion that indicates they lack full worth as equal human beings. Although this aspect will apply to any person regardless of familiarity, the more familiar we are with a person, the easier it will be to say or do things that discount their worth, and so the greater the burden is not to disrespect them in these ways. As a final aspect, we can respect a person not just by recognizing their worth, but also by seeing the value in their important projects while also accepting that these projects are theirs, not ours. Onora O'Neill points to the need to give proper distance for people to choose and pursue their life projects by neither trying to take over those projects nor disparaging them.[19] For this third aspect, greater interaction leads to greater risk of disrespect since interaction creates room for possibly taking over or disparaging someone's life projects.

My initial claim is simply that just as these three aspects of respect are applicable to almost every context of life, they apply to hooking up. It would be very strange to think that while we must normally respect each other, we need not respect people with whom we hook up. Yet, David Archard disagrees:

> This is not to say that we should not be alert to the dangers of coercion, manipulation, deception, exploitation, and abuse of power in any sexual relationship which falls seriously short of the 'mutual ends' ideal. But in the absence of these defects, we are left with failures of love and respect. Sexual relationships which fail in this regard are less than perfect. They are not impermissible.[20]

Thus, Archard thinks that a sexual exchange that fails to be loving and respectful is less than perfect, but is morally permissible – Archard explicitly denies that respect is necessary for permissibility. It is not clear whether Archard thinks that respect is generally too much to ask for, or whether it is only too much in sexual encounters. He does seem to accept this lower standard as simply a necessity for real life, as he explains this position by saying that, "We inhabit and negotiate an imperfect world in the awareness of its defects. Our encounters within it can surprise, disappoint, but also frequently please us."[21] Archard may be thinking that we have to settle for disrespectful sexual encounters because they are largely the norm.

However, morality can surely make demands that go beyond social conventions. For example, it might fit within social norms to treat waitresses at Hooters with a lot more disrespect than waitresses at Olive Garden. Surely waitresses at Hooters actually receive much less politeness. They also certainly receive much more undesired flirting that interferes with their work. It might be objected that Hooters waitresses were adequately informed and yet consented. However, this returns to the distinction made earlier in this chapter. They consented to waitress in skimpy uniforms. The fact that they work in skimpy uniforms does not entail that customers should treat them disrespectfully. What was consented to (waitress in skimpy uniforms) does not cover the manner in which customers may treat them (respectfully or disrespectfully). The point here is that morality requires respectful treatment, regardless of what action agents consented to perform. It also isn't clear that one could consent to being treated disrespectfully insofar as consent entails creating moral permissions, but you cannot gain the moral permission to treat someone disrespectfully. While Hooters waitresses certainly consent to waitress in skimpy outfits, their consent to work in that fashion does not license their customers to disrespect them. As it happens, it feels more socially acceptable to disrespect a Hooters waitress because of their job, but the fact that many people typically act poorly in certain contexts does not justify their disrespectful treatment of others.

Respect is owed to a person just because they are human, and circumstances (such as what kind of restaurant the person works at) cannot undermine the need to respect a person. It doesn't matter whether you are at a Hooters or Olive

Garden, you owe respect to your waitress. Similarly, it doesn't matter whether you are going on a date to a museum or hooking up with someone, you owe him or her respect just because of his or her humanity. It might be that people are more accustomed to showing respect on a museum date, but that doesn't affect whether respect is morally owed.

Respecting a hook up partner goes beyond merely obtaining consent in a few ways. First, morality requires a certain respectful manner of treatment, and rules out disrespectful manners of treatment. If consent were sufficient, then it would not matter whether hook up partners were polite or considerate to each other, or whether they were indifferent, rude, or insulting. Since it is immoral to treat someone disrespectfully, consent doesn't ensure moral permissibility.

Second, a respect requirement would demand that agents not be chastised or disparaged for their sexual proclivities, habits, or preferences. Whether it is within the consensual discussion prior to consent or the sexual activity itself, hook up partners expose themselves to unexpected vulnerabilities since they are engaging in a practice that is socially treated as quite private and intimate with persons whom they barely know. If the agents meet their moral requirement of respect, then they would not abuse any exposed vulnerabilities, but would instead give their partners the opportunity to feel safe in their sexual space. That does not mean that they have to sexually try out anything the other person would like. It means that within their sexual encounter, they must make sure that the other person has no fear that their sexual ideas will be disparaged, insulted, or ridiculed. Thus, respect provides a moral response to the possibility of unexpected vulnerabilities since respected agents feel less vulnerable due to the fact that any exposed vulnerabilities will neither be abused nor vilified by a respectful person.

Third, respect is also responsive to the objectification and sexism of the hook up practice. The fact that both objectification and sexism pervade the entire hook up practice entails that any particular hook up can, whether intentionally or unintentionally, convey signals of disrespect. That is, if you just take part in an objectifying and sexist practice, then you risk sending signals that you disrespect your partner, regardless of whether you intend to send such signals. After all, your partner can (mistakenly) read those signals in the practice's social conventions. To use one possibility, the partner may look at hook up social conventions and reasonably assume, "in spite of our consent, this near stranger will probably brag to their friends after our hook up."

Morality requires silencing these signals of disrespect through clear signs of respect. This is a minimal, but completely necessary response to objectification and sexism. Consent alone will not necessarily perform this function because it is possible for two people who completely disrespect each other to come to a consensual agreement. They merely have to meet the requirements of consent, which can be met without signals of respect: for example, you can use insulting and rude language as long as that language is non-threatening, non-frightening, and adequately informative. As another example, the profit motive will often suffice to get two people who openly disrespect each other to come to a consensual business agreement.

Where the social conventions provide good reasons to infer strong indicators of disrespect, the minimal moral solution must involve providing as strong or stronger indicators of respect so that the other person does not conclude that they are likely being disrespected (which would be quite reasonable without the countervailing respect signs). Thus, moral agents who want to engage in a practice that is objectifying and sexist have to make sure that their potential partners do not feel disrespected. To this end, they will do everything they can to show their respect (use the proper language, be open-minded, not say anything negative) to counter the inherent sense of disrespect.

Hence, respect is clearly required for morally hooking up. Even though respect is a standard part of ordinary moral engagement, different people in different situations find a wide variety of ways to show respect for each other. Parts of respectful treatment, as we have seen, are fairly standard: politeness, open-mindedness, avoiding clear signals of disrespect, etc. Nevertheless, hooking up morally may require additional, more specific avenues to be respectful. I will argue that being beneficent in the face of exposed vulnerabilities and providing a basis for trust supplement and expand the respect requirement.

Beneficent Hook Ups

I have thus far argued that consent and respect requirements for hooking up are not overly burdensome since we are required to obtain consent and be respectful in most aspects of life. As we turn to requirements for beneficence and trust, we will be looking at two moral requirements that are sparser in ordinary life, but that will be specifically necessary to be moral and respectful in hook ups. While I must respect my waitress, I can do so without having to be overly beneficent to her (politeness and tipping are minimal signs of respect for service rendered) or having to establish that she can trust me beyond our current interaction. To hook up morally, however, beneficence and providing a basis for trust will be necessary.

What I mean by "beneficence" is the moral duty to help another person who is in need. It is important that I am using "beneficence" to refer to a moral duty. Sometimes we are helpful to strangers or friends because we are being kind or friendly. Such help is not morally required, but is just a nice thing to do. Beneficence is a moral duty that requires you to help someone because their need is significant, your burden in helping is not nearly as significant, and you have some relation where you are the *right* person to help. We can distinguish two duties of beneficence: a duty with wide scope and one with narrow scope. What it means for a duty to have wide scope is that it is completely up to the agent when and how to meet the duty. A duty of narrow scope requires the agent to meet the duty all the time (do not murder) or at specific times (be honest with your friends when they are looking out for your best interests). A wide duty of beneficence would require giving to charity at some point in your life, finding general ways to help others, etc. Here, I am only interested in a narrow duty of beneficence, which requires helping people when situations and relations specifically require doing so. That is why it matters, for the narrow duty of beneficence, that you are the right person to help.

The duty of beneficence is a part of being respectful because sometimes it is disrespectful not to help another person in serious need when you can easily do so. You fail to recognize that person's worth as a human by refusing to help them in such a situation. It is basically like saying to a person, "Sure, I see you are in dire trouble and I am the only one who can help, but helping you would inconvenience me, and your life is just not worth that much to me." That is plain disrespectful.

How we measure the significance of need and burden are somewhat subjective, but the existence of a duty of beneficence is established by showing there can be cases where the other person's need is so clearly significant and your burden is so clearly insignificant that it would be disrespectful not to help. Imagine a stranger has fallen in a hole, is about to get attacked by snakes, and you just happen to have a ladder that you could easily save them with. Clearly, it is not merely nice, but is morally obligatory that you provide the ladder for as long as it takes for them to get out, so as to save their life. You would be a horrible person, morally speaking, were you to refuse to do so.

What it means to be the "right person" can likewise be seen in that example: you were the closest person and had the ladder. It may also be that in a crowd, multiple people are the right person. It could also be that a person is the right person because they are connected to the person in the hole: out of a crowd, the right person may be someone who happens to have a ladder, someone who knows the person in the hole, someone who failed to warn the person who fell in, etc. So, while I will not attempt to get into specifics of when the duty of beneficence kicks in, I have at least given reason to believe there is one and there are clear cases where we recognize that this duty applies.

My reasons for requiring beneficence derive from Onora O'Neill's requirement of "love,"[22] but there are two important differences. As a reminder from Chapter Six, O'Neill argues that treating persons as ends requires both respect and love. Love, which is relevant here, means helping them to meet their own ends, without overly interfering with their right to autonomously set and pursue those ends – giving them this distance is her requirement of respect.[23] The first difference between O'Neill's view and mine derives from my hope to avoid the unfortunate terminological baggage that comes with the term "love." I would agree with others that casual sex does not require the kind of love that is usually reserved for people in romantic relationships.[24] O'Neill has a different kind of love in mind, which can be confusing within hook up discussions. Fortunately, "beneficence" allows me to make a similar point.

Second, O'Neill's love seems to have a much larger domain as it requires that as an agent, I would "make the other's ends, whose achievement would constitute his or her happiness, in part my own."[25] My use of "duty of beneficence" only applies when someone has his or her vulnerability exposed. Where O'Neill's love requirement might apply to all hook ups, the duty of beneficence only applies to hook ups where something goes wrong where it would be morally required to respond to the wrong, even though this requirement does not derive from consent. Beneficence is a more limited duty, but one that is nonetheless essential given the need to help when problems arise.

As mentioned, the duty of beneficence may depend on the relationship the agent has with the person in need. For example, if a certain person has a relationship with you, then you may have to respond to their need directly, when it arises, without having the ability to defer to a later time. When you see a stranger crying on a park bench, you personally do not have to check on that stranger – it may even violate their privacy for you to pry into their saddened state. However, if it were your brother crying on that park bench, then walking away would clearly be a failure of beneficence.

Engaging in sexual activity with a person, such as in a hook up, surely creates the kind of relation that generates the duty of beneficence. That is because the hook up entails proximity. There is a physical proximity because the participants have to be near each other, and almost certainly near no one else. There is also the proximity generated by the sexual activity: they are not two strangers who happen to be sharing a cab, but two people who are interacting in sexual ways with each other. Further, it is the kind of proximity that enables vulnerability: hook up partners expose themselves to each other in private ways that they do not wish to become public. Since the hook up generates this kind of close proximity, it is the kind of relation that places one partner in a position where they are best suited to help the other party if a vulnerability, especially a sexual vulnerability that is directly connected to the hook up, is exposed. Further, these vulnerabilities are more likely to come up and be emotionally significant because we live in a world where sexuality is uncomfortable, where women can especially be judged negatively for what happens in the hook up, and where a prudish society considers it very important, especially for women, to keep sexual activity private. Because our hook up practice exists within a sexist world that makes it quite difficult to alleviate the disrespectful message that inherently comes along with objectification, it is essential that agents respond to unexpected vulnerabilities by being beneficent.

In particular, a person actually has to be nice and helpful. Being nice may sound simple enough – part of being a decent human really – and it certainly should be everyone's response to someone's need arising in a sensitive situation. Yet, the point here goes a step further to argue that it is a moral duty to be nice and helpful in this situation. Consider the various things a person might say when first seeing their hook up partner nude. Let's first note how unlikely it would be for hook up consent to cover what is stated. Pretty much no one would likely ask that both parties agree in advance to what they will say when they see each other naked. Consent is likely to be silent on this issue. General respect would rule out the stating of mean comments. It would clearly be disrespectful to say something about the other person's nude body that could hurt their feelings. The duty of beneficence, in particular, would require saying something positive, to ensure that person feels good prior to the start of the sexual activity. Beneficence goes the last step and asks that you say or do something nice to help the other person feel good about themselves prior to the upcoming hook up.

Merely obtaining consent and exhibiting general signs of respect are not enough to show your hook up partner that you do not intend to contribute to his or her disrespect that comes along with his or her objectification (which both persons face) and the adherence to sexist norms (which raises a greater risk of disrespect for women). If someone does not respond to your vulnerability in a nice, kind, and generally benevolent way when you are already in danger of feeling disrespected, that lack of beneficence will likely indicate any other moral treatment (the work to obtain consent and/or the general respectful treatment) was perfunctory. The unexpected vulnerability that is not responded to with an act of beneficence shows the lie to a non-beneficent agent's hard work to obtain consent and appear to be respectful. Therefore, the moral agent would do what she can to be beneficent to his or her hook up partners.

A Basis for Trust

We thus far have three tools in the moral hook up agent's belt, all of which could be substantially valuable in ensuring that his or her hook up occurs in a morally permissible way. The agent must obtain consent before beginning the hook up, must be generally respectful throughout the pre-hook up conversation and the hook up itself, and must be beneficent in case any need or vulnerability arises for his or her partner. While I believe that these tools are sufficient to ensure the morality of the hook up itself, they do nothing to ensure moral relations post-hook up. There is nothing inherent to these three moral tools that ensure that hook up partners will feel comfortable that they will not be harmed post-hook up. One common post-hook up practice, bragging to one's friends, challenges the morality of the entire hook up experience. This practice of bragging is inherently disrespectful. In the face of such a disrespectful social convention, it is respectful to give your hook up partner some kind of assurance that it will not happen. For this reason, it is also morally important for agents to provide their hook up partners with a basis for trust.

It is a fairly common part of our society's typical hook up practice for men to brag about the women with whom they've hooked up, which has a tendency to ruin those women's reputations – due in large part to the double standard where only women are judged for their number of hook ups.[26] Bragging, though, does not necessarily undermine consent since it seems to happen after the terms of the consensual exchange have expired. Yet, bragging is disrespectful and furthers the person's objectification past the hook up. The braggart acts like it is okay to say harmful things about a person after their interaction with them – thus undermining that person's worth as a human and acting as if that person can be summarized just in terms of how they performed as sexual bodies. Bragging is completely inconsistent with the worth of people who deserve high regard just in being human. Hence, insofar as bragging is both routine and disrespectful, respect requires taking measures so that hook up partners do not need to worry about being disrespected in this way.

Howard Klepper agrees with this idea that bragging after sex is disrespectful.[27] He thinks that bragging after the fact is degrading to the other person because it involves making public a kind of information that is culturally taken to be private.[28] In other words, the person would prefer not to have their sexual proclivities discussed with others, but bragging treats their sexual proclivities as something that it is okay to share and even open up to the mocking of others. Thus, bragging is disrespectful for Klepper because it takes a kind of information, sexual information, that is supposed to be private in our culture, and shares it with other people, whose use of that information cannot be trusted.

Importantly, bragging is not only disrespectful because it can harm reputations or due to social norms that we keep sex lives private. I hold that bragging is disrespectful because it communicates to others a reduction of a unique, multifaceted person to solely their physical body and sexual activity. In hook ups with near strangers, the partners know little about each other going into the hook up, and coming out of it they merely know each other in a physical/sexual way. The act of conveying that sexual information to others involves treating the hook up partner as if they can be reduced to their physical body and sexual activity, which is then put on display for the sexual imagination of others. The moral depravity of bragging does not depend on social customs. It is disrespectful just because it fails to respect the other person as a fully worthy human who should not be reduced to just a sexual body.

Bragging, then, combines the problems of unexpected vulnerabilities, objectification, and sexism (since it usually harms women), and it raises these moral problems after the fact, when the person being put on display may not even realize it or be aware of it. Consent is irrelevant since consent will not apply past the expiration of the activity consented to, unless those terms are explicitly discussed (which seems unlikely). It is true that if a person were respectful and beneficent, then they would not brag, as boasting would be disrespectful and sometimes even cruel. The problem, nonetheless, is that someone being respectful and beneficent during the hook up offers no assurance that they will continue that moral behavior after the hook up. In fact, respect and kindness could be used as a strategy to secure and complete the hook up, regardless of whether the hook up partner intends to continue that moral behavior when it is no longer necessary to hook up. Further, in real-life hook ups, there is a general lack of trust. Sociologist Lisa Wade discusses how the subjects of her hook up study felt that they could not trust their hook up partners, and they saw trust as something that would be necessary for good hook ups. As one subject said, "Love is not as important as trust."[29]

Moral hook up partners would seek ways to imbue their hook ups with trust. Let's examine trust for a moment here. Trust is partially cognitive, but also largely a feeling.[30] To feel trust for others is to have a sense that though you have opened up vulnerability to other people, you neither feel nor think that those others will harm you.[31] Trust is in part cognitive because you could have some evidence for your belief that the others will not harm you. Yet, it is not wholly cognitive because that evidence is always insufficient to support your belief. That is, trust lacks guarantees: if you had guarantees, you are not placing trust but are simply relying on the guarantee.[32] Second, trust often involves insufficient evidence because we trust in situations where people had previously let us down, we trust people we don't know at all, and we trust in situations where people are likely to let us down.[33] We should note briefly that hook ups sometimes involves the first (when you hook up with someone who has previously bragged, let's say), often involves the second (when you hook up with near strangers or total strangers), and almost always involves the third (since hook up norms allow for untrustworthy treatment after the fact, such as bragging). Hook up situations are ones where trust is almost never rationally placed. Trust, then, is not entirely cognitive and is largely a feeling that people will not let us down, even if the evidence is uncertain or even indicates that they probably will let us down.

Insofar as trust is a feeling, we simply cannot help placing our trust. It could be claimed that trust is often irrational, but this misses the point. Trust is not meant to be entirely rational – it is meant to allow us to act in situations where we have to depend on others.[34] The fact is that our dependence on others is so ubiquitous that we simply must do it at times when trust is not entirely rational or else we would not be able to live our lives. We have to trust numerous people and institutions everyday of our lives to get through the day: we trust people to not cheat us when we shop, not to hurt us when we walk down the street, not to tell lies about us behind our backs, etc. Since we must trust others to live our lives, we cannot wait for the evidence to make trust rational.[35] We must go on our feelings, and trust even when the evidence does not warrant doing so.

Since we trust without sufficient rational basis, trust is not exactly the correct basis for moral evaluation. We sometimes might say of someone, "You were wrong to trust him [or her]." And what we might be saying in such a situation is that the evidence did not warrant trust, but we must trust with insufficient evidence throughout our lives. So, it is not exactly right to blame someone for trusting with insufficient evidence – doing so is a misunderstanding of how we place trust. Perhaps we should only blame people for placing trust if the evidence is overwhelmingly against trust: "You were wrong to trust him because he has exposed your vulnerability nine times out of ten instances." Of course, even though we can think of instances of completely misplaced trust, such cases are rare and often point to more significant issues (misplaced trust of this kind may result from Stockholm syndrome or similar trauma). Though it is possible to legitimately blame someone for their trust, we often are blaming people wrongly because of our own tendency to forget that trust is so often placed with insufficient evidence.

While we should be very careful when blaming people for placing trust, morality should attend much more to giving others a basis for trust.[36] We know that everyone must trust much of the time with insufficient evidence. Consequently, when people trust us, they are often doing so in ways that are not warranted. That puts the other person in a less powerful position, leaving them with room for fear or at least concern that we might not be trustworthy in spite of them needing to trust us. Moral agents would try, where feasible, to give some basis to be trusted. This point does not apply to distant or quick interactions. When two people are engaged in an interaction where vulnerabilities are significantly exposed and where trust is very important because a good deal is at stake, moral agents would try to make sure they provide a basis of trust to the person whose vulnerabilities are exposed to them. A hook up is exactly this kind of situation: vulnerabilities are significantly exposed, trust is very important, and the partners are very unlikely to have sufficient evidence to warrant their trust. In exactly this kind of situation, moral agents would provide each other with a basis for trust.

A basis for trust is needed for this specific problem that cannot be adequately dealt with through these first three moral tools (consent, general respect, and beneficence). I will argue that while there are no guarantees, first, respectful and beneficent hook up behavior are a part of establishing trust. Second, trust can sometimes be aided through methods that make it easier to trust. Third, moral agents would show receptivity to what the other person may need to secure their trust. While these three aspects will not combine to assure there will be no bad behavior, such as bragging, after the hook up, trust exists independent of guarantees and this method will be the best one available to provide a basis for trust in a hook up scenario.

Before looking at hook up trust, I will note that the usual basis for trust, i.e. showing that you are a trustworthy person through shared experiences over a significant period of time, would be unavailable in hook ups. At the same time, we often have to trust people in one-off situations where a great deal is at stake. We have to find ways to trust doctors who we are meeting for the first time. We also sometimes have to trust strangers in emergencies because there is no choice. Even in fairly mundane scenarios, we trust restaurant staff not to poison us or spit in our food. We can trust people we barely know, so the question is how moral agents can show their hook up partners that they themselves are trustworthy.

Trusting relations, whether between people who have long known each other or people who have just met, primarily depend on evidence of character.[37] Moral hook up participants can start to provide a basis for trust by acting in virtuous and trustworthy ways in both securing the hook up and engaging in the hook up. They show they are trustworthy by not only seeking consent but also by making clear that they are not satisfied with just consent. As we have seen, consent can be secured in ways that allow each person to merely look out for themselves – you can even gain someone's unwise consent in a way that allows you to take advantage of the terms they accepted later on. Moral agents, though, would seek to look out for their partner as well as themselves – they would secure consent terms that worked out best for all parties. They would likewise wish to hook up in a way that was about mutual satisfaction. They would not think that because it was a hook up, only their pleasure should be sought. They instead would also want to please the other person. That is, moral agents would seek consent, be respectful, and be kind (and not just kind in response to exposed vulnerabilities, but in general). Such behavior does not guarantee trustworthiness, but it would provide a good basis for trust in a brief time period.

A second way that moral agents could work to provide a basis for trust would be through creating circumstances where trust is implied through the way the hook up occurs. For example, the possibility of stigmatization from after the fact bragging depends on the participants being members of the same social group where information is shared. Moral agents could drive some distance to hook up in places where bragging to the same social group would be less likely due to the distance. They also could save hooking up for vacations or road trips. Ethically hooking up may require some extra work to ensure there is no reason to think sexual reputations are on the line. Since we are living in a non-ideal, patriarchal society, we have to work to protect people's reputations from unfair smearing.

This initial idea is open to objections. First, it makes hooking up much less practical. Second and more importantly, it pushes people out of their emotional comfort zones: hook up participants would no longer be seeking out near strangers, but true strangers in areas they do not know well. Third, this response may push both sides (people who are likely to brag and people who fear bragging) out of that comfort zone, where fairness would seem to concentrate on pushing only the potential braggarts away. Yet, pushing away the braggarts alone makes less sense since the people who fear bragging will not know for sure that their potential hook up partner is from a different area (unless they just trust them to be honest, which is difficult since they have yet to establish a basis for trust). For these reasons, this basis for trust may work for some people, but it will not work for everyone.

There may be other routes for moral agents to create circumstances where trust is more easily given. They could make use of institutional means, such as hook up apps or hook up clubs that have strict privacy rules. There the basis for trust would derive from the app's or club's rules and enforcement policies. For example, the app could have a system for rating hook up partners as untrustworthy. Similarly, the club could kick out people who are caught bragging. Therefore, people would be motivated to be trustworthy. That way, the people using the app or going to the club would have a basis for trust.

None of these answers are for everyone. As mentioned, some people will not wish to go far away to find hook up partners. Hook up clubs do not yet exist, nor would entering one automatically license the assumption that a person has consented to hook up – though, quite unfortunately, that is likely to be a lot of people's unwarranted and highly dangerous assumption were hook up clubs to exist. Anything that would likely be considered a hook up app today would not likely be a moral hook up app. Even if someone developed hook up apps that were geared towards moral hook ups, they could still be misunderstood, misused, and could not assure trustworthiness.

None of these first two sets of answers would apply to everyone – providing a basis for trust is surely messy in this regard. For some people, moral behavior will be sufficient for establishing trust. Some people would prefer trusting people who are moral and who have traveled. Some people would find special apps or clubs would work best. Other people would be completely different in how they come to trust their hook up partners. For this reason, the third way to provide a basis for trust is to be open to what your hook up partner needs.

A good part of trusting people, especially ones who we do not know well, is that they listen to and respond to our trust-based needs. For instance, it is commonly known that hook up partners do not always learn each other's names. For people who enjoy hooking up with partners whose names they do not know, that practice is perfectly fine. Nevertheless, other people may be unable to trust someone whose name they do not know. If a moral agent would not hook up with someone who knows their name, that would probably be a piece of information that should be shared in the pre-hook up conversation. Otherwise, this request seems like a reasonable thing to be open to: if your partner cannot be comfortable trusting you without knowing your name, then you should give your name. Likewise, it could reasonably make some people more comfortable hooking up with someone whose cell phone number they have (so they can rest assured they can find the person again). Some people may only feel comfortable hooking up in their own homes, or at least hooking up in homes (and not in cars or restrooms).

These requests are not meant to merely be grounded in sexual appetites (though they could be). The requests being discussed here are ones that are necessary for one hook up participant to trust their partner. It is not that they are turned on by hooking up in bed (though they could be), but that they are not comfortable trusting someone who wants to hook up in a car. Therefore, the third way to establish trust is to be attentive and responsive to what the other person reasonably needs, whether that's a name, a phone number, a bed, cuddling, or some other reasonable demand. Of course, if the demand is not reasonable, then it is not necessary to be open to it. The point of this third way is that we are all unique when it comes to trust. There is nothing that ever guarantees trust since trust means that you cannot be sure (or else trust is not necessary). We all differ in what we need to trust someone. A moral agent who is about to hook up with someone will make sure to provide what that person says they need, within reason, to give their trust. And studies on trust likewise indicate that "the greater the amount of communication there is between the players … the greater the likelihood of there being a mutually beneficial outcome."[38] Thus, it will be imperative for moral agents to discuss what they need to trust each other prior to hooking up, and to be open to giving each other what is necessary so they can each feel more trusting.

To sum up, providing the basis for trust requires a variety of actions, some of which have already been established through the moral behaviors that were utilized in meeting the requirements of consent, respect, and beneficence. That is, the first way to establish trust is through acting in an honest and reliable fashion in securing the hook up as well as within the hook up itself. Second, the moral agent also may find they can make use of special circumstances that make it easier to trust, such as traveling, using a moral hook up app, or going to a hook up club. Finally, the trust requirement asks moral agents to be open to doing whatever else is necessary to help their hook up partners trust them. There is nothing that can guarantee trustworthiness, but moral agents realize that providing a basis for trust is important, and so they are disposed to do what is necessary to help others trust them. Providing a basis for trust does not seem to be easy, but the goal here has never been to maintain the ease of hooking up regardless of moral considerations. Moral agents should take extra steps to ensure their hook ups are morally permissible. One of those steps is to provide this basis for trust.

Conclusion

There are some quite serious moral problems within the hook up practice that do not seem to be solvable by consent alone. When unexpected vulnerabilities arise in a hook up, moral agents must respond to them, even if there is no way to understand their consent as committing them to such responses. Instead, they must respond to those vulnerabilities in a respectful manner. Further, the hook up, which occurs within morally risky terrain due to the inherent objectification of each person and the sexism of the practice, provides a context where the vulnerability must also be met with beneficent action. Finally, where the vulnerabilities may come up after the fact, the agents require a basis for trust, which can be provided not by the nature of the partners' relationship (which surely would not give reasons to trust each other), but by general moral behavior, possibly hooking up within special contexts (such as through a hook up app, in a hook up club, or in social circles that both partners do not belong to), or by a receptivity to what the other person needs to be able to give their trust.

Hooking up is inherently objectifying since partners are chosen neither for their intelligence, personalities, nor who they authentically are as persons. Hook up partners are almost always chosen for their sex appeal. Thus, it is nearly essential to hooking up that agents objectify each other. Objectification is disrespectful unless there are positive methods of countering that disrespect. Hence, moral agents must respond to objectification by signaling that they respect the other person in spite of objectifying them. Respect, beneficence, and giving a basis for trust are all necessary to show the other person that you fully respect him or her even while you objectify him or her.

The hook up practice is also inherently sexist. The practice treats men better than women, just because of their socially designated genders. That puts an extra burden on men to establish not only that they are not sexist – which the woman they are hooking up with would not know if they are near strangers – but also that they do not seek to contribute further to the sexism of the practice by taking advantage of their male privilege. To do this, men also must clearly be respectful, beneficent, and shoulder the weight of giving a basis for trust since they are the ones in a greater position to ruin the other person's reputation (since male reputations are bolstered by people hearing about their sexual exploits).

Therefore, while there are severe problems within the hook up practice that consent does not resolve, those problems are well responded to by respect, beneficence, and trust. The moral agent then has a four-part goal in every hook up. He or she must obtain consent, in the robust fashion laid out in previous chapters, be generally respectful, be beneficent if something comes up, and provide the other person with a basis for trust. While doing these things may not be easy, they are both feasible and necessary for morally permissible hook ups.

Notes

1 Jesse J. Owen *et al.*, "'Hooking Up' Among College Students: Demographic and Psychosocial Correlates," *Archives of Sexual Behavior* 39 (2010); Jesse Owen and Frank D. Fincham, "Young Adults' Emotional Reactions after Hooking Up Encounters," *Archives of Sexual Behavior* 40 (2011); Anne Barnhill, "Bringing the Body Back to Sexual Ethics," *Hypatia* 28, no. 1 (2013), 6; Lisa Wade, *American Hookup: The New Culture of Sex on Campus* (New York: W. W. Norton & Company, 2017), 134–135.
2 Wade, *American Hookup*, 41–48, 133–157, 170–176.
3 Ibid., 45–48.
4 Ibid., 170–176.
5 Ibid., 174.
6 Ibid., 133–157.
7 Ibid., 143.
8 Ibid., 175.
9 Raja Halwani objects to the view that casual sex is inherently objectifying since, "… in *most* casual sexual encounters no objectification occurs because sex partners do not treat each other with disrespect or by neglecting each other's sexual desires and needs," see Raja Halwani, *Philosophy of Love, Sex, and Marriage: An Introduction* (New York: Routledge, 2010), 191–192. However, this argument strays from the meaning of "objectification" as any act that treats a person as an object. Insofar as hook up partners are primarily interested in each other's bodies, and not at all interested in who the person is qua person, it is nearly constitutive of hooking up that it is objectifying.

10 Martha Nussbaum, "Objectification," *Philosophy & Public Affairs* 24, no. 4 (1995): 251, 271–273, 275, 289–291.
11 Ibid., 256–257.
12 Ibid., 257.
13 Ibid., 275, 290.
14 Patricia Marino, "The Ethics of Sexual Objectification: Autonomy and Consent," *Inquiry* 51, no. 4 (2008): 349–355.
15 Ibid., 355–361.
16 Ibid., 356.
17 Ibid., 358.
18 Howard Klepper, "Sexual Exploitation and the Value of Persons," in *The Philosophy of Sex: Contemporary Readings*, eds. Alan Soble and Nicholas Power (New York: Rowman and Littlefield, 2008), 254.
19 Onora O'Neill, "Between Consenting Adults," *Philosophy and Public Affairs* 14, no. 3 (1985), 265, 271.
20 David Archard, *Sexual Consent* (Boulder: Westview Press, 1998), 79.
21 Ibid., 79.
22 O'Neill, "Between Consenting Adults," 265, 271–272.
23 Ibid., 263–266.
24 Alan H. Goldman, "Plain Sex," *Philosophy and Public Affairs* 6, no. 3 (1977), 272–275; Raymond A. Belliotti, *Good Sex* (Lawrence: University Press of Kansas, 1993), 56–85; Raja Halwani, "Are One Night Stands Morally Problematic?" *International Journal of Applied Philosophy* 10, no. 1 (1995), 62; Alan Soble, *Sexual Investigations* (New York: New York University Press, 1996), 17–20; Archard, *Sexual Consent*, 79–80; Alan Wertheimer, *Consent to Sexual Relations* (Cambridge: Cambridge University Press, 2003), 136–137.
25 O'Neill, "Between Consenting Adults," 265.
26 Kathleen A. Bogle, *Hooking Up: Sex, Dating, and Relationships on Campus* (New York: New York University Press, 2008), 88–89, 96–127, see esp. 112–115; Norval Glenn and Elizabeth Marquardt, *Hooking Up, Hanging Out, and Waiting for Mr. Right: College Women on Dating and Mating Today*, An Institute for American Values Report to the Independent Women's Forum (2001), 16–17, 21–22; Elizabeth Paul, Brian McManus, and Allison Hayes, "'Hookups': Characteristics and Correlates of College Students' Spontaneous and Anonymous Sexual Experiences," *The Journal of Sex Research* 37, no. 1 (2000), 80–82; Ayres A. Boswell and Joan Z. Spade, "Fraternities and Collegiate Rape Culture: Why Are Some Fraternities More Dangerous Places for Women?" *Gender and Society* 10, no. 2 (1996), 134, 141; Eleanor Maticka-Tyndale, Edward S. Herold, and Martin Oppermann, "Casual Sex Among Australian Schoolies," *The Journal of Sex Research* 40, no. 2 (2003), 165; Wade, *American Hookup*, 34.
27 Klepper, "Sexual Exploitation," 251–254.
28 Ibid., 251–252.
29 Wade, *American Hookup*, 156, also 155–157.
30 Karen Jones, "Trust as an Affective Attitude," *Ethics* 107, no. 1 (1996); Lawrence C. Becker, "Trust as Noncognitive Security About Motives," *Ethics* 107, no. 1 (1996); Annette C. Baier, *Trust* (Princeton: The Tanner Lectures on Human Values, March 6–8, 1991), 137–142; Bernd Lahno, "On the Emotional Character of Trust," *Ethical Theory and Moral Practice* 4, no. 2 (2001); J. M. Bernstein, "Trust: On the Real but Almost Always Unnoticed, Ever-Changing Foundation of Ethical Life," *Metaphilosophy* 42, no. 4 (2011).
31 Baier, *Trust*, 113, 137; Lahno, "On the Emotional Character of Trust," 171; Bernstein, "Trust," 395, 400–404.
32 Partha Dasgupta, "Trust as a Commodity," in *Trust: Making and Breaking Cooperative Relations*, ed. Diego Gambetta (New York: Basil Blackwell, 1988), 53; Niklas

Luhmann, "Familiarity, Confidence, Trust: Problems and Alternatives," in *Trust: Making and Breaking Cooperative Relations*, ed. Diego Gambetta (New York: Basil Blackwell, 1988); Baier, *Trust*, 110; Onora O'Neill, *A Question of Trust* (Cambridge: Cambridge University Press, 2002), 6, 24; Thomas W. Simpson, "What Is Trust?" *Pacific Philosophical Quarterly* 93, no. 4 (2012), 565.

33 Dasgupta, "Trust as a Commodity," 51–52; O'Neill, *A Question of Trust*, 24.

34 David Good, "Individuals, Interpersonal Relations, and Trust," in *Trust: Making and Breaking Cooperative Relations*, ed. Diego Gambetta (New York: Basil Blackwell, 1988); Baier, *Trust*, 110; O'Neill, *A Question of Trust*, 23; Lahno, "On the Emotional Character of Trust," 172; Bernstein, "Trust"; Simpson, "What Is Trust?," 551, 556–559.

35 Bernstein, "Trust," 405–407.

36 Baier, *Trust*, 112, 120; Bernstein, "Trust," 415.

37 Dasgupta, "Trust as a Commodity."

38 Good, "Individuals, Interpersonal Relations, Trust," 36.

8

MORAL HOOK UPS

The central question of this book was: what should moral agents do to ensure that their hook ups are morally permissible? This book presented many challenges to the morality of current hook up practices, but at each step I followed the challenges with possible paths for hooking up permissibly. The result, which I will discuss in this last chapter, is a practice that looks entirely different from current, and even best, hook up practices. The point, however, is that this altered practice would allow individuals to hook up in morally permissible ways. A commitment to morality does not, in the end, require abandoning hooking up, but it may require a completely different, and perhaps practically much more difficult, hook up practice.

In response to the moral problems that the hook up practice currently presents, I argued for four requirements for hooking up morally: consent, respect, beneficence, and trust. With these requirements in hand, the next step is to look at how moral agents would work to meet the requirements. To this end, I will present a general methodology that makes use of clear communication, potentially of technology as well, and a commitment to value the humanity of one's hook up partners. That there needs to be clear communication has been seen throughout the discussions concerning consent. To avoid too much aggression, too much alcohol, or too little information, hook up participants need to communicate clearly and effectively with each other. We will later consider whether this communication requirement can be met more easily through mobile apps that connect hook up participants. While such technology can help with the morality of the practice, it cannot completely remove the need for in-person communication. Importantly, it will be morally essential throughout the hook up practice that participants treat each other primarily as humans, by being kind, respectful, and establishing a basis for trust.

The moral hook up practice that I argue for is substantially different than current practices. This result might raise a significant objection, namely that I am saying that ethical hooking up is impossible. I do not believe that I am arguing that ethical hooking up is impossible, but that it does require significant changes to be possible. Yet, if this response is not convincing, then I am willing to accept that I have argued that current hook ups are inescapably unethical, which would require building a new practice that could be ethical. It won't matter, I believe, whether I am arguing for substantial changes or for a new practice. I do believe I have shown that the current practice is not one that moral agents would take up, and so it is important, in this chapter, to present an alternative for moral agents who wish to have casual sex.

Hook Up Problems and Requirements

From the beginning, we saw that hooking up as currently practiced leads to numerous moral difficulties. For most of these problems, I have left open the possibility that hook up participants could luckily avoid the moral pitfalls and have numerous hook ups that are not blameworthy. However, the position of this book is that an agent who is trying to be moral would not rely on luck and would instead seek out a way to ensure their hook ups are morally permissible – especially since immoral hook ups are more common than people think and can be gravely wrong. We can quickly summarize those problems here to see how the requirements presented in earlier chapters help to overcome them.

One potentially serious difficulty with hook ups is the tendency, especially for men, to become aggressive, especially in the face of rejection. Since it is still unfortunately common for men to think that "no" means push further, numerous men throughout hook up culture have become accustomed to using aggressive techniques to obtain hook ups. Of course, some passive individuals may wish for someone to use aggressive techniques with them, and so aggressors could get luckily matched and face no moral problem. On the other hand, an aggressor may deploy these techniques on someone who is unsuspecting, does not wish for this type of encounter, and does not know how to get the aggressor to stop. In such a case, an aggressive hook up could easily become non-consensual while the aggressor assumes that both participants are willingly having an aggressive hook up.

Since a moral agent would not want to risk pushing someone into fearfully submitting to aggressive techniques, which would amount to a non-consensual hook up and even a rape, the moral agent would ensure they would not use aggressive techniques without permission. Thus, the moral agent would seek to have a conversation where aggressive techniques are agreed to in advance of the hook up. That open, non-manipulative, sober conversation would help ensure that the moral agents obtain the freedom required for consent.

The moral agent would not wish to have this pre-hook up conversation merely to discuss the possibility of aggression. Another common problem with contemporary hook up practice is that actual hook up agreements are rarely well-informed. So, moral agents would include in that pre-hook up conversation any significant factors that the other person may need to know to decide whether they wish to hook up. To avoid hooking up with a partner who has received insufficient information to consent, moral agents would make sure that they discuss anything that they believe could likely undermine the other person's consent. That way, the hook up participants would have the information they would likely need to make sure they are receiving consent prior to hooking up.

Another very common difficulty in the hook up practice is the habit of becoming intoxicated very early in the hook up process. Agreements cannot count as consensual if the people making them are too intoxicated to think clearly. No moral agent would rely on the agreement made by a person who is quite likely intoxicated beyond the point of reason-impairment. So, if a moral agent wishes to have an intoxicated hook up with a near stranger, the only way to accomplish this goal is to have a sober conversation about whether both people wish to have an intoxicated hook up. While this sober conversation may remove some of the reasons why people hook up while intoxicated, it cannot be morally permissible to hook up with a near stranger when you have no idea if they would consent to it while sober. To avoid the risk that their intoxicated hook ups are not consensual, moral agents must have a sober conversation to ensure consent.

Through these pre-hook up conversations, moral agents can do quite a bit of work to ensure they obtain consent prior to hooking up. The agents meet the freedom requirement by ensuring that if they are going to do something that could cause fear, such as being aggressive, they alert their partner to that plan in the pre-hook up conversation. The agent meets the information requirement by telling their partner about anything that has a reasonable chance of changing their partner's mind about hooking up. Finally, the agent meets the competence requirement by having the pre-hook up conversation prior to becoming intoxicated if they both wish to hook up while intoxicated.

Even when hook ups are consensual, there are still problems as consensual hook ups can be disrespectful, unkind, and lack any basis for trust. Just by engaging in a hook up, the participants risk devaluing each other since they are being objectified within a practice that is generally sexist. Thus, they must engage in the hook up with all the proper signs of respect so that they combat any potential disrespect. Consequently, in addition to consent, so as to be respectful, hook up partners are morally obligated to treat each other with common decency and politeness, just as one ought to behave within any human interaction. Although that level of respect is required in any human interaction, hook ups nevertheless involve heightened vulnerabilities both during the hook up and afterwards. So, additional manners of respect will be required for hooking up, namely being beneficent and doing what you can to provide a basis for trust.

Hook ups provide a context where agents may become morally required to fulfill their duty of beneficence. Hook ups are locales where vulnerabilities may become unexpectedly exposed. Obtaining consent and even being generally respectful would not be sufficient if a person was not helpful and kind when a hook up partner became vulnerable. To ignore a call for help in such a situation, or to respond less than favorably when a person is embarrassed or confused, can amount to treating the other person disrespectfully and even cruelly given how sensitive we can all be in sexual situations. Moral agents would thus make sure to be beneficent when it was called for in a hook up.

Finally, the potential problems for a hook up do not end when the hook up does. Hook up participants can become vulnerable or disrespected after the fact through the social convention of bragging about sexual conquests. Moral agents would want to provide their partners some kind of basis for trusting each other. Of course, it can be difficult to provide a near stranger with a basis for trust. But if a moral agent wishes to hook up with a near stranger in a morally permissible fashion, they would have to meet that difficulty. Moral agents can accomplish this task by doing what it takes, in the situation, to show that they are trustworthy. At a minimum, that means doing the moral activities in the manners we have discussed: they must secure consent, be respectful, and be kind both in general and in response to any exposed vulnerabilities. They could also seek out circumstances where trust comes more easily, such as using an app or meeting people at locations where they feel safer. If providing a basis for trust requires more, then the moral hook up participant will be open to additional avenues for providing a basis for trust as well. That might mean they would be open to sharing their name, providing a cell phone number, or even cuddling. But since trust differs from person to person, the moral hook up participant would simply be open to what their partner reasonably needs from them to be able to give over their trust.

Moral Hook Up Methodology

These requirements then led to a general methodology for establishing a moral hook up. As we have seen, many of the moral hook up requirements amount to necessitating a conversation prior to the hook up. So, this pre-hook up conversation is the first central part to ensuring a hook up is morally permissible. We should also consider the extent to which technology, such as a hook up app, could be a second part that assists with the conversation as well as with possibly providing more basis for trust. The answer will be that an app can help, but cannot be sufficient on its own. As a third part of the methodology, there must be a general commitment, in all parts of the hook up, to treat each other in ways that respect humanity. Such a moral commitment would go without saying if it were not for the fact that there are social conventions that treat hooking up as an exception to the more general rule that one must respect everyone else's humanity. One result of this book is that we can now dispel this myth that there are lower moral standards when hooking up with near strangers. Instead, moral work is required to hook up ethically, and that work is not necessarily easy.

Communication and Technology

Numerous problems with current hook ups can be addressed through sober, respectful, and open conversations prior to the hook up. These conversations are crucial to establishing free, informed, and competent consent. Hook up partners often have separate ideas of what they intend to do, and those separate ideas could work out felicitously, but they also could turn everything in a tragic direction where consent is undermined. Hence, it is imperative for hook up partners to discuss anything that can reasonably undermine the consent that is required for the hook up to be morally permissible. As we saw, there are multiple issues that need to be discussed in this fashion, variously including whether participants want to use aggressive techniques, whether they would like to become intoxicated, as well as health status, relationship status, possibly illicit motives, and the sex act itself.

That is a lot to discuss. There is a concern here that it could be too much to reasonably expect any near strangers to discuss. As I have stated in previous chapters, one response, which I would be willing to take if it were the only one that were plausible, is that if agents do not feel comfortable having these discussions, then they are not prepared to have moral hook ups. That is, these discussions are *morally required*, but the fact that they would be uncomfortable, which is undeniably true, still does not mean they can be skipped. Instead, if someone feels they must skip them, then their hooking up simply is immoral.

This result should not be that surprising. The way in which hooking up currently occurs is quite morally problematic, where grave wrongs are being risked by continuing the current practice. There should be an inclination to change to a moral way to hook up, especially to avoid these potentially grave wrongs. That moral way cannot be expected to be as easy as the current practice: some work will be required to make the practice more permissible. So, I acknowledge that having the pre-hook up conversation makes the new practice more difficult than the current practice. Yet, some increased difficulty should be expected as we work to make hooking up morally permissible.

On the other hand, the difficulty of this discussion is probably less than many would imagine. First, not all of these things have to be discussed: only the ones that are relevant and that could potentially undermine someone's consent need to come up. If neither partner wishes for an aggressive nor intoxicated hook up, and they are healthy, single, have no illicit motives, and they neither plan nor wish for anything out of the ordinary in the sex act, the conversation will be incredibly quick. The conversations would range from very simple to very complicated, depending on how much needs to be discussed. I would guess that most conversations will land closer to the simple and quick side because most people will just be happy to have uncomplicated hook ups that are morally safer because everyone is well-informed about what is happening.

Second, even the complicated conversations need not, and probably should not, be long. The moral agents are attempting to have a moral hook up, so they are mentioning things they would like to do in the hook up. If they are both into the same things, then they can get through discussing them quickly. If they are not into the same things, then one person turns them down and they can decide if they would like to hook up without that technique or style being involved in the encounter. Perhaps some things would have to be described or explained. But most will be straightforward and quick: "I'd like to get intoxicated first, that okay?" That question can be followed by a yes or no, with only a small chance of needing additional discussion. Then limits and safe words can be established to help with revoking consent if necessary.

Third, because these conversations are largely straightforward, they could potentially be eased through technology, such as a phone app. I am not going to speak towards any currently existing app as they are not, as far as I am aware, currently designed to facilitate *ethical* hook ups. Yet, we can imagine apps that were designed for moral agents who wanted to ensure their hook ups would be permissible. These apps could match people who are geographically close and have similar hook up interests. Thus, people who wish to have aggressive, intoxicated, and/or kinky hook ups could signal such desires on the app, and then find matches in these regards. In other words, the app would facilitate the pre-hook up conversation as its users already know that they match in the relevant respects.

Even though we can imagine ways in which such an app would be useful, we must be careful here not to overstate how much a moral agent could rely on such an app. As we saw back in Chapter Two, sexual consent is contemporaneous, and is not advance consent. That means that, for sexual contexts, you can always change your mind and withdraw your consent at any time, for any reason, without doing anything morally wrong. By the nature of contemporaneous consent, no one is bound by what they say on a phone app: they have the right to change their mind when they meet their potential partner or at any time. That is reason enough that the phone app cannot be taken as definitive: the hook up partners still need to have a conversation on whether they are still happy with what they said that they wanted to do on the phone. Because they have previewed this discussion, it can occur quite quickly, especially if no one is changing their minds. It might also be easier for people to say things on an app that they would feel uncomfortable saying in person, but they would still have to confirm those things in person. Yet, through saying them on the app first, they are less likely to face a potentially embarrassing rejection when they state what they are sexually into. The app has already matched them sexually, and so this makes things less awkward when they meet up. For these reasons, a phone app can facilitate but cannot replace the in-person conversation.

To add to this issue with an app, we also must remember that sexual consent can be vacillating in a perfectly reasonable way. Someone who agrees to certain things within a hook up on an app can easily change their mind when they meet up with their potential partner in person. As we saw previously, we should be highly suspicious of any theory that implies that people generally consent in advance to hook up with just anyone. Perhaps some people do that, but surely many people want to be picky about the people with whom they hook up. There are a myriad reasons why someone might change their mind after agreeing on the app. As we have seen throughout this discussion, hook ups are about physical attraction. So, no one can object, provided that everyone is being respectful and as beneficent as possible, if someone wants to withdraw consent once they see each other for the first time. People can look very different in person than they do on an app, and people may interact in face-to-face meetings differently than one assumed while interacting on an app. People might get a feeling in person about a potential partner that is disquieting to them in some way, but was not possible for them to gauge while on the app, etc. So, it is perfectly reasonable for people to change their minds from the app stage to the face-to-face stage. Again, an app cannot be sufficient on its own, even if it can ease the overall process.

Further, we must remember, as we saw in Chapter Two, that hook up consent has propositional content: the consent is to sentences that are meant to convey what people mean in their heads when they think they are agreeing. That means that we can make mistakes because our words do not always accurately convey our meanings. With a phone app, this problem is even more severe: people can click on the same box in an app, but think the box means different things. Since it is just an app, such confusion is less likely to be apparent than in a face-to-face conversation. So, the app can only start the conversation, but can never complete it. Instead, moral agents would want to talk about what was agreed to on the app to try to rule out as much confusion as possible.

An app, then, can be generally useful, but moral agents need to be aware of the limits of that usefulness. Hook up apps could be used to match people who have generally similar interests, but these individuals would still need to work out the specifics in person and ensure that they obtain consent in person. Of course, they are still perfectly free to take back their consent in person, and at any point in their hook up. The app would simply facilitate the communication that is needed. The app could also establish some basis for trust since the users need not be in the same social circles, but they can also be held accountable to a certain extent since they are tied together through the use of the app. Unlike strangers whose names you do not know and who you may never be able to find again, people on an app can have a trustworthy rating or can even be punished by the app with low ratings on the trust scale. In the end though, no app can possibly replace the need for moral agents to have a real conversation that helps establish the moral permissibility of their upcoming hook up.

Respecting Humanity

The next point is that hooking up morally requires treating hook up participants in a fully human way. As I will discuss shortly, this seems trivial, but – unfortunately – the social conventions surrounding hooking up treat it as a practice that allows for moral standards so low that it does not feel like a practice where one must treat people in a fully human way. Instead, I have argued that hooking up is not an exception to our moral rules and so treating people as fully human is required. As we have seen, treating hook up participants in a fully human way means establishing meaningful consent, and not mere agreements, and being respectful.

In addition to needing a conversation prior to hooking up, another common trend throughout this discussion has been that hooking up has somewhat higher standards (and not much lower standards as others may believe) than most moral interactions. Social conventions for hooking up suggest multiple ways in which standards might be treated as lower for hooking up than for other, everyday interactions. For instance, people may believe that consent should be easier to come by in a hook up: that the participants need not be sober, need not be adequately informed, or need not take refusals at their face value. But we have seen in each of these categories that these lowered requirements for consent cannot be rationally maintained, and moral agents would act according to higher requirements to ensure they are obtaining hook up consent. In Chapter Three, we saw that aggression can lead to sufficient fear to undermine consent, and so we cannot assume that aggression is consistent with hook up consent. In Chapter Four, we saw that we cannot relax the information requirement for consent since hook up participants often could require information that is not typically offered. Finally, in Chapter Five, we saw that hook up consent needs to be sufficiently sober for participants to be able to make their own, reasoned out decisions – just as all consent requires.

As an additional problem, social norms treat consent as sufficient in the area of hooking up, but as we saw, in both Chapters Six and Seven, hooking up requires going beyond consent, just as we must do in all other areas of life, especially whenever vulnerabilities are exposed. The general problem is the assumption that hooking up allows people to lower their moral standards. This assumption is false since hooking up failures are severe wrongs, sometimes amounting to rape, and these failures cannot be overlooked because the evidence (as provided by social scientists) shows that they are not as rare as people assume. So, in addition to obtaining robust consent, we then have reason to be respectful, beneficent, and provide a basis for trust while hooking up, to do our best to avoid immoral activity within or surrounding hook ups.

The point, then, is that we ought to treat our hook up partners as if they are fully human and deserve moral treatment like any other humans with whom we interact. This point may seem so obvious as to not need to be stated. Alas, we have seen, in each of the various attempts to lower the moral requirements for hooking up that I challenged in each previous chapter, there is a social tendency to act as if moral standards can be lowered for hooking up. There is a social tendency to think that if two people are hooking up, then they really do not have to obtain meaningful consent (even if they do have to agree, perhaps even verbally), do not have to be respectful, do not have to be kind, and neither have to be trustworthy afterwards nor provide solid indications of being trustworthy. In all of these cases, the previous chapters have argued the social trends are wrong and hook up moral standards should be no less stringent than moral standards in other areas of life.

Thus, the methodology to ensure one is hooking up morally requires seeing potential hook up partners as fully human and deserving of respectful treatment. Though social trends make this position seem controversial, it really is trivial. Hook ups are locales where there is heavy risk of grave moral wrongs. Even consensual hook ups can involve significant disrespect or exposed vulnerabilities. Since hook ups provide potential for grave wrongs, and one can treat hook up partners respectfully and with beneficence, morality surely requires doing so.

The Possibility of the Moral Hook Up

Given the acknowledgement that these moral changes require a hook up practice that looks very different than the current practice, it is important to consider the possibility that the practice that I recommend is simply not possible. Let's have a look at some of the required changes. In a typical hook up, the participants drink alcohol first, figure out what they are going to do through non-verbal communication, become aggressive without warning such as through refusing to accept a refusal, and often brag after the fact. In a moral hook up, agents must have a sober conversation where they reveal their intentions and anything that could change the other person's mind, ensure they have robust, meaningful consent prior to starting the hook up, try to be respectful throughout the process, respond to any exposed vulnerabilities in kind and helpful ways, and seek out ways to provide a basis for trust. These two processes, I readily admit, look very different from each other.

So, we can imagine an objection that claims that the moral process I have outlined here is one that no real hook up participants would follow. The communication is too awkward, the alcohol is necessary to initiate the sexual activity, aggression is not fun if you signal it in advance, being disrespectful and unkind come too naturally in hook ups, etc. Someone might object that the moral hook up is simply impossible. It is not something that people, in our society at least, are capable of.

My first response to this objection is that this book would still show that typical hook ups in today's culture are morally problematic, such that moral agents would avoid them. It could be a consequence of this work that there is no realistic way to morally engage in hook ups. The fact that current hook up practices are immoral does not imply that they can be practically fixed. Perhaps they cannot be. But even if there were no realistic fix, that would not imply that the hook up, as currently practiced, is morally acceptable. Maybe we should simply give up hooking up as a hopelessly immoral practice.

Yet, I do not think I need to go with that initial response. I accept that moral hook ups are quite different than typical hook ups today. I also accept that many current participants would be unable to change for the various reasons given. I do believe however that moral agents, especially if pushed to see the wrongness of the current practice, would find ways to change to a morally preferable practice. After all, being moral is very important to people, and moral hook ups allow almost all of the same fun as current hook ups. To obtain guilt-free hook up fun, a lot of people would probably be willing to accept some awkwardness and some loss of risky spontaneity.

The real question is whether people would choose moral hook ups over what is currently typical. The only way to find out is to spread the word that there is need for an alternative, morally permissible practice. Certainly the changes begin with people willing to seek out sober conversations about hooking up prior to taking significant risks of committing grave moral wrongs. Or perhaps there will be no moral hook ups, but then that would just mean that hook ups are not morally permissible. It is also worthwhile to keep in mind that we should not bemoan the fact that it would be hard to engage in this new practice, but rather that, as moral agents, we should work to lay the groundwork to ensure consensual, safe, and moral hook ups.

The Moral Hook Up

If the points in this book are correct – or even if a good number of them are – then hooking up permissibly is possible, but surely not easy. Moral hook ups require a good conversation, resisting the urge to engage in risky techniques, and being respectful of and sensitive to the other person's needs, goals, and feelings. Following these prescriptions may make it difficult to hook up as easily or as frequently as is now common. Nevertheless, these prescriptions may help individuals ensure that their hook ups are consensual, respectful, and morally permissible. In the end, individuals may have even more enjoyable hook ups by leaving behind the reasonable worry of violating the other person's autonomy or rights. In other words, these prescriptions can make hooking up ethical without necessarily taking away the fun. And normalizing these techniques could only lead to more positive outcomes in terms of casual sex encounters.

BIBLIOGRAPHY

Abrams, Kathryn, "Sex War Redux: Agency and Coercion in Feminist Legal Theory," *Columbia Law Review* 95, no. 2 (1995), 304–376.

Adams, David M., "Date Rape and Erotic Discourse," in *Date Rape: Feminism, Philosophy, and the Law*, ed. Leslie Francis, University Park: The Pennsylvania State University Press, 1996, 27–40.

Adetunji, Jo and Harriet Sherwood, "Arab Guilty of Rape after Consensual Sex with Jew," *The Guardian* (20 July 2010), Last accessed 11 August 2018 at: www.guardian.co.uk/world/2010/jul/21/arab-guilty-rape-consensual-sex-jew.

Allison, Rachel and Barbara J. Risman, "A Double Standard for 'Hooking Up': How Far Have We Come Toward Gender Equality?," *Social Science Research* 42 (2013), 1191–1206.

American Dialect Society, "2015 Word of the Year is Singular 'They'," Last accessed 4 January 2019 at: www.americandialect.org/2015-word-of-the-year-is-singular-they.

Andrews, Travis M., "The Singular, Gender-Neutral 'They' Added to the Associated Press Stylebook," *The Washington Post* (28 March 2017), Last accessed 4 January 2019 at: www.washingtonpost.com/news/morning-mix/wp/2017/03/28/the-singular-gender-neutral-they-added-to-the-associated-press-stylebook/?noredirect=on&utm_term=.59bbcca64a4d.

Archard, David, *Sexual Consent*, Boulder: Westview Press, 1998.

Armstrong, Elizabeth, Paula England, and Alison C. K. Fogarty, "Accounting for Women's Orgasm and Sexual Enjoyment in College Hookups and Relationships," *American Sociological Review* 77, no. 3 (2012), 435–462.

Bachtel, Molly K., "Do Hookups Hurt? Exploring College Students' Experiences and Perceptions," *Journal of Midwifery & Women's Health* 58, no. 1 (2013), 41–48.

Backstrom, Laura, Elizabeth A. Armstrong, and Jennifer Puentes, "Women's Negotiation of Cunnilingus in College Hookups and Relationships," *Journal of Sex Research* 49, no. 1 (2012), 1–12.

Baier, Annette C., *Trust*, Princeton: The Tanner Lectures on Human Values, 6–8 March 1991.

Balhorn, Mark, "The Rise of Epicene They," *Journal of English Linguistics* 32, no. 2 (2004), 70–104.

Barnhill, Anne, "Bringing the Body Back to Sexual Ethics," *Hypatia* 28, no. 1 (2013), 1–17.

Bauer, Nancy, *How to Do Things with Pornography*, Cambridge: Harvard University Press, 2015.

Beauchamp, Tom, "Autonomy and Consent," in *The Ethics of Consent*, eds. Franklin G. Miller and Alan Wertheimer, New York: Oxford University Press, 2010, 55–78.

Becker, Lawrence C., "Trust as Noncognitive Security About Motives," *Ethics* 107, no.1 (1996), 43–61.

Belliotti, Raymond A., *Good Sex*. Lawrence: University Press of Kansas, 1993.

Benatar, David, "Two Views of Sexual Ethics: Promiscuity, Pedophilia, and Rape," in *The Philosophy of Sex: Contemporary Readings*, eds. Alan Soble and Nicholas Power, New York: Rowman and Littlefield, 2008, 325–336.

Bergelson, Vera, "Consent to Harm," in *The Ethics of Consent*, eds. Franklin G. Miller and Alan Wertheimer, New York: Oxford University Press, 2010, 163–192.

Bernstein, J. M., "Trust: On the Real but Almost Always Unnoticed, Ever-Changing Foundation of Ethical Life," *Metaphilosophy* 42, no. 4 (2011), 395–416.

Bersamin, Melina M., Mallie J. Paschall, Robert F. Saltz, and Byron L. Zamboanga, "Young Adults and Casual Sex: The Relevance of College Drinking Settings," *Journal of Sex Research* 49, no. 2–3 (2012), 274–281.

Bix, Brian H., "Contracts," in *The Ethics of Consent*, eds. Franklin G. Miller and Alan Wertheimer, New York: Oxford University Press, 2010, 251–279.

Bogle, Kathleen A., *Hooking Up: Sex, Dating, and Relationships on Campus*, New York: New York University Press, 2008.

Boswell, Ayres A. and Joan Z. Spade. "Fraternities and Collegiate Rape Culture: Why Are Some Fraternities More Dangerous Places for Women?," *Gender and Society* 10, no. 2 (1996), 133–147.

Bradshaw, Carolyn, Arnold S. Kahn, and Bryan K. Saville, "To Hook Up or Date: Which Gender Benefits?," *Sex Roles* 62 (2010), 661–669.

Bussel, Rachel Kramer, "Beyond Yes and No: Consent as Sexual Process," in *Yes Means Yes: Visions of Female Sexual Power & A World Without Rape*, eds. Jaclyn Friedman and Jessica Valenti, Berkeley: Seal Press, 2008.

California Rape Law, "CA penal code section 261," Last accessed 17 August 2018 at: http://codes.lp.findlaw.com/cacode/PEN/3/1/9/1/s261.

Crawford, Mary and Danielle Popp, "Sexual Double Standards: A Review and Methodological Critique of Two Decades of Research," *The Journal of Sex Research* 40, no. 1 (2003), 13–26.

Dasgupta, Partha. "Trust as a Commodity," in *Trust: Making and Breaking Cooperative Relations*, ed. Diego Gambetta, New York: Basil Blackwell, 1988, 49–72.

Dir, Allyson L., Melissa A. Cyders, and Ayca Coskunpinar, "From the Bar to the Bed via Mobile Phone: A First Test of the Role of Problematic Alcohol Use, Sexting, and Impulsivity-Related Traits in Sexual Hookups," *Computers in Human Behavior* 29 (2013), 1664–1670.

Dougherty, Tom, "Sex, Lies, and Consent," *Ethics* 123 (2013), 717–744.

Dougherty, Tom, "Yes Means Yes: Consent as Communication," *Philosophy & Public Affairs* 43, no. 3 (2015), 224–253.

Downing-Matibag, Teresa M. and Brandi Geisinger, "Hooking Up and Sexual Risk Taking Among College Students: A Health Belief Model Perspective," *Qualitative Health Research* 19, no. 9 (2009), 1196–1209.

Draeger, John, "Can Girls Go Wild With Self-Respect?," in *College Sex: Philosophy for Everyone*, eds. Michael Bruce, Robert M. Stewart, and Fritz Allhoff, West Sussex: Wiley-Blackwell, 2010.

Dressler, Joshua, *Understanding Criminal Law*, Albany: LexisNexis-Matthew Bender Publisher, 2006.

Easton, Dossie and Janet W. Hardy, *The Ethical Slut: A Practical Guide to Polyamory, Open Relationships and Other Adventures*, Berkeley: Celestial Arts, 2009.

Ellis, Anthony, "Casual Sex," *International Journal of Moral and Social Studies* 1, no. 2 (1986), 157–169.

Epstein, Marina, "'Anything From Making Out to Having Sex:' Men's Negotiations of Hooking Up and Friends with Benefits Scripts," *Journal of Sex Research* (2009), Last accessed 17 July 2011 at: http://findarticles.com/p/articles/mi_m2372/is_5_46/ai_n42276082/.

Eshbaugh, Elaine M. and Gary Gute, "Hookups and Sexual Regret Among College Women," *The Journal of Social Psychology* 148, no. 1 (2008), 77–89.

Esterich, Susan, *Real Rape: How the Legal System Victimizes Women Who Say No*, Cambridge: Harvard University Press, 1987.

Falk, Patricia J., "Rape by Drugs: A Statutory Overview and Proposals for Reform," *Arizona Law Review* 44, no.1 (2002), 131–212.

Feinberg, Joel, "Victims' Excuses: The Case of Fraudulently Procured Consent," *Ethics* 96, no. 2 (1986), 330–345.

Fielder, Robyn L., Jennifer L. Walsh, Kate B. Carey, and Michael P. Carey, "Sexual Hookups and Adverse Health Outcomes: A Longitudinal Study of First-Year College Women," *Journal of Sex Research* 51, no. 2 (2014), 131–144.

Finch, Emily and Vanessa E. Munro, "The Demon Drink and the Demonized Woman: Socio-Sexual Stereotypes and Responsibility Attribution in Rape Trials Involving Intoxicants," *Social Legal Studies* 16 (2007), 591–614.

Flack, Jr.,William F., Kimberly A. Daubman, Marcia L. Caron, Jenica A. Asadorian, Nicole R. D'Aureli, Shannon N. Gigliotti, Anna T. Hall, Sarah Kiser, and Erin R. Stine, "Risk Factors and Consequences of Unwanted Sex Among University Students: Hooking Up, Alcohol, and Stress Response," *Journal of Interpersonal Violence* 22, no. 2 (2007), 139–157.

Foertsch, Julie and Morton Ann Gernsbacher, "In Search of Gender Neutrality: Is Singular 'They' a Cognitively Efficient Substitute for Generic 'He'?," *Psychological Science* 8, no. 2 (1997), 106–111.

Fortunato, Leanna, Amy Young, Carol J. Boyd, and Courtney E. Fons, "Hook Up Experiences and Problem Behaviors Among Adolescents," *Journal of Child & Adolescent Substance Abuse* 19 (2010), 261–278.

Friedman, David D. *The Machinery of Freedom: Guide to a Radical Capitalism*, Kindle Edition, Chu Hartley LLC, 2014.

Gardner, Susan and Laura Choate, "The College Experience for Women: Progress and Paradox," in *Girls and Women's Wellness*, ed. Laura Choate, Alexandria: American Counseling Association, 2008.

Glenn, Norval and Elizabeth Marquardt, *Hooking Up, Hanging Out and Hoping for Mr. Right: College Women on Dating and Mating Today*, An Institute for American Values Report to the Independent Women's Forum, 2001.

Goldman, Alan H., "Plain Sex," *Philosophy and Public Affairs* 6, no. 3 (1977), 267–287.

Good, David, "Individuals, Interpersonal Relations, and Trust," in *Trust: Making and Breaking Cooperative Relations*, ed. Diego Gambetta, New York: Basil Blackwell, 1988, 31–48.

Gorr, Michael, "Toward a Theory of Coercion," *Canadian Journal of Philosophy* 16 (1986), 383–405.

Gunderson, Martin, "Threats and Coercion," *Canadian Journal of Philosophy* IX (1979), 247–259.

Gute, Gary and Elaine M. Eshbaugh, "Personality as a Predictor of Hooking Up Among College Students," *Journal of Community Health Nursing* 25 (2008), 26–43.

Hall, Wendasha Jenkins and Amanda E. Tanner, "US Black College Women's Sexual Health in Hookup Culture: Intersections of Race and Gender," *Culture, Health & Sexuality* 18, no. 11(2016), 1265–1278.

Halwani, Raja, "Are One Night Stands Morally Problematic?," *International Journal of Applied Philosophy* 10, no. 1 (1995), 61–67.

Halwani, Raja, "Virtue Ethics, Casual Sex, and Objectification," in *The Philosophy of Sex: Contemporary Readings*, eds. Alan Soble and Nicholas Power, New York: Rowman and Littlefield, 2008, 337–349.

Halwani, Raja, *Philosophy of Love, Sex, and Marriage: An Introduction*, New York: Routledge, 2010.

Haslanger, Sally, "On Being Objective and Being Objectified," in *A Mind of One's Own*, eds. Louise Antony and Charlotte Witt, Boulder: Westview Press, 1993.

Hayek, F. A., *The Constitution of Liberty*. Chicago: University of Chicago Press, 1960.

HelmJr., Herbert W., Stephanie D. Gondra, and Duane C. McBridge, "Hook-Up Culture Among College Students: A Comparison of Attitudes Toward Hooking-Up Based on Ethnicity and Gender," *North American Journal of Psychology* 17, no. 2 (2015), 221–232.

Herman, Barbara, "Could It Be Worth Thinking About Kant on Sex and Marriage?," in *A Mind of One's Own*, eds. Louise Antony and Charlotte Witt, Boulder: Westview Press, 1993.

Hsiao, Timothy, "Consenting Adults, Sex, and Natural Law Theory," *Philosophia* 44 (2016), 509–529.

Hurd, Heidi M., "The Moral Magic of Consent," *Legal Theory* 2 (1996), 121–146.

Husak, Douglas, "Paternalism and Consent," in *The Ethics of Consent*, eds. Franklin G. Miller and Alan Wertheimer, New York: Oxford University Press, 2010, 107–130.

Husak, Douglas N. and George C.ThomasIII, "Rapes without Rapists: Consent and Reasonable Mistake," *Philosophical Issues: Social, Political, and Legal Philosophy* 11 (2001), 86–117.

Indiana Code for Rape, 'IC 35–42–4-1,' Last accessed 11 August 2018 at: www.in.gov/legislative/ic/code/title35/ar42/ch4.html.

Jensen, Robert, *Getting Off: Pornography and the End of Masculinity*, Cambridge: South End Press, 2007.

Johnston, David, "A History of Consent in Western Thought," in *The Ethics of Consent*, eds. Franklin G. Miller and Alan Wertheimer, New York: Oxford University Press, 2010, 25–54.

Jonason, Peter K., Norman P. Lin, and Margaret J. Cason, "The 'Booty Call': A Compromise Between Men's and Women's Ideal Mating Strategies," *Journal of Sex Research* 46, no. 5(2009), 460–470.

Jonason, Peter K., Norman P. Lin, and Jessica Richardson, "Positioning the Booty-Call Relationship on the Spectrum of Relationships: Sexual but More Emotional than One-Night Stands," *Journal of Sex Research* 48, no. 5 (2011), 486–495.

Jones, Karen, "Trust as an Affective Attitude," *Ethics* 107, no. 1 (1996), 4–25.

Kalish, Rachel, "Masculinities and Hooking Up: Sexual Decision-Making at College," *Culture, Society & Masculinities* 5, no. 2 (2013), 147–165.

Kalish, Rachel and Michael Kimmel, "Hooking Up: Hot Hetero Sex or the New Numb Normative?," *Australian Feminist Studies* 26, no. 67 (2011), 137–151.

Kalven, Harry and Hans Zeisel. *The American Jury*. Boston: Little, Brown, 1966.

Kant, Immanuel, *Groundwork. Practical Philosophy*, ed. and trans. Mary J. Gregor, Cambridge: Cambridge University Press, 1785/1996, 43–108. Standard Pagination Abbreviation: G.

Kant, Immanuel, *Metaphysics of Morals. Practical Philosophy*, ed. and trans. Mary J. Gregor, Cambridge: Cambridge University Press, 1797/1996, 353–603. Standard Pagination Abbreviation: MS.

Katz, Jennifer and Monica E. Schneider, "Casual Sex During the First Year of College: Prospective Associations with Attitudes About Sex and Love Relationships," *Archives of Sexual Behavior* 42 (2013), 1451–1462.

Katz, Leo, "Choice, Consent, and Cycling: The Hidden Limitations of Consent," *Michigan Law Review* 104, no. 4 (2006), 627–670.

Kettrey, Heather Hensman, "What's Gender Got to Do With It? Sexual Double Standards and Power in Heterosexual College Hookups," *The Journal of Sex Research* 53, no. 7 (2016), 754–765.

Kimmel, Michael, *Guyland: The Perilous World Where Boys Become Men*, New York: Harper Collins, 2008.

Kleinig, John, "The Nature of Consent," in *The Ethics of Consent*, eds. Franklin G. Miller and Alan Wertheimer, New York: Oxford University Press, 2010, 3–24

Klepper, Howard, "Sexual Exploitation and the Value of Persons," in *The Philosophy of Sex: Contemporary Readings*, eds. Alan Soble and Nicholas Power, New York: Rowman and Littlefield, 2008, 249–259.

Kramer, Karen M., "Rule by Myth: The Social and Legal Dynamics Governing Alcohol-Related Acquaintance Rapes," *Stanford Law Review* 47, no. 1 (1994), 115–160.

Kristjansson, Kristjan, "Casual Sex Revisited," *Journal of Social Philosophy* 29, no. 2 (1998), 97–108.

Kuflik, Arthur, "Hypothetical Consent," in *The Ethics of Consent*, eds. Franklin G. Miller and Alan Wertheimer, New York: Oxford University Press, 2010, 131–161.

Kukla, Rebecca, "That's What She Said: The Language of Sexual Negotiation," *Ethics* 129 (2018), 1–28.

Lahno, Bernd, "On the Emotional Character of Trust," *Ethical Theory and Moral Practice* 4, no. 2 (2001), 171–189.

Lambert, Tracy A., Arnold S. Kahn, and Kevin J. Apple, "Pluralistic Ignorance and Hooking Up," *The Journal of Sex Research* 40, no. 2 (2003), 129–133.

Larson, Jane E., "Women Understand So Little, They Call My Good Nature 'Deceit:' A Feminist Rethinking of Seduction," *Columbia Law Review* 93, no. 2 (1993), 374–472.

LaScotte, Darren K., "Singular They: An Empirical Study of Generic Pronoun Use," *American Speech* 91, no. 1 (2016), 62–80.

Lewis, Melissa A., David C. Atkins, Jessica A. Blayney, David V. Dent, and Debra L. Kaysen, "What is Hooking Up? Examining Definitions of Hooking Up in Relation to Behavior and Normative Perceptions," *Journal of Sex Research* 50, no. 8 (2013), 757–766.

Louisiana Simple Rape Law, 'LA RS 14.43.,' Last accessed 19 August 2018 at: http://law.justia.com/louisiana/codes/146/78531.html.

Luhmann, Niklas, "Familiarity, Confidence, Trust: Problems and Alternatives," In *Trust: Making and Breaking Cooperative Relations*, ed. Diego Gambetta, New York: Basil Blackwell, 1988, 94–107.

McGregor, Joan, *Is It Rape? On Acquaintance Rape and Taking Women's Consent Seriously*, Burlington: Ashgate, 2005.

Mackenzie, Catriona and Natalie Stoljar, eds., *Relational Autonomy: Feminist Perspectives on Autonomy, Agency, and the Social Self*, Oxford: Oxford University Press, 2000.

MacKinnon, Catharine A., "Feminism, Marxism, Method, and the State: An Agenda for Theory," *Signs* 7, no. 3 (1982), 515–544.

MacKinnon, Catherine A., *Toward a Feminist Theory of the State*. Cambridge: Harvard University Press, 1989.

Manning, Wendy D., Peggy C. Giordano, and Monica A. Longmore, "Hooking Up: The Relationship Contexts of 'Nonrelationship' Sex," *Journal of Adolescent Research* 21, no. 5 (2006), 459–483.

Manson, Neil and Onora O'Neill, *Rethinking Informed Consent in Bioethics*, Cambridge: Cambridge University Press, 2007.

Manthos, Megan, Jesse Owen, and Frank D. Fincham, "A New Perspective on Hooking Up Among College Students: Sexual Behavior as a Function of Distinct Groups," *Journal of Social and Personal Relationships* 31, no. 6 (2014), 815–829.

Mappes, Thomas A., "Sexual Morality and the Concept of Using Another Person," in *The Philosophy of Sex: Contemporary Readings*, ed. Alan Soble and Nicholas Power, New York: Rowman and Littlefield, 2008, 229–249.

Marino, Patricia, "The Ethics of Sexual Objectification," *Inquiry* 51, no. 4 (2008), 345–364.

Maticka-Tyndale, Eleanor, Edward S. Herold, and Martin Oppermann, "Casual Sex Among Australian Schoolies," *The Journal of Sex Research* 40, no. 2 (2003), 158–169.

Menegatos, Lisa, Linda C. Lederman, and Aaron Hess, "Friends Don't Let Jane Hook Up Drunk: A Qualitative Analysis of Participation in a Simulation of College Drinking-Related Decisions," *Communication Education* 59, no. 3 (2010), 374–388.

Millar, Thomas M., "Towards a Performance Model of Sex," in *Yes Means Yes: Visions of Female Sexual Power & A World Without Rape*, eds. Jaclyn Friedman and Jessica Valenti, Berkeley: Seal Press, 2008.

Miller, Franklin G. and Alan Wertheimer, "Preface to a Theory of Consent Transactions: Beyond Valid Consent," in *The Ethics of Consent*, eds. Franklin G. Miller and Alan Wertheimer, New York: Oxford University Press, 2010, 79–106.

Monto, Martin A. and Anna G. Carey, "A New Standard of Sexual Behavior? Are Claims Associated with the 'Hookup Culture' Supported by General Social Survey Data?," *The Journal of Sex Research* 51, no. 6 (2014), 606–615.

Moore, Monica. "Courtship Signaling and Adolescents: 'Girls Just Wanna Have Fun'?," *The Journal of Sex Research* 32, no. 4 (1995), 319–328.

Muehlenhard, Charlene and Lisa Hollabaugh, "Do Women Sometimes Say No When They Mean Yes? The Prevalence and Correlates of Women's Token Resistance to Sex," *Journal of Personality and Social Psychology* 54, no. 5 (1988), 872–879.

Narveson, Jan, *The Libertarian Idea*, Ontario: Broadview Press, 2001.

Nozick, Robert, "Coercion," in *Philosophy, Science, and Method: Essays in Honor of Ernest Nagel*, eds. Sidney Morgenbesser, Patrick Suppes, and Mary Terrell White, New York: St. Martin's Press, 1969.

Nozick, Robert, *Anarchy, State, and Utopia*, New York: Basic Books, 1974.

Nussbaum, Martha, "Objectification," *Philosophy and Public Affairs* 24, no. 4 (1995), 249–291.

Nussbaum, Martha, "'Whether from Reason or Prejudice:' Taking Money for Bodily Services," *The Journal of Legal Studies* 27, no. S2 (1998), 693–723

Olmstead, Spencer B., Patricia N. E. Roberson, Kay Pasley, and Frank D. Fincham, "Hooking Up and Risk Behaviors Among First Semester College Men: What is the Role of Precollege Experience?," *The Journal of Sex Research* 52, no. 2 (2015), 186–198.

O'Neill, Onora, "Between Consenting Adults," *Philosophy and Public Affairs* 14, no. 3 (1985), 252–277.

O'Neill, Onora, *A Question of Trust*, Cambridge: Cambridge University Press, 2002.

O'Neill, Onora, "Which Are the Offers You Can't Refuse?," in *Bounds of Justice*, Cambridge: Cambridge University Press, 2005, 81–96.

O'Sullivan, Lucia F. and Elizabeth R. Allgeier, "Feigning Sexual Desire: Consenting to Unwanted Sexual Activity in Heterosexual Dating Relationships ," *The Journal of Sex Research* 36, no. 3 (1998), 234–243.

O'Sullivan, Lucia F. and Sandra Byers, "Eroding Stereotypes: College Women's Attempts to Influence Reluctant Male Partners," *The Journal of Sex Research* 30, no. 3 (1993), 270–282.

Oswalt, Sara B., Kenzie A. Cameron, Jeffrey J. Koob, "Sexual Regret in College Students," *Archives of Sexual Behavior* 34, no. 6 (2005), 663–669.

Owen, Jesse and Frank D. Fincham, "Young Adults' Emotional Reactions after Hooking Up Encounters," *Archives of Sexual Behavior* 40 (2011), 321–330.

Owen, Jesse, Frank D. Fincham, and Jon Moore, "Short-Term Prospective Study of Hooking Up Among College Students," *Archives of Sexual Behavior* 40 (2011), 331–341.

Owen, Jesse J., Galena K. Rhoades, Scott M. Stanley, and Frank D. Fincham, "'Hooking Up' Among College Students: Demographic and Psychosocial Correlates," *Archives of Sexual Behavior* 39 (2010), 653–663.

Paul, Elizabeth, Brian McManus, and Allison Hayes, "'Hookups': Characteristics and Correlates of College Students' Spontaneous and Anonymous Sexual Experiences," *The Journal of Sex Research* 37, no. 1 (2000), 76–88.

Paul, Ellen F. and Fred D.Miller, Jr., eds., *Autonomy*, Cambridge: Cambridge University Press, 2003.

Pennsylvania Consolidated Statutes: Rape, 'Title 18, Section 3121,' Last accessed 19 August 2018 at: www.womenslaw.org/statutes_detail.php?statute_id=4203#statute-top.

Pineau, Lois, "Date Rape: A Feminist Analysis," in *Date Rape: Feminism, Philosophy, and the Law*, ed. Leslie Francis, University Park: The Pennsylvania State University Press, 1996, 1–26.

Primoratz, Igor, *Ethics and Sex*, London: Routledge, 1999.

Primoratz, Igor, "Sexual Morality: Is Consent Enough?," *Ethical Theory & Moral Practice* 4, no. 3 (2001), 201–218.

Raz, Joseph, *Morality of Freedom*. Oxford: Oxford University Press, 1988.

Reid, Julie A., Sinikka Elliott, and Gretchen R. Webber, "Casual Hookups to Formal Dates: Refining the Boundaries of the Sexual Double Standard," *Gender & Society* 25, no. 5 (2011), 545–568.

Remick, Lani Anne, "Read Her Lips: An Argument for a Verbal Consent Standard in Rape," *University of Pennsylvania Law Review* 141, no. 3 (1993), 1103–1151.

Rhode, Deborah L., "Perspective on Professional Women," *Stanford Law Review* 40, no. 5 (1988), 1163–1207.

Rhode, Deborah L., "Feminism and the State," *Harvard Law Review* 107, no. 6 (1994), 1181–1208.

Richards, Janet Radcliffe, "Consent with Inducements: The Case of Body Parts and Services," in *The Ethics of Consent*, eds. Franklin G. Miller and Alan Wertheimer, New York: Oxford University Press, 2010, 281–303.

Roberson, Patricia N. E., Spencer B. Olmstead, and Frank D. Fincham, "Hooking Up During the College Years: Is There a Pattern?," *Culture, Health & Sexuality* 17, no. 5 (2015), 576–591.

Rocha, James, "Aggressive Hook Ups: Modeling Aggressive Casual Sex on BDSM for Moral Permissibility," *Res Publica* 22, no. 2 (2016), 173–192

Roiphe, Katie, *The Morning After: Sex, Fear, and Feminism on Campus*, Boston: Little, Brown, 1993.

Rosin, Hanna, "Boys on the Side," *The Atlantic* (September 2012), Last accessed 1 August 2018 at: www.theatlantic.com/magazine/archive/2012/09/boys-on-the-side/309062/.

Russell, Bertrand, *Marriage & Morals*, New York: Norton & Company, 1957.

Ryan, Cheyney C., "The Normative Concept of Coercion," *Mind* 89 (1980), 481–498.

Sanday, Peggy R., *Fraternity Gang Rape: Sex, Brotherhood, and Privilege on Campus*, New York: New York University Press, 1990.

Schulhofer, Stephen J., *Unwanted Sex: The Culture of Intimidation and the Failure of Law*, Cambridge: Harvard University Press, 1998.

Scruton, Roger, *Sexual Desire*. London: Continuum, 1986.

Shabi, Rachel, "Arab Rape by Deception Charge 'Was Result of Plea Bargain,'" *The Guardian* (8 September 2010), Last accessed 11 August 2018 at: www.guardian.co.uk/world/2010/sep/08/rape-by-deception-plea-israel.

Simpson, Thomas W., "What is Trust?," *Pacific Philosophical Quarterly* 93, no. 4 (2012), 550–569.

Soble, Alan, *Sexual Investigations*, New York: New York University, 1996.

Soble, Alan, "Sexual Use," in *The Philosophy of Sex: Contemporary Readings*, eds. Alan Soble and Nicholas Power, New York: Rowman and Littlefield, 2008, 259–288.

Sprecher, Susan, Elaine Hatfield, Anthony Cortese, Elena Potapova, and Anna Levitskaya, "Token Resistance to Sexual Intercourse and Consent to Unwanted Sexual Intercourse: College Students' Dating Experiences in Three Counties," *The Journal of Sex Research* 31, no. 2, 125–132.

Steinmetz, Katy, "This Pronoun Is the Word of the Year for 2015," *Time* (9 January 2016), Last accessed 4 January 2019 at: http://time.com/4173992/word-of-the-year-2015-they/.

Stinchcombe, Arthur L. and Laura Beth Nielsen, "Consent to Sex: Liberal Paradigm Reformulated," *The Journal of Political Philosophy* 17, no. 1 (2008), 66–89.

Strossen, Nadine, "A Feminist Critique of 'The' Feminist Critique of Pornography," *Virginia Law Review* 79, no. 5 (1993), 1099–1190.

Sutton, Tara E. and Leslie Gordon Simons, "Sexual Assault Among College Students: Family of Origin Hostility, Attachment, and the Hook-Up Culture as Risk Factors," *Journal of Child and Family Studies* 24, no. 10 (2015), 2827–2840.

Taylor, James Stacey, ed., *Personal Autonomy: New Essays on Personal Autonomy and Its Role in Contemporary Moral Philosophy*, Cambridge: Cambridge University Press, 2005.

Taylor, Kate, "Sex on Campus: She Can Play That Game, Too," *New York Times* (12 July 2013), Last accessed 1 August 2018 at: www.nytimes.com/2013/07/14/fashion/sex-on-campus-she-can-play-that-game-too.html.

Thomas, Laurence, "Sexual Desire, Moral Choice, and Human Ends," *Journal of Social Philosophy* 33, no. 2 (2002), 178–192.

Todd, Brenda K., Rico A. Fischer, Steven Di Costa, Amanda Roestorf, Kate Harbour, Paul Hardiman, and John A. Barry, "Sex Differences in Children's Toy Preferences: A Systematic Review, Meta-Regression, and Meta-Analysis," *Infant and Child Development* 27, no. 2 (2018): e2064.

Troost, Hazel/Cedar, "Reclaiming Touch: Rape Culture, Explicit Verbal Consent, and Body Sovereignty," in *Yes Means Yes: Visions of Female Sexual Power & A World Without Rape*, eds. Jaclyn Friedman and Jessica Valenti, Berkeley: Seal Press, 2008.

Tyler, Kimberly A., Rachel M. Schmitz, and Scott A. Adams, "Alcohol Expectancy, Drinking Behavior, and Sexual Victimization among Female and Male College Students," *Journal of Interpersonal Violence* 37, no. 15 (2015), 2298–2322.

Tyndale, Eleanor Maticka, Edward S. Herold, and Martin Opermann, "Casual Sex Among Schoolies," *The Journal of Sex Research* 40, no. 2 (2003), 158–169.

Wade, Lisa, *American Hookup: The New Culture of Sex on Campus*, New York: W.W. Norton & Company, 2017.

Wells, Catharine Pierce, "Date Rape and the Law: Another Feminist View," in *Date Rape: Feminism, Philosophy, and the Law*, ed. Leslie Francis, University Park: The Pennsylvania State University Press, 1996, 41–50.

Wentland, Jocelyn J. and Elke D. Reissing, "Taking Casual Sex Not Too Casually: Exploring Definitions of Casual Sexual Relationships," *The Canadian Journal of Human Sexuality* 20, no. 3 (2011), 75–91.

Wentland, Jocelyn J. and Elke D. Reissing, "Casual Sex Relationships: Identifying Definitions for One Night Stands, Booty Calls, Fuck Buddies, and Friends with Benefits," *The Canadian Journal of Human Sexuality* 23, no. 3 (2014), 167–177.

Wertheimer, Alan, "Intoxicated Consent to Sexual Relations," *Law and Philosophy* 20, no. 4 (2001), 373–401.

Wertheimer, Alan, *Consent to Sexual Relations*, Cambridge: Cambridge University Press, 2003.

Wertheimer, Alan, "Consent and Sexual Relations," in *The Philosophy of Sex: Contemporary Readings*, eds. Alan Soble and Nicholas Power, New York: Rowman and Littlefield, 2008, 289–317.

West, Robin, "Authority, Autonomy, and Choice: The Role of Consent in the Moral and Political Visions of Franz Kafka and Richard Posner," *Harvard Law Review* 99, no. 2 (1985), 384–428.

West, Robin, "Submission, Choice, and Ethics: An Rejoinder to Judge Posner," *Harvard Law Review* 99, no. 7 (1986), 1149–1456.

West, Robin, "Comment on 'Beyond Rape'," *Columbia Law Review* 93, no. 6 (1993), 1442–1459.

West, Robin, "The Harms of Consensual Sex," in *The Philosophy of Sex: Contemporary Readings*, eds. Alan Soble and Nicholas Power, New York: Rowman and Littlefield, 2008, 317–323.

West, Robin, "Sex, Law, and Consent," in *The Ethics of Consent*, eds. Franklin G. Miller and Alan Wertheimer, New York: Oxford University Press, 2010, 221–250.

Wiederman, Michael W., "The Gendered Nature of Sexual Scripts," *The Family Journal: Counseling and Therapy for Couples and Families* 13, no. 4 (2005), 496–502.

Wolf, Allison B., "A Hookup of Her Own," *International Journal of Applied Philosophy* 30, no. 2 (2017), 191–200.

INDEX